Application of Holistic Engineering to Sensitive Systems Analysis and Design: Example of E-Business

Alexander Vengerov

To order additional copies of this book, contact:
Xlibris Corporation
1-888-795-4274
www.Xlibris.com
Orders@Xlibris.com
15936

Contents

Chapter 4

PART 4

HOLISTIC ENGINEERING

I DEDICATE THIS BOOK TO MY WIFE SANDY WHOSE SUPPORT AND UNDERSTANDING MADE THE WHOLE PROJECT POSSIBLE, TO MY SONS, STEVEN, SCOTT, AND DAVID, RELATIVES AND FRIENDS FOR THEIR FAITHFUL AND STIMULATING ATTENTION. I OWE SPECIAL THANKS TO MY SON DAVID, FRUITFUL CONVERSATIONS WITH WHOM GREATLY HELPED IN KEEPING MY THOUGHTS ON TRACK. I ALSO WANT TO EXPRESS GRATITUDE TO MULTIPLE VISIONARIES, THINKERS, AND RESEARCHES THAT LAID THE FOUNDATION FOR THIS WORK EVEN IF SOMETIMES I WAS NOT ABLE TO EXPLICITLY TRACE THE ORIGIN OF SOME IDEAS TO THEIR EFFORTS.

Part 1

E-BUSINESS AND E-ECONOMY

Chapter 1

GENESIS. E-BUSINESS EVOLVING

Situation

Complexity, Uncertainty, and Instability

> *The pace of change in our world is speeding up, accelerating to the point where it threatens to overwhelm the management capacity of political leaders. This acceleration of history comes not only from advancing technology, but also from unprecedented world population growth, even faster economic growth, and the increasingly frequent collisions between expanding human demands and the limits of the earth's natural systems. (Brown, 1996)*

Not only is the natural environment being rapidly destabilized by human activities, but also artificially created systems of all kinds are becoming extremely sensitive to each other, and to their own components. Practically all areas of human interests are affected by these changes: health, economics, politics, environmental and socio-economic systems, etc. "In just 10 years from 1985 to 1995 world economy grew by $4trillion—more than from the beginning of civilization until 1950" (Brown, 1996).

Ability for continuous change in such an environment is becoming more important for organizations than is excellence. Return on investment, cash flow, market share, product leadership, technological renewal, all of these and a number of other concepts are understandable corporate concerns and concentrations; but, at the highest level of strategy, they are no more than means to the supreme, institutional imperative—to secure continuing existence as a viable, independent, economic entity. Transformations, transitions, reengineering and start-up evolving are everyday issues. Growing complexity, uncertainty and instability (CUI) are becoming fundamental properties of the modern organizational environment.

CUI properties are mainly the result of higher sensitivity of various types of organizational structures and substructures to their external and internal environments with extremely high degrees of freedom in assuming possible future states. "Uncertainty has been introduced formally into the model of *Theory of Value* by recognizing that the primitive data of *environment*—in particular resources, tastes and technology—are not known and given, but are part of the unfolding history of the world" (Dreze, 1987).

Instability adds a new dimension to these problems when even statistical models of uncertainty become unstable, often referred to as *model drift*. Model drift does not allow for the development of compact descriptions without increasing the risk of extrapolating the validity of the model beyond the past behavior.

Complexity is a phenomenon with two major features:

1. Large number of components and their interactions are increasing computing complexity often beyond the

ability of handling it in acceptable time and with existing resources.

2. Constant self-organization and the evolving of new entities and their relations have to be considered in analysis and forecast, which often makes models of the previous system states obsolete.

CUI Pressures as a Trend

Electronic commerce and technology proliferation stimulated rapid expansion of the new breed of socio-economic relationships based on strong, fast and rich connectivity built around Internet and other communication standards and technologies. The invisible hand of mutual connectivity, sensitivity and evolving economic self-organization started becoming more visible and physically real. Such a situation leads to new types of businesses and technology interdependence when parts of the whole stimulate and speed up changes in each other and are also influenced by the evolution of the whole.

Are growing CUI-properties of modern organizational environments a temporary problem and will they go away soon? Interconnectivity of organizational network structures and their increasingly distributed performance is not the only factor supporting high sensitivity of system components to each other and their environments in general. The more difficult it is to control the situation (or even to remain viable), the more sensitive organizations have to be to their external and internal environments. But the more sensitive they are, the more CUI-like the environment becomes just because of that. Everybody is playing the same look-around-and-change-faster game which, in its turn, dramatically increases the interconnectivity of distributed events. Small change in one place can turn out to be a big deal in hundreds of others. Growth of sensitivity leads to higher CUI requiring higher sensitivity to the environment and faster response, which in turn . . . Such a positive feedback loop is just springing up.

The old business model and the old economy were based on the idea of *stabilization* of various deviations from the course through use of *control* methods. Such a method of operating inevitably meets Ashby's (1958, 1964) *Law of Requisite Variety,* which posits the necessity of a controlling system having a variety of actions at least as great as the variety of possible controlled states. But the development of controlling abilities and complexity of systems makes the whole environment even more complex, requiring additional controlling abilities (variety), and so on. This coincides with the "Red Queen Principle" (Van Valen, 1973), which requires continuous system development just in order to merely *preserve* an entity's fitness in the environment it co-evolves with.

Some of the main components of a rapidly changing environment include:

- Changing patterns of demand in volume, time, distribution and specific product/service features;
- Changing market valuation of organizational effectiveness, which is very important at times when business is largely driven by borrowings from the market, based on market perception of the possible success, and its scale reflected in huge market to book-value ratios;
- Changing patterns of competition/cooperation among major players, arrival of new players and modification of the market involvement of the existing players;
- Constant innovations in technology and information architectures changing models of information/ knowledge processing, models of processes and control;
- Innovations in service methods, product design and presentation, and customer relationships leading to new expectations and constantly changing culture of business transactions and relationships in general;
- Changing patterns of the supply and distribution chain

organization, relationships and functionality reflecting in addition to above mentioned factors ongoing internal transformations in models of participating businesses;

- Changes in employee expectations with growing knowledge, skills and battles for the best people.

Old Economy and New I—and E-Economies

Speaking of the old economy . . . Already for a while there has been a growing perception of dramatic economic changes happening nowadays. As Jorgenson and Stiroh (2000) put it: *"a consensus is emerging that something fundamental has changed"*.

Important extensions have been developed to the classical Solow model of economic growth. They show the growing influence of knowledge, learning and network externalities, according to Romer (1989), as well as the explosive innovations and growing effectiveness of technology and information systems, as pointed out by Aghion and Howitt (1992), upsetting traditional model behavior.

Metcalfe's Law and the so-called "network externalities" show the counterintuitive paradox of growing value with the scale of sales. This is the result of value simplification which before was almost identical to products and services as self-contained value carriers that could be exchanged for other value containers. At that time, the value math was linear to the amount of value containers on the market. The price could fluctuate because of competition and production costs, but basically that was it.

Network economies that are rapidly transforming into *sensitive economies* under explosive growth of connectivity and sensitivity of their elements and processes have started showing growing non-linearities in all previously existing simplifications. Sensitive economies pushed further connectivity effects of network economies to the level where emerging sensitivity started exposing serious non-linearities. We will focus here on several of the most important factors of changing economic dynamics under the described conditions.

First, if one is to start inquiring deeper into the nature of created value—is the growing complexity of value structure and its dynamics. Increased sensitivity has another result: complexity, which includes the emergence of complex needs requiring complimentarity. Complimentarity (Economides, 1995) reflects the situation within which customers demand either a combination of two goods or when the sale of good A stimulates the sale of complimentary good B and vise-versa. Such complimentarity could be generalized into *complex patterns of value composition* when even the structure of such complimentarity is unknown and often unpredictable. The term "value" more and more started being associated not with particular goods or well-definable value containers but with patterns of creatively combined activities capable of satisfying customers. An almost invisible switch from "value production" to "customer satisfaction" in value analysis has serious consequences symbolizing the end of production of value as the kinds of objects and the beginning of more active customer participation in value creation and perception. This, in turn, required bigger connectivity with customers, where new connectivity technology sharply increased customer sensitivity to market processes and . . . consumption trends. Because of that, value as customer satisfaction started being not only more complex (requiring various combinations and aggregate types of *complementary activities*) but also more dynamic, causing frequent changes and modifications in value design.

Second, complimentarity requires compatibility in order to be realized, according to Katz and Shapiro (1985), which, if offered at sufficiently low cost, can move the industry toward collaboration in achieving such compatibility. Internet efficiency was that trigger that, with its simplicity and ubiquity, offered the possibility of an incredible explosion of *creative complimentarity*. Otherwise, many value models (as value designs) would have not been realized, remaining just a social dream which didn't come true because of economic inefficiency. Satisfaction of the problem of this kind of inefficiency (versus demand/supply balancing) is another task of the new economy.

The third aspect comes naturally as the result of the previous development. Balancing dynamic complex patterns of value/resource/compensation is impossible without advanced *intelligence* of the economy. The "invisible hand" of self-organization on the production/demand balancing level is one thing, and another is the recognition (and preferably forecast) of complex value patterns and the ability to creatively and quickly restructure resources to match such needs. Where can this level of intelligence come from? Is there any guaranteed market strategy for it? These and many other questions stemming from this discussed situation require answers that do not exist in the "old economics."

Hence, the fourth aspect is in the complex and adequate market reaction to complex and dynamic value patterns imposed in real time by user—and not manufactured according to the prescription for happiness of mass production facilities. Increased connectivity and sensitivity, spelling trouble by increasing CUI properties of the economic environment, at the same time offer the remedy. Already Cournot (1838) showed that an integrated monopolist producing two complementary goods would charge less than two vertically-related monopolists, each producing one type of goods only. Economides (1994) and Economides and Lehr (1995) also showed that "an integrated monopolist also provides a higher quality than the two independent monopolists." Using new means of communications and IT, market participants started moving away from isolated microeconomics to network microeconomics and, finally, to dynamic pattern systems reminding weather patterns.

Analyzing features of the new economy, Kelly (1998) pointed out the dominating importance of the management of opportunities and creative forces, compared to conformist efficiency requirements. Such an unleashing of creativity can only be based on 'soft' relationships and not on conflicting ones. The needs for growing market intelligence, especially with respect to pattern selection and recognition, are becoming paramount.

Increased sensitivity leading to the "Edge of Chaos" dynamics of the *market system* allows for much *more intelligent self-organization* than before. Unlike in a network economy, the very structure and richness of connections in a *sensitive economy* started fluctuating, exposing complex dynamic behavior and evolution of various types of attractors as discovered regularities matching market pressures. Inability to develop a sensitive enough system fitting the lifestyle of the new economy throws companies out of this economy into old-style stiff relationships. But the more organizations and mini-markets succeed in this new direction, the higher will be the challenge for the old economy, which will have to join the march along this path.

Economics of the Internet (I-economics), which belongs to the economics of communications, should be distinguished from the economics of electronic business or E-economics. I-economics deals with network resource economies that play a role of a carrier for E-economies. Some of the problems involved include service pricing, resource allocation, supply/demand dynamics of Internet traffic, effectiveness and efficiency of communication markets and signaling, taxation, investment effectiveness, ownership, congestion externalities and regulatory efficiencies.

Opinions on relationships of both types of economies

vary from trends to merge them, overemphasizing the role of the Internet as the main feature of electronic commerce and business, to attempts to count the Internet out as a simple carrier, which has nothing to do with innovative ways of doing modern business and developing modern organizations. The meaning and the future of the Internet long outgrew the idea of packet switching communications using the TCP/IP family of protocols and related technologies. We already can see a fast evolution of protocols and the changing role of the WWW as it becomes able to carry multimedia, interface file transfer and client-server communications. With XML, Java, scripting languages and other add-ons as well as technologies supporting services, messaging, queuing, transactions, sessions, intelligent trafficking and distributed computing, with rapid addition of wireless and mobile connections and increasing communication efficiency, the Internet is becoming a Universal Communication Machine. Given its growing processing power and memory, it is also becoming a Universal Living Space (World) capable to perform complex vital functions and to support the dynamic co-evolution of this environment for all participating agents.

From our point of view, the relationship between I— and E—economies is based on the situation where the I-economy services the needs in **connectivity** for the E-economy (its client), which tries to harmonize its **sensitivity.**

The emergence of the I-economy indicates the new type of demand, and its scale is an indicator of the speed and degree of the shift to the new methods of organizational adaptability. Combining needs in connectivity and sensitivity into the term "Internet Economy" allows estimation of the scale of changes along the lines of the discussed trends and brewing catastrophes.

The Internet Economy Indicators Review (June 2002) offers the following statistics:

According to the study, the Internet Economy now directly

supports more than 3.088 million workers, including an additional 600,000 in the first half of 2000. This is about 60,000 more than the number employed in insurance industry and double the real estate industry. These jobs were created both by the explosion of the Internet and by companies shifting workers to take advantage of the benefits created by embracing the Internet.

Employment in Internet Economy is growing much faster than employment in the overall economy. Total employment at Internet economy companies grew 10 percent between the first quarter of 1999 and the first quarter of 2000. Internet-related jobs at Internet Economy companies grew 29 percent during the same period. Both of these figures far exceed the growth of non-Internet related jobs in these same Internet Economy companies, which grew 6.9 percent during the same period. The Internet Economy generated an estimated $830 billion in revenues in 2000, a 58 percent increase over 1999. The $830 billion in revenues is a 156 percent increase from 1998, when the Internet accounted for $323 billion in revenues.

Internet economy revenue is growing twice as fast as Internet Economy employment. In 2000, for example, second quarter revenue grew 58.8 percent over the second quarter of 1999. Meanwhile second quarter employment grew 22.6 percent over 1999.

Role of Technology: Information and Communication Systems

The Information and Communication Systems (ICS) innovation explosion and proliferation became a catalytic phenomenon for the new economy's evolution. Communication efficiency and universal acceptance of Internet standards and formats were initially used in evolutionary ways as merely more efficient tools of information delivery. However, growing efficiency and the effectiveness of communication networks and enhancement of multimedia types of content led to the new business environment. Remembering the history of computing, we can see that availability of computers with large storage, effective data organization and retrieval mechanisms led to the Information Systems Revolution.

First, huge expenses in information collection were leveraged with the increased value of vast collections of data. This led to a rapid evolution of ways of using such collections. Transaction Processing Systems (TPS) were augmented with Management Information Systems (MIS), then Executive Information Systems (EIS), Decision Support Systems (DSS) or even group DSS (GDSS) and finally data warehouses making access to any part of such a collection available not only to top management but to all participants of organizational processes. Given storage effectiveness and efficiency function domination, the whole process of system design was based on determining all stable data structures and relationships and then implementing them for decision-making and control processes.

Then, when transactional efficiency and ease of connectivity with any desirable party exceeded a certain threshold level due to Internet technologies, communication function started playing a more and more important role until it overshadowed data storage and the retrieval function of information systems. Already in 1998 most surveys showed that management considered communication effectiveness and efficiency as the biggest value gained from information technologies (this is when we stopped using exclusively the term *Information Systems* but started using *IS/IT* and, with the constantly growing role of communications, just *information technology* or simply *technology*). Microsoft, reflecting these changes, was the first company announcing universal connectivity as its cardinal direction. The Internet, intranets and extranets, became the foundation of new business communication systems.

Low cost of communications and ease of connectivity establishment have had a great influence on business transactions. Take an example from banking, where actual money transfer among banks is happening mainly on books with just information exchange of data *about transactions*. The same idea started proliferating in other business processes, when the dynamics of actual transactions have been largely replaced with information about them. Finally, separation in e-business of the actual physical transaction from its distributed information processing has led to the possibility of totally new ways of doing business. Much richer communications among parties on pre-transactional, transactional and post-transactional stages allow for the most of business work to be done on levels of information processing and communication. Search, advertising and marketing, dynamical pricing, shopping and haggling, customer relationship management and corresponding enterprise modifications can all be done electronically with only a small part—actual delivery of a physical product—to be done offline (still with a lot of information processes happening during distribution management and control).

Thus, the main volume of transactions has turned into communications and information processing, which has changed enterprises focus from the huge engines and pumps that were pushing physical product exchanges down expensive system of predesigned pipelines to switchboards and clubs opened for fast mingling of the general public into dynamic opened marketplaces. The importance of this feature and its influence on e-business development leads to definitions of e-commerce and e-business as business systems with automated commercial transactions done over modern communication networks. The authors of such definitions, though recognizing the importance of electronic transactions, still consider e-business as a mere continuation of automation of former business systems, as a way of more efficient lubrication of existing business wheels. However, from the point of view of the evolving sensitive economy, it is the main factor of the future evolution in e-economic dynamics. We can say that it is just the beginning of the end of the business world as we knew it during the last several centuries . . .

Electronic Business Phenomenon

The role of sensitivity among system components as the main factor leading to the increasingly complex behavior of the whole system is specifically studied in Dynamic Systems Theory and the Theory of Complexity. The sensitivity growth in economic and social environments tends to be initially self-supporting but later can be stabilized by forces of self-organization (which is also self-stabilization). Although the complexity of controlling highly sensitive systems is exponentially growing, self-adaptability (versus external control and decision-making) is developing also quickly, allowing at some level of system sensitivity to rely on it. Such a level of sensitivity is called the "Edge of Chaos" (Kauffman, 1995) and it has been shown that the living systems (animals, plants, bio-ecologies) all display certain stability of the "Edge of Chaos" state balanced with tamed sensitivity. It looks like as if it is very difficult for any system to stay at medium levels of sensitivity where control methods already do not work and self-organization has not yet started. The two stable states are high-stability and control based structures and high-sensitivity and self-organized systems. Staying between frozen overstabilization and random hysteria, such systems show an ultimate richness, intelligence and adaptability. Our economic and business environment has brought modern organizations to such a middle ground from where there are two ways to escape.

E-business is actually the first phenomenon in the latest economic developments which chooses the second way of high sensitivity and is trying to thrive on CUI properties of the business environment (Vengerov, 2001). Its main attraction is not in a cool way of shopping using the Internet but in the ability to effectively cope with vast variety of changes, with life fluidity of the market, business, technology, culture, politics, etc., staying adequately fluid and yet organized. For the first time, people realized that business as well as organizational development and management might not be about making continuous chains of decisions and following their implementation, as it is required by corporate job descriptions, but about caring and letting go . . . Huber (1990) suggested that advanced information technology is capable of influencing the patterns of organizational dynamics. In his view, enhanced communication abilities and shared resources can allow leaders of insufficiently centralized (in terms of decision-making) organizations to regain influence by being informed and having access to everybody, while empowering employees of over-centralized organizations, moving them to a more distributed structure. As a result, the organization self-regulates in its position toward the necessary proportion of centralization/ decentralization.

Technology proliferation created a new opportunity, allowing use of the increase of mutual sensitivity of system components to the level of their self-adaptability without control interference, creating effective "self-running" business. However, if the sensitivity stays below the necessary level and control remains weak, then organizations find themselves falling between the hands of control/stability and sensitivity/self-organization, and not being supported by either one. This is the point of separation of a successful electronic business from the one which ventures into the area of high sensitivity to customers and other business needs without the ability to handle it.

The first wave of dot-com catastrophes showed the necessity of understanding the new laws and principles of *sensitive systems* (SS) and their survival. Once the electrical current of e-commerce cable bringing in the energy of thousands and even millions of connected customers and businesses is turned on, the organization can either burn or shine depending on the readiness of its architecture and processes, the readiness to live in the world of high sensitivity and constant changes in the world of complexity, uncertainty and instability.

Trends in E-Organizations and E-Markets

As a result of the discussed CUI dynamics with a catalytic influence of technology, the transformation of traditional organizations into e-organizations started with simple communication enhancements, but rapidly continued into a much broader area of changes than was initially thought. Below, we will discuss the main trends in such changes, focusing on the method of conducting business, the form and the values of economic activity.

E-Organizations Strike Back

Method: Continuous Dynamic Relations

The method of organizational self-realization, the major patterns of socio-economic and technological activities undergo significant changes with further development of the New Economy. The general trend is toward increased connectivity and sensitivity of all business processes and entities. For example, ERP development supports growing internal interdependence of all organizational units and processes. In supply and sales chain management, CRM tasks require dismantling of the Great Chinese Wall around the organization and all internal and external systems, connecting them together in order to support the growing complexity of transactions involving multiple economic agents. Instead of concentrating mainly on the expansion of the spheres of their influence and stabilization of operations, the companies in their holistic behavior are consciously choosing the areas of external changes they want to make their business processes sensitive to.

Furthermore, instead of economics of networks with value exchange in the form of products, services and financial equivalents they are becoming *networks of continuous relations* requiring constant and fast harmonization until a more stable state of joint satisfaction is achieved. Such a trend can also be seen in terms of transactional dynamics between and within organizations.

Another effect of holism is the so-called *product convergence.* Amount and speed of changes led gradually to the erosion of the idea of product stability. First, it started as requirements for fast design changes as a result of the struggle for quality management and dynamic customer satisfaction. Then came the concept of product generations, then continuous improvement . . . Such changes reflect the increase in product design and supporting service sensitivity to its utility environment. This sensitivity could be managed only through the increased information component in the product/service life. Lately, intensive research and development efforts have been made in Internet appliances—a growing class of products responding to changing utility situations by using Internet connectivity and virtual flexibility. For example, TV sets could be gradually changed to new models by just automatically downloading different software and supporting information. In their approach to XML services, Microsoft attempts to turn all their products into services provided over the Internet.

Since growing information content in different products is basically treated the same way (generated, delivered, and consumed) the difference among various products from the point of view of the main cost component design and management is disappearing. Potentially, we will see many products that can become something totally different from an application point of view based on the received information. Products served by one of the most universal product generators—computers—can be seen as examples. You can see and feel a telephone on the screen with all the buttons, a book with pages turning, a music player, but you also can change the "skins" of the design, change functionality and so on.

The growth of the information dynamics of products and services has led to another effect—the disappearance of product objectivity as physical boundaries and contained value. Products became more like information services without final and stabilized quality and value. They started stretching in time, becoming more like continuous relationships of need and of its continuous satisfaction. They are becoming product-patterns of need-satisfaction dynamics in changing environments.

Form: Integration of Producers and Consumers

The rapid transformation of the causal logic of business relationships to pluralistic and then holistic ones has a serious impact on all major components of the economic mechanism. One of them is the trend toward the disappearance of differentiation between producers and consumers that represents one of the most profound changes. This concerns B2C and B2B relations as well as so-called "value chains" in general. Chains are becoming networks that are then becoming hubs of joint activity as a new form of relationship. Such a form supports parallel multiparticipant evolving processes as coevolution of the whole cluster where states (as stable configurations) are not individual but represent joint coevolution. Since everybody working simultaneously in the same space collaboration does not result in sequential cause-effect chains, this should be resolved in some form of results, milestone dates and responsibility synchronization. Everything is happening in parallel at the same time. Who is producer and who is consumer of intermediate material and information flow is irrelevant. They all are co-producers and co-consumers with simultaneous exchange activities.

The Ford Motor Co. uses real-time design sessions with suppliers on a project Web site to reduce design costs and time. Electronic manufacturer Adaptec, which competes in an environment of shrinking product life-cycles, uses Extricity's technology to participate in internal processes of its suppliers, including forecast sharing. This allows knowledge of possible delays or deviations from the planned processes and for taking compensatory actions. As an example, through the use of Extricity the company was able to decrease development time by 50% and reduce inventory levels by 25% and provided for bottom-line savings of $2 million per year (Extricity Software, 2002).

The future extension of collaboration hubs will result in multilevel hubs with different rights when, after the product-service is shaped in B2B format, it becomes available for customer participation in B2C format. Such multilevel hubs will be especially popular in the knowledge industry, e-learning, product-service knowledge, and skills support and training. The same kind of Hub2Hub (H2H) cooperation will be developed as a learning/knowledge supplemental services to physical product development. Later, information and learning services will be integrated more and more into H2H and H2C.

Such hubs are not stable structures but are created dynamically as clusters of mutual sensitivity to each other's needs and possibilities. They are increasingly losing various attributes of organizational identity, like in case of multiple "peering" into hubs. The connectionist network of multiple relations oscillates in its dynamics until it reaches some temporary stable state. Such a state becomes a joint state of coevolution of the participants.

Value: Sensitivity and Harmony

Current trends show certain changes in approaching the problem of system valuation. First, it was a deviation in the understanding of the term "Organizational Designers," which originally represented a narrow group whose goal is to collect, systematize, and approve all the requirements and then design the system matching these requirements as close as possible. Such a match was the ultimate value that originally was supposed to be captured in the requirements. Two schisms started developing in this area:

1. Growing connectivity of all entities led to the broadening of the entitled designers, ultimately including all kinds of actors including buyers and suppliers across all existing connections;
2. Inability to "capture" requirements that became very dynamic forms of the continuously changing ways of customer satisfaction.

Such change from value, based on measurable deviation from the model (requirements), to complex and dynamic pattern of customer satisfaction led to the rise of Customer Relationship Management (CRM) as a function responsible for creation and maintenance of customer "value chains." CRM is positioned to take the leading role in redesign and management of such functions as knowledge management (KM), organizational learning (OL) and enterprise resource planning (ERP).

In the past, approach to value was quite simple, including the following ideas (Porter et al, 1985):

*   the firms' output was considered "value to the customer";
*   the value created by a firm can be measured by the amount that customers are willing to pay for it;
*   the value-for-business of value-for-customer creation

is obtained if the value a business creates exceeds the cost of the value production.

With the form of business outputs more and more resembling continuous services, new approaches to "value-as-output" have been developed, seeing it rather as "value-as-kinda-behavior." For example, the SERVQUAL framework (Parasuraman, A., V. A. Zeithaml, and L. L. Berry, 1988) of measuring the quality of service saw the following aspects of value: reliability, responsiveness, assurance, empathy and tangibles (appeal of physical appearance of service components). Here we also see an interesting understanding of assurance as **"knowledge and courtesy of employees and their ability to convey trust and confidence"** and reliability as **"the ability to perform the promised service dependably and accurately."** Such terms differ a lot from the prior view of value as a well-defined product and service output. They started more and more resembling the features of desirable . . . *relationship*, stopping short of *friendship*.

The growing importance of relationships at the time of a growing fuzziness around the dynamics of changes of previously known and used economic elements based on object-oriented finality, stability and definability can be seen in the influence of trusted members of relationship clusters on choices and actions of other members (Rosen, 1987; Price et al 1984; Ardnt J., 1967). Such influence has an informational basis as "influence to accept information from others as evidence about reality" and normative basis as "influence to conform to some expectations of other individuals through reward/punishment relationship or a desire on the part of the person to identify with the other individuals or their point of view" (Pincus, 1977)

The growing sensitivity of all actors and elements of economic processes and the shifting of the main method of organizational existence to creation and maintenance of internal and external relationships started refocusing e-business toward the value of such relationships. Increased sensitivity to multiple external agents creates a switch from the term "shareholders" to the term "stakeholders" all as actors, sensitive to organizational behavior. Products and services, through a continuous fight for quality, started redefining quality as continuous customer satisfaction and finally as satisfying relationships. Erosion of the differences between producers, consumers and all involved parties *in general* (across all aspects of mutual sensitivity) creates understanding of harmonic and mutually satisfying relationships *in general*. The information character of resources, with the disappearance of physical scarceness and the arrival of the idea of mutual *resource creation* as mutually agreed patterns of relationship harmonization, has led to the new value and goal of **moving to higher volume and quality of relationships**. Relationships as mutually produced/consumed resource/product are becoming more like the adequacy and harmony of coevolution.

E-Markets Join The Game

Form: E-Societies

The economics of relationships has led to the arrival of specific markets (vertical and horizontal) that later started becoming hubs of collaboration and relationship—all self-balancing as good markets are supposed to be. The growing non-industrial character of information exchange and processing is converting these mini e-markets into e-societies of relationships.

The extremely active position of e-business and its models spreading outside the pure economic domain can be explained by the growing connectivity with environmental, social and political issues. Such a transformation is happening not only on the business side. Consumers, or rather participants in e-relationships, are increasingly treating them as parts of their everyday life functionality. More and more, we live, work, and get satisfaction/utility for our changing needs in the evolving virtual world. The emotional influence of multimedia Internet sources like music, TV and other forms, wearables and connectivity of home appliances, the possibility of participation in cultural, political, economic and other forms of society and individual development, access to knowledge, skills and educational power are all moving into this virtual reality, this Matrix. Therefore, the issues of fairness of connectivity, e-relationship distribution, ethics, etc. are becoming more and more important. Equilibrium, or rather harmony, in such e-societies is a much more complex task then demand-supply balancing.

Another aspect of this trend is due to the much stronger relationships and interdependencies among the economic agents that leads to the phenomena of *fuzzy identities*. The more sociable and connected with others the organization is, the more joint forms and traits influence its individual identity. The new joint identity emerges. At the same time, membership in such relationship markets is varying, with new members arriving and old disappearing. Such ID fuzziness, especially in peer-to-peer architectures, is being enhanced through the temporary nature of many relationships. The distributed, temporal, limited and fuzzy identities of actors and the results of their activities create growing accounting, legal and economic problems as deviations from the existing forms inherited from the times of Roman Empire.

Method: Market Communications

Traditional market allocation mechanisms are based on price signaling and the following harmonization using cost-revenue re-evaluation allowing for automatic adjustment of resource/product value and allocation. Such communications are usually enhanced by various intermediaries and push (advertising)-pull (shopping) information distribution. Growing customization of particular values based on attempts to avoid direct Bertrand price competition, which drives profit down, and proliferating mechanisms of first-degree price discrimination with individual pricing for each customer, decrease workability of the economics of price, demand, and supply based on price signaling.

The new e-reality of non-products, non-producers and non-customers simultaneously creating the new meaning and structure of information content as a new value leads to increased use of non-price signaling and feedback controls built into market self-organization capabilities. Non-price signaling devices, especially for customized products, include various means of sellers information (email, search, banners, web site pages, personalized and targeted advertising, etc.), means of customer information/experience exchange (forums, email, etc.) and third party signaling like specialized consumer-oriented newsletters and services of various intermediaries. In case of mass customization, advertising is leaning toward so-called informative advertising, which delivers information about product specifics and quality. Portals, intelligent agents and search engines do the job of informing the customers. Intrusive persuasive advertising, such as flashing the banners and spamming Internet or other unsolicited push-strategies, is becoming obsolete. Instead, New Organizations are switching to customer relationship management (CRM) that, instead of broadcasting attractive images and skillful brainwashing, uses everyday connectivity and responsiveness.

Another form of signaling is in device-mediated experience, when customers see and feel the product "first hand," like the multimedia experience of Honda's interior design with controlled focus change and viewing scope. Active research in remote sensors and sensor interfaces will definitely cover some part of the signaling needs or rather information "symmetrization" when the customer can obtain the same knowledge and experience as the local supplier.

The third option is in converting sales intermediaries into information intermediaries and customization intermediaries. In this case intermediaries play a very important and specialized role as the interface between suppliers and consumers, trusted by both sides and having intimate knowledge of both sides, capable of additional customization on both ends (affecting producing and packaging as well as delivery and consumption).

Ultimately, the New Organizations become more valuable because of consistent efficiency (min efforts for customers) of their responsiveness to customer needs and desires that can be discovered automatically even without special informing efforts of the customers. It means the trend is in enhancing signaling between all the parties to the extent that it is becoming not just signaling as information hints about the broader market situation but a specific flow of information capable of producing immediate changes in organizations and, hence, markets, as it flows. Markets have started changing from the balancing game to holistic evolution of relationship and value patterns.

Value: Harmonization of the Market

The goal and the value of traditional markets can be seen in proper resource allocation, where the price that the user of the resource paid should be adequate to resource usage. Deviations are considered diseconomies. The main problem here was imperfect competition, when resources cannot be allocated properly due to imperfect information and imperfect information distribution.

Just when the markets started increasing their quality in an information symmetrization sense, the question arose about what actually is being balanced. Now with infinitely continuous products-relationships and a disappearing idea of quantity, we need to use other areas and patterns of specific individual and group satisfaction. The ideas of *demand* and *supply* that could be averaged across the market are gradually being transformed into the need/value of full-scale relationship harmonization in all specific aspects.

The desire and value of stabilizing organizational dynamics, as well as its forms using various control methods, is increasingly substituted with the need to harmonize relationships with various external entities. Such approaches as Customer Relationship Management (CRM) and e-Procurement gradually substitute for methods of sales and supply chain control as product/service pipelines. Specific hub-style collaborative pattern matching has become the direct result and the sought value of e-economic functionality.

Such development has led to the emerging of the two new economies still coexisting with older forms. One is the **economy of connectivity** (which I-economy is evolving into) as a resource that has to be delivered when and where it is needed. Another is the **economy of sensitivity** (e-economy) leading to evolving/dissipating hubs and patterns of organizational behavior in search of relationship harmonization in all interwoven aspects of organizational sensitivity.

We see the shift in the understanding of market value and importance from balancing price/resource usage among well-defined elements of economic exchange to relationship improvement and harmony. Another shift is from the value of stability of functionality, processes of growth and profitability and existing organizational forms to the growing importance of coping with relationship management, which dictates the necessary changes.

Summary

The table below summarizes the discussed trends. Here we can see changes on organization and market level concerning the main parts of economic dynamics: form, method or mechanism and value of activities.

Table.1 Trends in E-organizations and E-markets

Entity	Method	Form	Value
Organizations	T1. Growing connectivity and sensitivity among participating economic entities with increasing fuzziness of boundaries and dynamics of evolving	T4. Transformation of value chains into simultaneous multifaceted collaboration hubs	T7. Growing complexity of using value as finite and measurable unit of exchange given the growing dynamics, continuity, and scope of relationships
	T2. Products and services as continuous relationships. Not only e-orgs assimilate consumers but consumers assimilate e-services as parts of their life functionality	T5. Increasingly fuzzy and dynamic boundaries of organizational actors	T8. Growing value of relationship harmonization
	T3. From transactions with individual entities to joint transactional states of connected entities.	T6. Information is becoming less of a product and more of a tool of mutual sensitivity; technology is less of a service and more as means of mutual connectivity in clusters of relationships	T17. From balance between supply and demand to harmonic coevolution of all clusters of sensitivity outside and inside organizations
Markets	T9. From use of signals (price, ads, etc.) for market balancing by independent agencies to continuous collaboration clusters in order to achieve it	T13. From markets of organizations as well-defined participants to evolving multilevel and multi context clusters of collaboration across corporate boundaries	T18. From supply/demand balancing to more complex forms of harmony as ultimate value
	T10. Role of intermediaries changes from connectivity of demand and supply to harmonization functions	T14. Growth of continuous non-transactional forms of relationships	
	T11. From resource distribution across markets to distribution of sensitivity and connectivity	T15. Includes less defined with blurred boundaries participants as clusters of actors with high mutual sensitivity	
	T12. Growing evolving on CS carrier without borders (holistic) versus competition of well-shaped actors	T16. Deterioration of market-organizational differences and boundaries	

All the described trends have the following features in common that constitute the underlying change processes:

- **Form**: High sensitivity and connectivity of system components (organizational, product, service, process) in a form of clusters of mutual sensitivity or hubs of relationships along a growing variety of interacting features with fuzzy permeable dynamically changing boundaries;
- **Method**: Use of sensitivity and connectivity as a resource for higher auto harmonization of relationships among parties in real time and along the whole spectrum of frequencies of mutual impact;
- **Value**: The growing value of improvement in relationships on all time horizons (including continuous current as well as the long term ones) leading toward more effective and efficient coevolution of harmony with each other and mutual environment. We also see the shift from the value of stabilization to the ability for dynamic self-organization

Chapter 2

APOCALYPSE. CHAPTER OF CATASTROPHES

The trends described in the previous chapter unfortunately are not the trends of gradual changes but ones leading to serious discontinuities. Organizations that can afford it should attempt not to cut into them by pieces but to do it all at once. There is no way around it. Switching to advanced e-business requires understanding of the degree of the changes that will be encountered on the way. The best term to apply to the most dramatic of them is the term *catastrophe*, taken in mathematical sense. "Catastrophe" means the serious discontinuity of a process or function leading to the progress in the opposite direction, usually caused by the initially innocent and smooth growth of some feature. For example, enjoyment by hamburgers grows with eating until suddenly you are fed up, and further insistence on eating by the host results in a growing hate of those hamburgers. Here, the satisfaction trend abruptly switches to hate, going in the opposite direction.

The growth of business component and process sensitivity

is reaching the moment when systems become holistic, with all the previously-discussed consequences. How would this affect the approach to the revolutionary e-business understanding, design and management?

Organizational Catastrophes

Catastrophe of the Form

Previously described trends T1-T4 of the disappearance of boundaries in products/services as well as production processes and organizational structures and the following movement toward developing relationships, instead of a product/service exchange, shift accent to enhanced communication systems as the mechanisms supporting the necessary sensitivity required for relationship harmonization. As an example, there are user groups such as Open Nap and Gnutella that also enable computer users to swap online music files, but they might be difficult to fight with, because unlike Napster, they are not companies, but just hubs of user interactions without formal representation as one economic agent. Increasing the role of channel organizations that rapidly become hubs of interconnections in some or all functions creates a very different approach to organizational development. Instead of analyzing existing strength stemming from organizational skills and asset structure in order to determine growth and development strategy as expansion of current business (growth "inside-out"), new organizations will place themselves in-between interacting agents with the purpose of assuming the controlling and organizing heat of relationship harmonization and will evolve accordingly. They become organizations-channels and organizations-hubs delivering the value of quality relationships for multiple entities from users and customers to business associates of all kinds. They will not know the direction and often even the type of internal processes required for such a mission, but will rather rely on increased external sensitivity using the advanced harmonization abilities of the dynamics of relationships between parties. Growth of such companies will stem from such external sensitivity, allowing them to feed on adaptive responses to it.

The pattern of such a type of organizational development can be called growth "outside-in" leading to emerging *inverted organizations.* They value sensitivity over stability and the dynamic evolving of internal architecture based on external needs over the planned models.

Catastrophe of the Method

Driving by the Rear Mirror

It took several decades to persuade management and accounting minds that information is an asset and may be so to a greater extent than equipment, materials, etc. Finally, almost nobody objects to this assertion at a time when it just stopped being an asset. This is true, at least, for old information, which is supposed to show the trends of this year by the analysis of the last year. Traditionally, management control was realized through extensive information collection, discovery of the models and making decisions or choices of the best actions, causing desirable outcome.

The beginning of the tide of organizational changes was well reflected in (Neef, 1998 p.21) as following:

- The Industrial Revolution at the beginning of the 18th century, which determined the shift from local skills to standardized and easily spread-around production technology. Management control here is very appropriate, as the decision to buy equipment, which one and how much, was based on simple and available information about possible factory location.

- The Productivity Revolution, symbolized in Taylor's system, which was the natural continuation of widely available production technology. Here control was applied to models of process organization and tool usage with the simple goal of producing more and cheaper. Information about the way various processes perform becomes even more useful for control here. But such information is still primitive enough that the control issue and the sufficiency of its power enforcing the necessary productivity is the main concern.

- The Management Revolution was the result of market restrictions when production stopped being the main goal since it encountered various market forces and became sensitive to competition, demand, and other forces described in Potter's model of competitive advantage. "The traditional "factors of production"— land (i.e. natural resources, labor and capital—have not disappeared. But they have become secondary. They can be obtained, and obtained easily, provided there is knowledge. And knowledge in this new meaning is knowledge as utility, knowledge as the means to obtain social and economic results." (Neef, 1998 p.30) He then continues "What we now mean by knowledge is information effective in action, information focused in results."

Information was supposed to reveal existing models of how things work, allowing for the best choice of actions. But it was more and more difficult to get such information because the data was too noisy and situations were too messy, not allowing for clear-cut modeling and it got worse and worse until environments started exposing strong CUI-features. However, when everything constantly changes, what is the use of old information? The less stable the discovered patterns are, the less valuable past information is until it becomes dangerously inadequate. Using such past information in rapidly changing situations is like driving the car on a mountain road by the rear mirror view.

On the other hand, current information is intensively used in "managing by the wire." It is a different kind of information from that which we use as inputs in classical decision-making systems. It is being counted not in bits, as messages to be processed in organizational models, but is considered to be a general sensitivity to the environment, automatically triggering an internal response. It becomes Vision.

Driving by the Windshield View

E-businesses are designed differently from traditional enterprises that are based on dedicated support of strategic stability. They do not use as much of old statistics to feed into old models but rather respond dynamically to new and future transactions, intelligently submitting themselves to environmental evolution. The new approach redirects organizations from the search for the most efficient way of maintaining control to the most efficient way of **losing control** with increased sensitivity or *organizational vision*.

This is the most important change in inverted organizations because it determines the foundation of communications and group decision-making/vision development based on commonly accepted vision and the methods of its development and integration. An unparalleled sensitivity of human individual and group body/ mind as a carrier, detector, and evolver of sensed patterns of situational dynamics already plays, and will play, an increasingly important role being properly included into the fast-paced organizational technology. At later stages, we will definitely see technology allowing externalization of these important human abilities and perceived patterns as well as providing additional support for their group processing and harmonization.

Managed Evolution

The dramatic coming change in decision-making orientation is based on the switch in management culture from thinking of what to influence **to the search of what to be influenced by** . . . We can say that this is also a change from management by control to management by submission and control elimination, from building and supporting stability to its destruction standing in the way of sensitivity.

The Evolution model applied to market dynamics is based on the idea that there is a process of trial and error leading to the survival of the fittest. The necessary speed of adaptability is already growing far beyond the capabilities of the Darwinian model. We cannot wait for generations to pass. Whatever didn't fit in the previous generation can be important in the next one and vise-versa. Fitness has to be obtained here and now. The new requirements include:

- Development based on continuous and always current vision sensitivity rather than on choices of the statistically most stable results of the past;
- Moving from attempts to survive as a living proof of the correctness of chosen business model to attempts of continuous change/evolving as a proof of ability to change models.

Managed Evolution can be described as a shift from evolution based on the decisions and choice with the following Darwinian selection of the best moves to managed favorable conditions of continuous coevolution with the dynamic patterns of environmental situations.

Catastrophe of Organizational Goal/Value

Trends T5 and T6 in the previous chapter show the increasing value of relationship harmonization based on increased sensitivity. Such sensitivity penetrates the organizational body, stimulating changes in all elements and processes that are in the way. Existing values of architecture and process stability and existence of control over vital processes will give way to the value of sensitivity and the resulting harmony. Instead of using technology for increased control, organizations will try to build means of enhanced connectivity and sensitivity to be ingrained into the structure and main organizational processes. Internal harmony and harmony with the environment substitutes for the value of gaining and maintaining control. This leads to changing short-term and long-term goals as directed to higher effectiveness in delivering stated values.

According to Metcalfe's Law the value of the networked system grows in proportion to the square of the additional number of its nodes. For example, in the case of fax machines, the value of one machine is zero since there is nobody to send faxes to. The more people who have fax machines, the higher the value of the machine. Of course, this is an experimental law, and a certain decrease in value growth might occur, but the general dynamics of it holds surprisingly well. But there is an important continuation of connectivity growth. After a certain level, sensitivity of the system is growing too, creating strange additional effects of growing instability and a variety of potential states of the system that start changing with the smallest impacts of localities transferred and multiplied across the whole system. Such a relationship of connectivity value with the scale of connectivity becomes an example of quantity-quality transition when the extra value of communications becomes a **different quality** of such a value.

It is important to note that there is no middle ground here. If sensitivity reaches sufficient levels, it triggers the processes of self-organization and self-adaptability. It means a fight against all existing controls and stabilities that are in the way of harmonization. However, if sensitivity does not reach the necessary levels but control is disbanded, then it might lead to chaos and self-destruction. This is the result of the attempts of many organizations to jump to the future through an e-business springboard, which only leads to bankruptcies or rolling back to old, more stable methods of operations. Inability to develop sufficient sensitivity and responsiveness in all internal operations to external changes leads to the large wave of crashes of such business and to the need for reassessment of what it really takes to be an e-organization.

Values of stability and control are being shifted to values of sensitivity and harmony. The catastrophic aspect here is in the change to the opposite strategy: from creating stability to fighting it (by enhancing sensitivity and connectivity), from creating and supporting control to fighting it in favor of mutual harmony.

E-Economy and E-Market Catastrophes

Traditional economies deal with the distribution of resources for effective growth of traditional goods and service exchanges for various payment instruments. The old economy was concentrating on such well-shaped carriers of value as products. This is why "productivity" was considered a value-creating ability. Such a type of value, easily accountable and transferable, could be measured by the amount of financial compensation given in exchange for it, or labor and other costs, or a chunk of obtained utility. Such monies could be further exchanged for other necessary goods of personal and organizational consumption. This consumption usually took a form of ownership and utility of these well-shaped products. The more products or capital you had, the more powerful in terms of value ownership and potential of its creation you had. Ownership and control were the natural strategies in such economies.

On the other hand, we know about a different type of

value, which is not well-shaped and usually is also non-transferable. This includes the health of the human body, smartness and orientation, market positioning, reputation and so on. There are systems (like the so-called connectionist systems) that are viable only because of the proper distribution of internal and external connections and their sensitivity that does not and cannot use well-shaped objects like "prepackaged" value products (inputs/outputs) for their benefit. For such systems, mechanisms of proper distribution of connectivity and sensitivity is the only value and need. It is the juice of their life and . . . its flesh.

The higher connectivity and sensitivity is introduced to organizational and market development the more they resemble the described systems. The more important are becoming such features like the number of customers, web site hits (as a measure of connectivity to customers), effective collaboration with other organizations and internal process integration and mutual sensitivity. Such entities are stepping into situations with the new type of rules that we can describe as e-economies.

Ownership and control cannot be the strategic interests anymore because of the non-transferable character of the new "assets." More and more, *mutual harmony*, alignment with environment, adequacy and harmonic coevolution are becoming the behavioral goals of such entities. This shift in our view constitutes the catastrophe of economics as an adequate vision and measure of ongoing developments. E-economies have yet to be shaped and pick up strength, but their influence is seen in Wall Street shifts in company valuations, in corporate strategies of dot-coms, in evolution of payment methods and collaborative approaches as adjustments to new values.

Catastrophe of Market Form

The traditional market economy consists of two

components: stability (architecture, actors) and sensitivity (signaling). Architectural stability is supported by value chains that stabilize and protect relations among market entities (objects). The value chain was designed as a restricted channel of product/service and information transfer clearly separated from the environment by security measures, planned content of flows, fixed source/destination structures, and some other means. Sensitivity to the world outside of value chains was obtained through largely predetermined signals captured by connected economic entities with periodic channel readjustment. Such signals are mainly delivering supply-demand information and information about the periodical emergence of new market entrants, products and services delivered by intermediaries. Fixed entities/channels and more fluid intermediaries and directly gathered signals determine the proportion between market stability and sensitivity. This is shift from markets of objects to markets of relationships.

Trends described in the previous chapter lead to new requirements and pressures on the market organization, driving them away from existing object-orientation as fixation on stable and well defined entities, content of economic and information exchange, value channel architecture. With the deterioration of organizational boundaries by dynamic integration with customers and other organizations, the difference between organizations and other economic actors and markets is disappearing. Organizations-hubs and specialized organizations-mini markets are spreading around. The market is becoming more of a mechanism used on all levels and in all localities and less of a particular entity. The content of economic and information exchange is also changing to a more diverse and more dynamic and flexible form, becoming more of a relationship or means of joint coevolution/harmonization. Value chains become less often structured and protected channels and more often opened gates to whatever good can come from the outside and increase the value. Multiple outsiders and even customers should be able to penetrate and reshape value chains via opened channels-gates.

Such evolutionary changes lead to the revolution of market form, transforming largely controlled and structured market architectures to opened clusters of internal and external sensitivity with much higher dynamics of exchange-reconfiguration and potential effectiveness and efficiency. The need to distinguish between organizations and markets is becoming more of a multilevel pattern design and recognition when bigger market clusters contain several organizational sub clusters of mutual connectivity and sensitivity. Market influence on organizations as whole entities is spread across all organizational functions and internal areas, temporarily merging them into clusters whose parts can belong to several organizations. We see a change from the market being a form of organizational connectivity to organizations becoming a form of market connectivity, processes of which penetrate e-businesses all across the board.

The organizational role as a container-prison trying to maintain and repair its walls will change to one promoting the destruction of the walls, allowing for better direct collaboration between internal parts across the borders of corporate identities. The change in the level of stability of produced market forms shifts from markets of organizations as well-defined and rather stable participants to easily evolving/dissipating multilevel clusters of collaboration across corporate boundaries.

Markets offering a balancing game to players-organizations are giving way to specific patterns of collaboration/mutual sensitivity, harmonizing their relations in small clusters of particular relationships ("small" here doesn't mean geographically small but rather indicates narrow specificity). Direct pure price competition is becoming suicidal . . . and more a piece of a passing era. There are always specific needs for specific value patterns or patterns of satisfaction that are becoming the focus of economic activities.

On the other hand, global clusters are becoming increasingly non-transactional, looking more like mini-cultures or mini-societies. Such global clusters include a number of interwoven subpatterns of particular contexts of relationships. Here, the discontinuity is in the switch from the choice of either one (specialization or generalization) of the options of development to both: specialization and generalization at the same time but in different and mutually-connected contexts. This is a move from structured hierarchies of specialized markets to e-societies with roles, relationships, influences, trust, and other broad sensitivity problems combined with all kinds of smaller clusters-contexts of the relationships populating such e-societies.

Catastrophe of Market Method

The change in market form creates a new understanding of market evolution moving away from the vision of emerging, surviving and dying organizations, increasing market fitness to fluid clusters of sensitivity with constantly **changing features**. Again, we see a shift from Darwinian adaptability of survival of the object-oriented well defined fittest to the continuous evolution of the features and behavior of the market as one organism. This, of course, does not prevent old-type organizations from dying out fast . . . Dynamics of traditional organizational development cannot match time requirements for reorganization. Dynamic enterprise and interorganizational forms (like the "liquid metal" body in film *Terminator*) should rather emerge under the simple pressure of environment then be "planned" and "implemented."

Market processes have started changing from creative selection to selection of creativity (and its support). We can formulate this change as selection by evolution replacing evolution by selection. It means that winning forms are not selected for further breeding but their immediate evolution selects them as winners.

The traditional mechanism supporting market balancing and harmonization effectiveness was in sensitivity as information symmetrization when information about mostly supply-demand and price imbalances was delivered by intermediaries or captured directly from sources. Future development shifts toward redistribution of sensitivity itself versus information delivered by stable channels. Market behavior is changing from being based on organizations attempting to penetrate the market to the market attempting to penetrate organizations. This shift feeds the Internet Economy and investment in all types of networking technologies. A long economic boom in the 90's was a result of the huge new demand in means of connectivity and sensitivity versus information as a product. It was a period of the market reshaping itself into a butterfly from a caterpillar, and is not finished yet, and we can expect another long period of economic growth in the direction of building efficient sensitivity clusters and economics of harmonization of such sensitivity.

The days of the trivial price signaling controlling the volume of the production and distribution are coming to an end. Market of the future has to be able to assist in creative reshaping of the product/service patterns matching the structure and dynamics of the current patterns of demand. This can be achieved with market effectiveness measured by the optimality of the distribution and of connectivity and sensitivity as well as the dynamics of satisfaction in their level and presence in the right place at the right time. Compare to the distribution of products and services (treated as products) . . .

Catastrophe of Market Goal/Value

Understanding the value of markets and their importance in a pragmatic way as they are seen by the government, which supposedly wants to enhance this value for the nation's sake, have to have a catastrophic change which will also require a big change in thinking and in governmental regulatory and support functions. This is an interesting byproduct of the new and old economy coexistence, when switch from control to harmonization in the new economy will require changes in remaining global control functions and goals that have to support both economies with different values and goals at the same time. This problem has been reflected in the arguments of both sides in the Microsoft case.

The possibility of engineering markets on organizational and macro levels using means of modern technology allowing for changing the distribution of connectivity and sensitivity across the market and organizations leads to redefinition of the value of the market and market improvement goals. The market value catastrophe can be seen in the change from effectiveness in stimulating competitiveness to effectiveness as stimulation of creative cooperation. Such a change becomes a basis for a number of various aspects of value and goal discontinuity.

We are moving away from balancing supply-demand to dynamic and content-rich harmonization of relationships. These relationships, instead of allowing the fittest to survive, are directed toward collaboration in the design of the mutual harmony of relationships based on the coevolution of all clusters of sensitivity the economic entities participate in.

This is similar to the goal of the whole organism, of achieving a long-term internal and external harmony—not at the expense of new organ growth and old organs dying out (which can be only an interpretation on long-time intervals), but in collective harmonization of functionality of all systems and changes in mutual sensitivity and responsiveness of parts, patterns and processes.

The revolutionary transformation of market goals dictates reorientation of the market as a tool rewarding and supporting the fittest in their deadly fight for control of the market as a means of collaboration and coevolution heading toward the search of mutual harmony of relationships across all aspects of life functionality. The goal of good market work switches from determining the winner as survived stability to creating the winner as a dynamic pattern changing as needed. This refers to winners as specific patterns of organizational cooperation and product/service design results as instant patterns of satisfaction.

Market intelligence should change from its learning abilities of how to distinguish the losers to learning abilities of how to create the necessary harmony in all its complexity and lifetime. It means that it has to switch from price/volume "solutions" for winning producers, consumers or products to an ability to create the proper patterns of their combination, including value pattern, pattern of consumption, pattern of production/cooperation, and pattern of delivery as a dynamic relationship pattern of all these aspects.

These changes are accompanied by the catastrophe of market value for organizations. Instead of rewarding winners with extra stability and reinforcement, the shift is to their fast deconstruction and loss of identity. The better the food is, the better its digestion. The dissipation of organizational boundaries is the symptom of its usefulness for the others that merge with it, attaching to its harmony and participating in it. Instead of evolution through generations, where the previous one clears the way to the next one, it becomes an evolution in the same generation. There is no time for new entities to grow—everything will be different then.

National "market and economy regulatory structures" have to understand such a catastrophe and seek actions rewarding creative complexity versus pitching players against each other in the search for the most antagonistic relationships. As a result, the pressure of deconstructing complex products/services into components (based on assumption that it is easier to compete against parts) should be substituted by the stimulation of competition against complexes by producing comparable complex value patterns. This shows a change from mass-competition in efficiency of production of simple products/services to competition in effectiveness of matching the complex value patterns (needs), which is the monopolistic packaging of bundled and mutually connected features in each offering. This will be a competition between giants capable of such integration and offering various types of complex value satisfaction (almost like choice of life styles). Whether such giants will be sole entities or clusters of relationships is a different matter. Ultimately, the market as we knew it, the market as a zero-sum game, will change to creative labs of mutual sensitivity (that can hardly be called markets).

The biggest problem of catastrophe lies in the coexistence of two economies where the old one will be hurt by such an approach. The decision should be balanced against the staged plan of switching the national economy to more progressive forms meanwhile using discretion and separate approaches to entities operating in the old and new economies. Hurting new economy in favor of good global numbers is hurting the future.

Summary

The evolutionary trends discussed in the previous chapter lead to coming revolutionary changes leaving a choice for modern organizations: to undergo a series of rapid and dramatic changes (but every time as half-measures attempting to change as little as possible) or transform to the new stage of this revolutionary process at once. The table below summarizes the radical changes discussed in this chapter.

Table. 2 The revolutionary changes in E-Business

Entity	Method	Form	Value
Organizations	C1. Driving by the windshield view instead of driving by the rare mirror C2. From management by control to management by submission C3. From building and supporting stability to fighting it	C4. Inverted organizations	C5. From value of stability to value of sensitivity C6. Connectivity is valued not as a service but as a resource C7: From value of control to value of harmony
Markets	C8. From organizations penetrating market to market penetrating organizations C9. From shaping organizational boundaries to blurring the differences between market and organizational processes C10. From Darwinian "win or die"—to mutual readjustment and harmony in the current generation C11. From market shaped by competition to market shaped by cooperation	C12. From markets of well-defined actors and entities to dynamic clusters of mutual sensitivity/relationships of various organizational contexts across organizational boundaries C13. From market being a form of organizational connectivity to organizations becoming a form of market connectivity. C14. Instead of growing antagonism between organizations and markets—disappearance of the differences into the same all-penetrating transformations of connectivity and sensitivity	C15. From markets supporting effective competitiveness to stimulation of effective collaboration C16. From rewarding the winners with extra independence from environment and stability - to their faster absorption into environment C17. From determining the winner (or the "real" value of the product/ service) to their creation C18. From competition in efficiency of mass-production to competition in effectiveness of unique complexes and systems matching the complexity of value pattern needs

The catastrophe section shows that, although certain features are evolutionary, further growth of the main variables of the change trend leads to certain catastrophes not allowing for a smooth transition. This situation creates growing difficulty in using the old vision for the new processes. **The existence of discontinuities signals an inadequacy of current ways of seeing the current situation**, of orientation in it, of planning the future.

The catastrophic character of organizational and market dynamics is based on the catastrophic nature of changes stimulated by growing sensitivity. There are only two viable options: either to go back to stability and control or move forward to higher sensitivity and self-organization. Nothing can survive in-between, no gradual improvement will work. The evolutionary approach has much shorter time and resource availability than it might seem. The economic downturn that started in Y2K was not a regular business cycle but a purgation for all those "in-between." Further economic growth requires continuous business improvement. At some point, organizations have to realize that the time for the jump into a different type of economic game has come.

Regardless of the choice (revolutionary switch now or continuation of the evolutionary process), which is based on available resources and needs in sustained viability, understanding of the direction and final forms of these processes is crucial. Such understanding should be based on the new **vision** allowing one to see the real processes and real actors, often invisible to traditional ways of focusing only on stable object-oriented values forms and methods.

The existence of gradual measures of success or directions of improvement is a very important requirement for successful orientation and adaptability. "Graduality" means the existence of meaningful vision. In the Theory of Catastrophes it is shown that there could be found variables allowing one to see catastrophic change or discontinuity as a continuous path using an additional dimension with the possibility of quality/value evaluation at every step. Such a process is called "catastrophe unfolding" and the possibility to do that in modern socio-economic environments makes the difference between meaningful and meaningless focus, effort mobilization, and resource allocation. The trend chapter shows the existence of such variables/features of change whose gradual growth determines the continuous path toward adequacy and including:

- Growing connectivity;
- Growing mutual sensitivity;
- The growing dynamic and fuzzy character of participating entities and processes turning into clusters of evolving/dissipating relationships;
- The growing importance of harmony of relationships as a value more and more substituting values of local "utility" and/or stability.

The ability to create a new clear vision as a process of orientation and action based on continuous measurements like the ones above determines the type of vision of the driver (DWI or sober) who relies more on driving by the windshield view than automated navigation by the rear mirror picture.

Part 2

VISION

Chapter 1

VISION REQUIREMENTS AND TRENDS

"Organizational vision is influential only to the extent that it connects with the personal visions of people throughout the organization. Building shared vision must be seen as a central element of the daily work of leaders. It is ongoing and never-ending." (Peter Senge)

E-business as a Sensitive System

What is this E-business?

The decimation of dot coms at the beginning of the new Millennium ended the naïve belief in the sole power of an Internet capable of creating business super players from basements and garages. Although some companies managed to collect funds and survive after all, many didn't. If the Internet is so good, why such different results? Maybe the trick is not in the Internet but in something else, which was missed in the tide of technology glorification. The approach of following successful, so-called, business models didn't work. They turned out to contain just surface features and fads where the majority failed even with the same models. Is there a fundamental knowledge allowing one to seriously increase chances of success of technology-based businesses? Is it possible to tell which e-business will be more viable? Is it possible to know when large-scale investment in technology will generate benefits justifying expenses and risk? In order to answer these questions we have to return back to the origin of the factors of e-business evolution.

Connectivity as Pain and Cure

Increasing connectivity among all entities and processes and, as a result, escalating their growing mutual sensitivity, creates a problem for planning and business development in general. How does the organization integrate various design solutions under complexity, uncertainty and instability (CUI) of external and internal environments? Any business design requires coordination of its components aligned around some architectural core. But any core traditionally based on asset, service/product structures, or areas of internal functionality is now constantly changing. Reengineering as organizational remodeling is meeting increasing resistance and is accompanied with the high rate of failure. Anything we fix and try to keep stable, as the best solution for the current situation, will be broken soon by the tide of new changes, defying the pain and expense of sweeping transformations.

But, as often happens, the solution was delivered by the problem itself. Growing connectivity has led to increasing communications among all parts of the system (including communications with customers, business partners, ASP support). Flexibility of well-supported communications compensates for the frozen stability of organizational structures, converting them to patterns of learning, knowledge management, and group decision-making (customers are usually included in such groups). More and more past information, which was residing in databases, is becoming the constantly flowing communication signals changing on the fly with changes in the situation at their origin.

In electronic businesses, these changes are built into the process itself as a varying volume, type, structure and behavior of constantly reconnecting the network of users, demands and business interactions. With their increasing importance in business adaptability, communications as a form of mutual sensitivity are becoming the foundation of organizational survival. It means that at the architectural core, around which business evolving is organized, we see communications and increased mutual sensitivity in a distributed process management context.

The effect of the high internal and external sensitivity of e-businesses can be seen in a much bigger and active role of buyers-users, which, as in the domino effect, penetrates the whole organization knocking down all the walls and barricades between entities and processes built in previous attempts to structure and stabilize system architecture and behavior. This gave a rise to such methods as customer relationship management or CRM (with an emphasis on "relationship"), enterprise application integration (EAI) and process management models dealing with the necessity to account for new connections and interrelationships. Growing influence of evolving and dissipating patterns of mutual sensitivity compared to predesigned architectures determine increasing interest in other types of systems with high levels of sensitivity (we will call them *sensitive systems* or SS and discuss in more detail later) like the ones seen in biology, ecology, sociology, politics, human body/mind and cognition processes.

Sensitive Systems and Vision

Sensitive systems differ from stable systems not only in

"shades of the color" but in major aspects of method, organization, and the intentionality of their very existence. The evolution of e-businesses as sensitive systems caused all those catastrophic changes discussed in the previous part.

The traditional efforts of system management were directed toward the supporting of systems viability and stability. These efforts were focused on the use of all kinds of stabilities around which they were built. We call it architecture, strategy, form, assets, models of control, etc. They are intended to "withstand environmental impacts," "filter the noise," "keep the form," "reuse the assets" and "stand the course." Orientation toward, search for and the cult of stabilities embedded in multiple models designed to control the overall system stability or stability of certain entities and processes resulted in the specific type of engineering discipline focusing on methods and tools designed to deliver stability as one of the major values.

SS uses sensitivity as the main method, form, and tool seeking the value in sensitivity preservation and enhancement. The big part of what was treated as "noise" is considered to be valuable inflows leading to the enhancement of internal adequacy, used to nurture proper internal patterns and weed out the inappropriate ones. The approach to sensitivity as the main value and its predominant use in designed systems supports a different type of engineering which we will call *holistic engineering* (HE).

Although sensitivity is always accounted for somehow, HE treats it differently, as a rich connection to the environment which collects information via external sensitivity and processes it via internal sensitivity. We will call such use of sensitivity as *system vision* (or just *vision*), emphasizing the major organizing role of sensitivity supporting systems' orientation and evolution in dynamic environments as a continuous non-interrupted holistic process.

Importance of Vision in Sensitive Systems

Vision was long considered in organizational and systems development as an important source and type of information, one which plays a special role in organizing, integrating and often transforming ways of adaptability, forms of dynamics and the direction of evolution. Ability to change types and forms of vision allows some SS to improve their adequacy in fast changing environments. A switch in Soviet companies from the vision of environment as a given 5-year plan detailed for annual production and accompanying reward of the controlling organization if the plan is met to the idea that there exist customers that want different things at different times, and only matching these wants in quality, quantity and price will allow for company existence, has significantly changed the structure and behavior of such organizations.

The importance of vision in sensitive systems stems from the necessity in growing orientation (remember the "driving by the windshield view") of all comprising entities as well as intensive communications between them. Communications between SS play a much bigger role than in stable systems. The behavior and evolution of SS is based on distributed communications and the ability to act on a constantly evolving meaning of the whole situation as a result of such communications exchanging with locally-made sense. The effectiveness of such holistic meaning-based dynamics of development and relationships with environment is the criteria of the properly organized communication and meaning evolving processes of vision.

The use of vision gives meaning and direction to smaller projects within the framework of orientation in a fast-paced turbulent environment. Being used to its fullest extent, vision encompasses functions of "thinking" allowing substitution of an old question about how people and organizations think with the question of **how they should think** . . . considering a number of possible types of vision and ways of their implementation.

Scientific Method as a Universal Communication System/Vision

The importance of vision in communications, meaning-making and resulting behavior especially grows for sensitive systems where communications is the mode of existence. In order to effectively communicate meaning among different SS, there is a need for some **common language**, communication system, or **vision** allowing for interpretation of all local specificity of the perception and sense-making onto a carrier capable to deliver the information to the recipient for adequate interpretation.

The incredible growth of scientific, technological and industrial development during the last three centuries was catalyzed by the development of the universal communication and meaning processing and integration system called the *scientific method*. The accompanying it *vision* is focused on the search for stabilities, based on beliefs that causal inferences on such stabilities sufficiently closely describe the real events, and looking for control in vision application based on the known logic of events, will be called Object-Oriented/Control basetl (OO/C) vision.

The main meaning-making concern of OO/C vision was in the possibility of synthesis of local meanings in a form of a discussion where the "right side" would be able to persuade the Gods. Logic seemed to be able to play such a role if the entities it operates with have certain properties allowing for logic application. Such properties include well-defined entities, causality and other features that we will analyze later in this part of the book. The whole complex of rules determining properties of entities and operations on them mapped onto a communication system allowed for a clear and universal method of understanding each other, obtaining local results and integrating them in some logic-based process. These features made OO/C vision a *Universal Communication and Meaning-Making System* allowing for effective communication of various entities, local analysis and global synthesis of orientation in complex situations. The rapid growth of multiple theories and their application in engineering and other applied sciences was a direct result of the possibility to effectively connect small local contributions in understanding to the global body of knowledge. Knowledge management as production, integration, and distribution of "knowledge objects" was the latest logical development in OO/C.

The problem emerged with the growth of connectivity and sensitivity leading to CUI-properties of environment that cannot be easily and uniformly mapped onto OO/C vision. In order to be able to make local sense and meaning, various disciplines dealing with SS had to deviate from the requirements of the existing Universal Communication System in favor of the effectiveness of local communications. This in turn led to further differences between local and global communication needs and finally led to the public outburst against the tyranny of OO/C vision in postmodern rebellion. In fact, meaning-making communications in various SS and Cartesian prescriptions started developing in almost opposite directions which contributed to what we call a the catastrophe of the old Universal Communication System.

EB Phenomenon as a Result of Vision Catastrophe

The series of coming catastrophes described before demonstrates, in fact, the main underlying phenomenon— the **catastrophe of OO/C vision** in the context of sensitive systems (SS). Modern evolutionary attempts to cope with dynamic reality have led to a growing role for connectivity and sensitivity leading to CUI environments. Proliferation of networking as the major IT expense suddenly exploded into e-business openness to Internet influences where the magnitude of external sensitivity suddenly greatly exceeded all previous levels. All the trends in electronic business discussed in the previous part of the book are, in fact, the grass-root developments of the new form of organizational existence as a sensitive system with a new type of vision allowing for effective orientation in the CUI environment and sharply increased mutual sensitivity of all components of such organizations.

Showing increasingly dominating features of sensitive systems, e-business systems and processes require a new type of engineering explicitly accounting for a holistic all-penetrating role of sensitivity in relationships. Definitive planning of the organizational mechanism and its control-flow logic do not stand a chance in the fast-paced and demanding situations. No matter how small the pieces of logic and objects of sense are in the puzzle of organizational design, no matter how easy it might seem to redesign such a grand plan—the dynamics of reality and the distributed character of modern organizational experience make such an approach not viable.

A dramatic change of vision came with Web services. The idea lay in enhancing the opposite features of organizational components: instead of determining the state space and control flow of elementary interactions, the components were set free to seek "employment" of their usefulness, offering it as universally acceptable Web services. You may ask where the need of their use will arise and why, if no grand control schema is determined. It might come from the outside of the system, from the users, and from neighbors as well as a part of the meaning-creation process which dynamically determines the pattern of necessary communications into a temporarily created function or form. Actually, the system or organization stops existing as a protected mechanism but is deconstructed into the market of services similarly available for internal or external users.

The increased sensitivity of components exposed as services waiting for calls continues the revolution of e-business vision against the tyranny of planned stability and control. Is it enough, and no real management is necessary, or will such openness destroy the last chances for orderly and meaningful functionality? This will depend not as much on Web services and many other technologies increasing system sensitivity but on the features of sensitive system survival defense substituting OO/C methods.

Vision Catastrophe Proliferation

History of Vision Evolution

The traditional modernist vision evolved as a result of multi-century training in symbolic vision, rationality and decision-making during the Enlightenment, which "coincidently" overlapped with the Age of Absolutism, sharply decreasing the CUI-properties of environment. Empiricism and mechanicism became a dominating foundation of vision, spreading from engineering and abstract science to the whole Universe, including all social and organizational systems. The natural science of Isaac Newton, social, political, psychological theories of Hobbes and Locke, and the scientific method of cognition laid out by Pascal and, especially, Descartes largely determined the specifics of the modern vision.

The main components of this vision include the following "commandments":

- See the world as fundamentally rational and open to proper empirical observation and experience processed by skeptical (no authority) reasoning as a tool of arriving at the meaning and truth;
- Social, psychological and organizational processes should be seen as mechanistic and controllable;

- Since engineering is the process of improvement, history has to be seen as constant progress;

Modernism of the twentieth century, often seen as the finalization of the logocentrism and rationality of Enlightenment, and based on the success of the technological and scientific revolution, became the last stage of the attempts of the described type of vision to expand to all areas of our lives. We saw the growing influence of structuralist methods in literary criticism claiming the structure of metalanguage as the ultimate form of meaning. Cubism, pointillism, and general analytic abstractionism attempted to break down the holistic experience of reality into structured subcomponents. We saw the domination of economic theories (vision) of mass production, valuation of mainly tangible assets, and beliefs in demand/supply equilibrium.

But despite of its natural tendency to proliferate to all areas of human orientation and experience, such vision was bound for growing difficulties and real problems later. As we saw in the discussion of electronic business, growing connectivity and sensitivity of multiple simple and seemingly mechanistic components suddenly has led to a strange effect of complexity and self-organization within and around growing sensitive systems. The whole became more than the sum of its parts and this "more" started seriously upsetting the results of rational reasoning as an inferential method of arrival at the meaning of the situation.

Such upsetting obtained the catastrophical proportions discussed in the previous part and, in fact, can be seen as the catastrophe of the Cartesian system of vision as a methodical foundation of orientation and cognition for SS. This catastrophe was perceived and reflected in the long fight against rationalism and determinism by modernism by postmodern thought/vision.

Postmodernism arrived in the twentieth century as a challenge to the logical, symbolic, and certain vision of modernism. The most dramatic fight has been put up in the poststructuralist philosophy and analytical practices. Deconstruction as one of the core components of this movement continues phenomenological inquiry mixed with hermeneutical problems into the field of signifier as a component of modern systems analysis and design. In this sense, signifier is a smallest piece of sense, combinations of which create whole meaning. The battle occurs in the moment of justification of sense and meaning as connection between the "real world" and the "text world".

The similarity of waterfall and later object-oriented methodology of systems analysis and design with structuralist and positivist platforms as well as with the first wave of cognitive science as application of symbolic methods to data input, processing and subsequent behavior is not incidental. Objectivist claims of modeling reality and deriving knowledge of the future situations from various types of "reasoning" or inferential processing of conceptual stabilities clash with interpretational problems as well as with problems of complexity, uncertainty and instability of the "real world." This dynamics of signifieds, their fuzziness and continuous evolution into different forms, creates a problem for adequacy and synchrony between rich dynamics of signified and system models of signifier. If we do not know the origins of this evolution and cannot clearly and logically describe them, then isolated abstract system of signs cannot demonstrate adequate and synchronous behavior.

There are multiple observations of the profound impact of the postmodern vision on the method, purpose, structure and behavior of designed systems, human organizations and cultural phenomena grown in the modern vision environment . . . Such influence of vision deserves special analysis and considerations in the context of business, organizational development and the engineering of sensitive systems.

Vision in Organizations

The conflict of vision and subsequent behavior based on the value of stability versus sensitivity could be also seen in organizational development. Managerial economics, financial management or engineering economics mainly deal with problem-solving. A management problem solution usually has two parts: finding the best course of actions (project) and implementing it. Implementation means design and initiation of certain structures and processes that will be able to hold the solution workable for the planned interval of time.

Concentrating more on the result of such actions rather than on decision-making process, we can generalize managerial problem-solving as a fight against unforeseen changes in attempts to control and stabilize the system. The more sensitive the system is, the more control we tend to implement to decrease such sensitivity or keep it under control. Policies, procedures, norms, regulations, organizational hierarchies and automation of routine processes are examples of some such tools of organizational control.

Stability achieved somewhere in the controlled system might be lost if the scope or amplitude of changes due to existing sensitivity exceeds the level of tolerance of some of the system components. Then new "fixes" are necessary to maintain the stability of the desirable state. The more changes are accounted for, the better is the solution. But how to account for the unknown? It can be done only through sufficient **current sensitivity** to the environment because the past knowledge is rapidly becoming obsolete. At this point, old stability and object-oriented vision starts conflicting with the necessity of seeking and value sensitivity as the only savior. This also means changes in orientation and behavior and calls for . . . fighting stability.

Such conflicting needs could be seen as two possible strategies competing with each other :

a) fixing or stabilizing the business process through *rigid structural components* or *standard operating procedures* (*SOPs*) in order to fight excessive sensitivity and the solution's increasing sensitivity in order to get better vision of the situation;

b) maintaining sufficient sensitivity to perceive changes and easily adapt to them.

Can we find the win-win point of equilibrium with enough control and sufficient sensitivity and hold it right there? Experience shows that the coexistence of both requirements does not have a stable solution. It seems that once variability of changes decreases, stabilization and control tend to take over, growing as much as possible, overstepping the point of desirable equilibrium. But once current sensitivity is lost, the amount of change grows with time to the level where in explosive manner it breaks all created walls and chains of stabilization.

Mike Davidson, analyzing the rise and fall of industry giants such International Harvester, American Can, Continental Group, RCA, Sperry, LTV and others, discovered strange cycles of their fitting into the environment from energetic beginning, developing a Winning Paradigm, Market Dominance and Control, and sliding into overcontrol and "perversion of the Winning Paradigm," loss of sensitivity, inability to create an adequate response, and demise.

This fight of control and stability with sensitivity is not only a general strategic approach, but it exists on all levels and in all parts of the system where problem-solving takes place. Thus *stability* versus *sensitivity* orientation could be seen as a key management choice.

The use of vision strongly affects the outcome of such a choice. Traditional stability/control domination is generally embedded in all aspects of vision implementation within most organizations, leading to major problems in CUI environments. The development and implementation of the organizational vision allowing for smooth balancing of stability and sensitivity benefits depending upon the current situation will offer the major competitive advantage of consistent adequacy.

Vision in Communications

Rhetoric

In our understanding of the importance of context sensitivity we find modern inference methods incapable of handling ill-defined context patterns and dynamic influence on the main models stemming out of the context. It is very difficult to build a context model without loss of valuable components and often is impossible. Usually the context of an analyzed entity is a much more complicated dynamic system than entity itself. Its complex, uncertain and very often chaotic behavior requires special evaluation techniques, like methods of dynamical complex systems analysis, perception and recognition methods based on the harmonization of internally-stored patterns with information collected from context/environment, and some others.

Such methods do not comply with pure inferential techniques and allow for fuzzy objects and classification, multimodal logic and probabilistic reasoning without "true" and "false" as the only options of statement assessment. Such methods have the group name *rhetoric* as a science and art of reasoning under the situation of extreme complexity, uncertainty and ill-defined context influence.

As an example of some rhetoric methods, we can use value and common-belief reasoning instead of logical "self-evidence," methods of minimizing structural asymmetries in information and mental model vocabulary, vision building and, respectively, vision recognition/satisfaction methods as utilization of context sensitivity. Further development of applications of rhetoric requires multidisciplinary efforts combining achievements and common approaches in various fields of *parallel knowledge processing* (PKP). Such development is not only important for organizational dynamics, but the very success of Democracy as creative and adequate integration of multiple visions is based on the ability to conduct an open, effective and efficient public discussion in all areas of sensitivity of society and its members.

Rhetoric and Probabilistic Reasoning

In a situation of chaotic sensitivity and instability, there is no conclusive evidence, like accounting for the past weather patterns in a monthly forecast. As Schum mentions in (Schum,1994): "The evidence is incomplete on matters relevant to our conclusions, and it comes to us from sources (including our own observations) that are, for various reasons, not completely credible. Thus inference from such evidence can only be probabilistic in nature, and our conclusions have to be hedged in some way." He distinguishes problems of evidence, saying that "No evidence comes to us with already-established "credentials", regarding its *relevance, credibility,* and *inferential force.*" A mixture of the various forms of reasoning and different kinds of judgments contributes to the complexity of the Rhetoric framework.

If we would construct an inference network like an expert system explanation of how we arrive at a conclusion, we would see that during the course of mutual analysis this network fluctuates, depending upon new facts and hypotheses. So, it is a theory opened for new experience and vision influence, allowing for a mix of hypotheses and evidential validation as harmonization with other visions and experience.

Semiotics

Semiotics essentially is the study of communicative objects and thus involves signs, symbols, and various codes as well as means by which they are produced and interpreted. So far, general knowledge is based mainly on written texts, where the process of PKP as group knowledge processing and development is seen by semiotics as analysis, interpretation, evaluation, and production of texts and its meaning. Although "interpreters are not free to make meaning, but are free to find it by following the various semantic, syntactic, and pragmatic paths that lead away from the words of the text" (Scholes, 1982). Having no instant control over readers' interpretations, authors had to rely on various techniques, guiding the trained reader through the process of meaning restoration (using various metaphoric riddles, for example).

Readers, or text receivers, on the other hand, have many choices for processing text. They can receive it lazily as a vague feeling, or actively decompose and reconstruct its meaning through the use of semantic, syntactic and pragmatic coding. Thus, group discussions based on text publications have problems of over—or under-interpretation unless they are based on linear logic using well-defined objects. This explains the domination of the scientific method and the wide use of publications in information exchange. Rhetoric and interpretational technology supporting these processes just could not provide viable solutions for more fuzzy objects and dynamical patterns of sensitivity. The old techniques of conversational rhetoric did not have good means of multiperson parallel communication support.

Saussure's distinction between *language* and *parole*, language and speech was further developed by Benveniste noticing a very important difference between them. Language is systematic, speech or utterance is situational. In speech, current context and patterns, if a particular interactive communication, shape the meaning. The latest development of powerful communication tools capable of using various types of information, including multimedia, experience of virtual reality, distributed parallel access to evolving meaning in various types of collaborative groupware, allow for the expansion of semiotics to parallel distributed knowledge and meaning development.

The meaning of any text may then be thought of as a consensual correspondence between the experience, the author and the reader, and between the producer and an interpretative community. It is a result of harmonization procedure of all these dynamical patterns. Such a conclusion sheds a different light on communications procedure. It cannot be seen any more as just an instrument of meaning delivery from point "A" to point "B," but becomes the place where meaning is created. It is a dynamical system with meaning as its harmonized evolving state. If it cannot be harmonized or serious problems are encountered then we say that messages arriving from local sensitivity and intentionality make no or little sense. Considering a new role of communications, let us take a look at some trends in communication theory extending ideas of semiotics.

Communication Theory vs. Semiotics

Communication Theory is an evolving multidisciplinary area embracing developments in linguistics, philosophy, social psychology, semiotics, literary theory and whatever else matters. Combined with another evolving field—Cognitive Science—it attempts to create a foundation for the new search of Truth,

Meaning, Cognition, Cultural Viability and Evolution under growing uncertainty, complexity and instability.

Communication Theory can be seen as semiotic concentration on the abstract signification process expanded to group and cultural interpretational networks. As Marcel Danesi notes, "communication theorists generally focus more on the study of message-making as a process, whereas semioticians center their attention more on what a message means and on how it creates meaning" (Danesi, 1994).

Evolving of Meaning in Group Communication

There are principally two different theories of linguistic signs, the *representational* and the instrumentational or *communicative*. Representational theories seek the meaning of a linguistic sign in its extralinguistic referentiality. It means that signs are supposed to represent various stable concepts, objects, etc. The adequacy of such representation and its verification is the area of the main suspicions.

Instrumentational approach, going back to Plato, sees linguistic signs as tools that serve or can be used to let the addressee know what the speaker wants him to know. The meaning of the sign is in its usability in effective communications, its usability as an instrument of communications.

Although original cognitive theories and methods of AI were based on the representational approach, the use of communication technologies, multi-agent systems, and distributed artificial intelligence, in general, started paying more attention to the evolution of the meaning in the process of communications. One of the most influential works in this direction was done by studying the problem solving and the evolution of the higher meaning in group communications among children (Vygotsky, 1978).

Hermeneutical Methods

"There are universal laws of thought which are reflected in the laws of change of meaning" Jespersen proclaimed in 1925. Most modern linguists—even those of different persuasion—would accept this suggestion, since it is possible to interpret *laws of thought* in several ways. One interpretation is the following: the manner in which knowledge is acquired and processed is basically common to us all. Given this assumption as well as the assumption that people instinctively know with fair accuracy the extent to which processing is common, it follows that the kind of thinking certain knowledge will provoke in certain circumstances is partially predictable. In other words, knowing what other people are informed about, we also know how this information is likely to be processed. We make use of this insight in making words mean what they never meant before. The importance of context when accounting for how words take on new meanings is therefore evident. The meaning of a word in context will not simply be retrieved from memory, but will be the result of mental processing involving both general knowledge and, in particular, knowledge of the context.

If meaning evolves in communication, how is it possible for all participants of communication to grasp it when they have different general and context knowledge and experience? Hermeneutics offers a partial answer, referring to a group of two participants and their understanding of each other. Schleiermacher and then Wilhelm Dilthey, in their attempts to establish hermeneutics as a universal methodological basis, saw the task of understanding as "to recover the original life-world they betoken and to understand the other person (the author or historical agent) as he understood himself. Understanding is essentially a self-transposition or imaginative projection whereby the knower negates the temporal distance that separates him from his object and becomes contemporaneous with it" (Gadamer, 1977).

But what about meaning evolving among many participants, or rather a pattern of meaning which can change with every word of any of them as a reaction of others? In such a situation who is the person (or a virtual person) we should reconstruct as a model of understanding? What are the tools and methods that can help to perform "sense making"? A pattern-oriented approach could be a base for such a search, but it will definitely need a common communication carrier where such patterns of meaning could evolve. Participants should have simultaneous parallel access to such patterns contributing to their further evolution.

Dynamic Patterns in Communication Framework

Harmonization as convergence of local meaning-sense is the essence of rhetoric. The development of group experience, logic, vision and cognition is seen as a goal of constructive rhetoric. It is broader than pure inferential methods since have to include ALL forms of individual connection with phenomenal life (life-world) as well as individual methods of perception and cognition!

The potentiality for communication amongst people who are physically separated defines the concept of computer-mediated communication, or CMC (Kiesler, et al, 1974). Considering its general repercussions, CMC impacts not only the way we think about possibilities for interaction, but also the forms we compose and use, written language (as presented by Murray (Murray, 1991), and the manner we interact through it, as was shown in (Wilkins, 1991).

In (Lotman, 1988) it is postulated that, in any communication process, each text has sociocommunicative functions, which are grounded in interrelationships between the context and its participants. These sociocommunicative functions not only emphasize the roles sender (writer), receiver (reader) and text (mediator) play, but also situate these agents in a communicative event that takes place in a cultural context which possesses a cultural tradition. Patterns of meaning evolving in such cultural contexts should be harmonized first locally and then globally. Global harmonization of local meaning allows for the creation of an adequate orientational model for the whole organization, which then could be decomposed into local requirements that have to be harmonized with local meanings.

Actually, some of such evolving patterns represent a discovery—the most uncomfortable event for scientific method. Its non-symbolic evolving nature, when small pieces of local evidence coherently interpreted and harmonized on all levels of abstraction can suddenly deliver a value much bigger then was contained in original information. More than a hundred years ago, John Stuart Mill was arguing that discovery cannot be stated in terms of rules (Mill, 1865). It can just evolve in a self-organized fashion when sensitivity between necessary components of discovery reaches the level sufficient for bringing it the Edge of Chaos—the situation broadly explored in Santa Fe (Kauffman, 1995).

Such bottom-up evolving of patterns of meaning and their multilevel harmonization is nothing else but creation of an adequate orientational model of Truth in response to challenges of CUI-environments. If the described harmonization could be completed when all the processes converge to certain equilibrium, then the adequate orientational model is likely to be discovered.

Application Features of Vision

The growing problems of interpretation of local vision systems by OO/C have common features and trends. In the cases of social and economic environments, the problem is in general human sensitivity and the sensitivity of small groups and organizations to non-rational choices and ill-defined situations. In cognitive science, this is the discovery of dynamic mapping procedures between different parts of the brain based on neural and psychosomatic sensitivity to each other. In ecologies, we start seriously considering the mutual sensitivity of various life forms. In weather systems, this is the sensitivity of gas dynamics to conditions in other parts of the atmosphere, on the surface of the planet, and sun activity. Many other examples of different sensitive systems show that growing sensitivity with accompanying connectivity, regardless of the underlying carrier, can produce similar types of dynamics.

Let us take a more detailed look at general OO/C features causing application problems in sensitive environments. We will call them *application features of vision* (AFV). Some of the most important of them are:

- object-oriented definitions that are self-contained and context-free;
- knowledge as a system of well-definable knowledge objects that can be stored or delivered to others during communications;
- communications as knowledge-object transfer attempting to preserve their meanings taking place between two rational model-based systems when knowledge objects are transmitted from a well-definable sender to a well-definable receiver, and the effectiveness of communications is in preservation of the meaning of the transferred knowledge object, which becomes a part of the knowledge system of the receiver;
- analysis and synthesis methods of knowledge acquisition;
- well-observed causality;
- control as engineering method of such vision utilization;
- harmony as logical consistency;
- some others.

What are the alternatives of these features that could be used in other vision types? These alternatives can be discussed in the two major groups of application features: object-orientation and control-based intentionality.

Object-Orientation versus Pattern-Orientation

Object-orientation, during the last decade of twentieth century, became widely accepted as an embedded vision for information systems and technologies supporting communications and decision-making processes and forms. In its generalized form, it includes:

1. Object-oriented definitions and search-focusing allowing for distinguishing such objects as entities and stable relations among them that could be assigned a symbolic name;
2. Independence of object existence from each other (including world from cognition);
3. OO-reflections that are either self-explanatory or could be reduced to a set of self-explanatory components in analysis and then explain higher forms in synthesis;
4. Communications as knowledge-object transfer attempting to preserve their meanings taking place between two rational model-based systems when knowledge objects are transmitted from a well-definable sender to a well-definable receiver, and the effectiveness of communications is in preservation of the meaning of the transferred knowledge object which becomes a part of the knowledge system of the receiver;
5. Abstraction from context and reductionism as methods of searching for object-like stabilities;
6. Analysis and synthesis along the borders of object stability as a method of cognitive distribution in time and space.

Aristotelian definitions should be supplemented by other methods, allowing for the use of dynamic pattern-context systems, indefinable in a clear, complete and permanent way. The new approach should allow for the process of pattern recognition as a method of flexible identification with various probabilities and fuzzy boundaries leading to the possibility of *identity drift* and new *concept evolving*. Such a method of dynamic identification is as temporal as a pattern itself and is sensitive to various vision systems performing recognition, which supports the requirement of vision sensitivity proposed above. Eventually, the boundaries of such entities as dynamic pattern-context systems are not firm but rather *permeable* allowing for the processes of *absorption* and *expulsion*.

Focusing should be guided not by the decision and object form as an easy focus but by changes in internal sensitivity to external areas. It means that after sensitivity guides vision connectivity or focusing, the latter changes the area and sensitivity itself, which gives rise to new mutually determined searches. In such case the stability of an "object" of vision can vary to its total dissipation. Internal interpretation is not preset by selected symbolic labels but evolves according to the stability of external area of focusing.

There are two main goals of utilizing analysis/synthesis as a method of knowledge engineering:

- Allow for step wise knowledge improvement acquired piece by piece;
- Allow for parallel distributed knowledge processing integrating later all discovered local truths into a bigger picture of the Whole Truth.

Several problems started arising from such an approach with increasing needs of handling systems in CUI environments:

1. Optimal solutions and the highest clarity of partial knowledge cannot guarantee better clarity or even consistency in the knowledge of the whole. Like James Martin notices, attempts to understand how each car part is supposed to be designed and taking the best from all known car designs does not guarantee high quality of the whole car once they all will be put together.

2. Synthesis as a sum of its parts does not explain and supports such phenomena as discovery or new knowledge evolution.

3. Different ways of performing analysis (analytical systems) often provide incompatible set of "Lego parts" for synthetic engineering. What is worse, internal consistency and isolation of various analytical systems, theories, disciplines call for specific synthetic systems not allowing for natural knowledge integration across discipline borders. Such skills and methods of multidisciplinary integration are becoming an object of special studies and experiential approaches.

4. Need in handling subjective knowledge, experience, perception that cannot be simply separated from the system/person they evolve in (human experience, artificial neural networks taught specific generalization or recognition lessons, some others).

On the other hand, the communication needs of SS include features allowing bypassing the named problems of analysis/synthesis:

1. Although possibility parallel distribution of gradual understanding of the whole is important to preserve, the parts should allow for *dynamic and fuzzy patterns* as well as stable objects with included *context sensitivity* at all

times. In other words, they are never totally disconnected and preserve sensitivity to their contexts and through them to the whole and its *evolving* understanding.

2. The process of integration of partial knowledge into something that can qualify as "the Truth, the Whole Truth and nothing but the Truth" should be based not on mechanical sum of parts but on their gradual *harmonization* and *evolving* in the *distributed parallel dynamical communicative process*. It leads us to the understanding of truth more often as dynamical evolving process then a stable object or a fact with clear boundaries.

3. Such constantly-running process of truth evolving and self-confirmation should be sensitive to various ways of seeing the area of interest. Changing points, angles, systems of view should meet a fast response in the presentation of the body of knowledge—may be reminding an OLAP-type method of coordinate changing, drilling down and rolling up. It will allow for comparison of various ways of analytical vision of parts of the whole and harmonizing such visions in a rhetoric-like communicative process.

Harmony Versus Control

The purpose of vision in traditional OO/C approach was in serving the desire to obtain control or to stay in control as a method of ensuring non-hostile development of events. Control-based intentionality of vision includes the following features:

1. Knowledge of causality and internal integration (internal control) based on logical consistency of self-evident objects (entities and processes) results in the most effective way of external harmonization—control (where without control all objects are independent);

2. Control could be enhanced through the use of knowledge objects that can be accumulated, transferred and reused as control models;

3. Behavior is rational (logical), has acquirable, definable and measurable goals.

Intensively connected and mutually sensitive networks of dynamical patterns obviously create problems for cause-effect models because of their simultaneous holistic nature. In such systems there should exist methods of distributed parallel harmonization allowing for various measures of its dynamics. Such measures could differ depending upon particular harmonization mechanisms (minimum internal energy, heat, maximum entropy, as examples).

In the absence of clear cause-effect connections and objects, "Control of what?" will be the question. What will be the goal of control in such a potentially stateless environment? The new paradigm should be able to supplement the method of control effective in deterministic systems with another engineering concept allowing for some meaningful activity supporting systems' viability. Viability here is actually the most general thing we can care about without the detailed and always truthful knowledge of the mechanics of the process. It becomes more like growing a plant without controlling every process of every cell in it. The best thing to do will be to support its natural harmonization by taking gentle care of some environmental holistic features (watering, supporting the right temperature, light, soil, etc.).

Summary

The table below summarizes the main AFV of OO/C and the alternatives found in the development of local visions dealing with SS.

Table 3. Comparison of OO/C and postmodern alternatives

OO/C	Alternative
Aristotelian type of *definitions* used for analyzed parts. Sometimes they are called inclusion/exclusion definitions because at first the defined term is included in some relevant category and then we try to exclude all the other members of this category (discriminate them).	*Pattern recognition* instead of clear object-type identification, where a more flexible mechanism of handling parts of the whole could be used. Patterns are supposed to be not defined but recognized as they evolve and change. Recognition method will allow for handling all types of entities from stable objects to fuzzy patterns and stochastic behavior by varying the degree of certainty and similarity.
Analysis as a method of obtaining knowledge about whole based on its parts (objects), where such parts are fully extracted and separated from the whole through the use of definitions. Such separate parts have their own truths that are possible to grasp fully. **Reductionism attempts to obtain meaning from lower level harmony**	Instead of analysis as full disconnection of a part from the whole, to use *dynamic pattern/context systems*. Explicit accounting for a context will provide for more adequate information and understanding as well as simplifies the task of a holistic vision development. **Holism attempts to obtain meaning from higher-level harmony.**
Synthesis as a method of integration of small truths obtained from isolated parts of reality, into knowledge about the whole based on the sum of partial truths. Complexity of the world is a result of a combination of objects, their associations with each other and behavior.	Gradual *harmonization* and *evolving* of knowledge of the whole from partial and local truths in the *distributed parallel dynamical communicative process*. Instead of clear-cut distinction between structure and behavior mutual sensitivity is used allowing for their smooth trasnfromation into each other.
Interdisciplinary and intertheoretical boundaries defending internal logical consistency and inferential derivation from uncontrollable external concepts. (Gödel's theorem made a hole in this defense anyway)	*Flexible readjustment of the vision* in various vision systems of interactive cognition. It is important for an entity of our attention to be able to play different roles depending upon the change in the point of view: from stable object-like forms to becoming an association or fuzzy context
Stable identity and constant firm boundaries of objects obtained in the process of analysis and synthesis	*Permeability* of emerging pattern boundaries with respect to their environment versus closed system's methods. Identity drift is allowed.
Any statement in such world should be logically consistent with acquired small truths and be inferred out of existing body of knowledge. No transformation of knowledge where something new in principle will *emerge* is possible	*Emergence* phenomena tends to work in the direction of minimum energy, tensions, and conflicts (maximum harmony).
Cause - effect associations between objects are a norm, when for every effect there is always a cause	Distributed parallel harmonization where most of the time the cause is coevolution
Control as the main engineering method utilizing cause-effect relations between objects. If we want to change some effect (the output) we just change its cause (input). Everything can be controlled this way if we have a model of system's structure and cause - effect behavior	Harmony as a method of supporting viability. Most of the internal states are unknown but the stability and quality of holistic harmonization can be measured and improved on.

The Way Out: Universal Vision Organization

The growing pressure of SS evolution (e-business is just one of examples) is based on the need for communication effectiveness. Postmodernism greatly contributed to the proof of incompetence of the systems and even cultural developments based on modernist OO/C vision. It gave rise to the ideas of meaning relativism in various localities, multiplicity of visions, and deconstruction of structural-logic based communication structures incapable of reflecting dynamic patterns of evolving sensitivity and fuzziness of conceptual boundaries. But . . . it did not offer alternatives to the effective communication development so necessary with growing speed of communications, discussions and sense-making in the Internet environment. Benefits of having multiple visions mutually validating each other started fading in the face of requirements of *effectiveness and efficiency* of communications and integral meaning-making. Too few people, let alone systems, were able to efficiently manipulate several visions, setting them against each other. The need for the **Universal Communication System** as an intermediary between local visions emerged with renewed strength. This covers not only human and group visions but also whole organizations, automated systems, disciplines and cultures.

The introduction and broad implementation of the OO/C approach to communications and meaning creation was based on new needs of a rapidly industrialized civilization. Engineering was seen as the development of various control mechanisms carrying human will and commands. With growing complexity of control devices from mechanical to electronic, the control function had to be supplemented by knowledge as a model supporting control variability necessary to handling variability of situational states. Further enhancements required knowledge processing which was successfully supported by the Turing machine implementation in computer architectures. Shannon's theory of information and communications was a useful finishing touch to OO/C proliferation.

The use of OO/C as a universal communication and meaning-creation system was based on the idea of a language as a communication and representation tool. This comes at no surprise, since the object-orientation allows for symbolic representation of objects by some names as indexes to those objects. Objects are seen as containers of self-evident truth or knowledge. The logic as a main communication and meaning-preservation foundation can be implemented in formal or not-so-formal languages with logic implemented in the structure of sentences, paragraphs, and whole documents. The possibility of using languages allowed delegation of most of modern communications to computers that also are capable of inferential processing of the logic of object relationships. The arrival of the new area of knowledge is resulting in the new language reflecting on specifics of object and logic patterns.

The latest attempt of OO/C to retain its position as a universal communicator can be seen in the proliferation of XML technologies capable of mapping object structures as ultimate stabilities. The benefit of such a communication platform is in its universality, when all participants see the ultimately stable components as having the same level of stability. The inevitable results of such an approach were the needs in controlling the structure as centrally governed schemas and controlling the uniqueness of object names by centrally-governed namespaces.

Understanding the limitations of such communications, when all less stable features are taken out, preventing from meaning integration and evolution according to the dynamics of local situations, the non-linguistic means have been covertly injected into the Grand Plan. Such non-linguistic means represent the main area of communication possibilities and future evolution allowing for local experiences to deal with objects in locally determined way. Such local technologies are hidden in object design and communication platforms insides organizations as well as in special types of "semantic processors" like BizTalk servers outside.

Temporarily, such an approach might take the heat of the overfreezing of communication language, but in a short while it will explode in thousands of local visions, becoming even more disconnected because of their local vision application specificity that, as we showed, cannot possibly fit OO/C methods as Universal Communicator. As a result, there will remain the only possibility of fitting obvious stable objects into such Global Fields, keeping the more fluid parts as single integral fields with no clues to their interpretation.

The alternative approaches to and requests for vision application characteristics shown in the previous section are grounded in the type of vision focused on constant interactive dynamics of sensitivity and stability, based on beliefs that holistic harmonization of perceptional patterns (not objects) is the true self-unfolding process, and directed toward the search of harmony. Such type of vision will be called Pattern-Oriented/Harmony based (PO/H) vision.

If one is to look at differences in the way various types of vision handle meaning integration, it is possible to notice that the toughest area for OO/C vision lies in the processing of the rich fuzzy and dynamic flows of sensitivity known as *experience*. Emotional orientation, imaging, empathy and other phenomena of communicating ill-defined information objects and process requires changing the term "communications" which usually implies messages for the term "vision" that creates a richer metaphorical content.

The PO/H vision builds upon several major contributions to the understanding of the dualistic insufficiency of signifier and signified symbolic model: deconstruction philosophy, the connectionist approach, dynamic systems theory, and the theory of complexity. In poststructuralist thought, the observation of higher evolutionary dynamics of reality then of the symbols that we try to capture led Derrida to the impression of dealing with traces of what has already left. Any stability imprinted in naming systems might not deserve such honor, and might disappear before the name has been reused.

The increased speed of evolution or the surrounding world put serious pressure on the whole postmodern perception and reflection system. The feeling that something vital is being thrown out as noise and fluctuations started growing until becoming realization of the major importance of the sensitivity and interactions among all system components in scientific, economic, political or art models/vision systems.

PO/H vision organization acknowledges the more important role of sensitivity versus stability. It studies major patterns of relations of mutual sensitivity and the resulting forms as most general system properties and applies the knowledge of such patterns to any cluster of sensitivity built on top of any system of interconnected and sensitive components or contiguous areas. Another important aspect of PO/H design is in its use not only by people, but also by whole organizations in their everyday distributed processes penetrating all aspects, times and locations of coevolution with their environment.

The PO/H vision existed for a long time and OO/C was developed because of the main flaw in PO/H which is . . . interpretation. The moment we relax OO/C's strict requirements for knowledge object stability and ability to carry self-contained meaning, we face the need of local interpretation (substituting the global rule of structure). Unlimited semiosis as infinite interpretational attempts to interpret interpretation and inability to find the way of meaning preservation, ensuring its transfer from one communicator to another was the weakness patched with OO/C strictness poorly but it worked on the global level.

The trick of OO/C was in the concept of self-evident truth, which does not require interpretational guidelines and was perceived by everybody as exactly the same. Once meaning is captured by such an assumption, then reductionism and context abstraction allows for meaning engineering in analysis (getting to primary, self-evident bricks) and synthesis (building a new logical structure of such bricks). Navigation of inferential trees by all parties together led to the possibility of getting to the lower level where everybody "gets the message" and then using step-wise logic check the presence of faulty inferences that led to a deviating conclusion. Although such a "truth capturing" mechanism more or less worked in environments with very low CUI, it caused objections and resentment with CUI growth. We all know examples of tricky rhetoric which uses OO/C in less stable and fuzzy environments and by initially building self-evident bricks that miss what they want to miss and contained what they want to be captured which were able later to build a persuasive inferential tree forcing opponents (and often jurors) to agree with what seemed wrong by holistic perception. So, the foundation of universality on OO/C is not so kosher at higher levels of CUI.

The first systematic attempt to create an alternative communication system based on PO/H vision was done through phenomenology, seeking *sense data* stability and objectivity without *a priory* meaning restrictions. Instead of

self-evident truth in elementary knowledge objects, it tried
to find the *shared immediacy* of *primary impressions* using various
methods of *phenomenological reduction* operating on harmony
and holistic unity of perception versus stabilized logic of later
relations.

But the problem of the proper interpretation was not
successfully solved by just referring to archetypical
impressions, similarity of human body-sensing or closeness
to the origin of impressions (immediacy, which supports
similarity of such impressions). It felt close, but not rigorous
enough. It worked in many situations when precision was
not important but similarity and synchronicity of emotions
was the goal. It worked even in stone-age dances around
the pictures of the tribal hunt uniting and synchronizing
the vision of the hunters and allowing for their more
synchronous and group-adequate behavior.

Hermeneutics made another attempt to increase the
precision of communications, the need for which started
growing with the industrialization of the economy, the
growth of organizations and distributed groups requiring
instructions for the proper synchronization of environmental
control actions. The need of precise and proper
interpretation has led Dilthey to support the immediacy of
impression with technology transferring such immediacy to
the receiver as a necessary context in which impression
blossoms into its full meaning. In his opinion, understanding
is essentially a self-transposition or imaginative projection
whereby the knower negates the temporal distance that
separates him from his object and becomes
contemporaneous with it.

Gadamer made, actually, the first serious attempt to avoid
the problem of subjectivity by . . . not fighting it. His position
that "understanding is not reconstruction but mediation"
of past subjectively obtained meaning into the future
indicates the direction of the PO/H-based universal
communicator development. We will just continue this line

of thought, expanding his "mediation" to the whole environment of the message receiver. The past problems of PO/H were in incomplete deviation from OO/C in a sense that the purpose of vision was still considered as control, which requires model precision and clearness of knowledge instructions to deal with specific "buttons" of environment. CUI of modern sensitive system developed so much that, with clear consciousness, it is possible to pronounce the **purpose of vision as harmony with the environment**. But then there is no need in the precision of interpretation that will not be used for mechanistic control, but rather applied to the general sensitivity of subject/organization increasing ITS OWN ways of harmonization, ITS OWN BEING with ITS OWN ENVIRONMENT.

Such an approach seems viable in high CUI environments populated by sensitive systems, but what about organizations in more stable situations, successfully exercising control and enjoying success as they see it? The remaining parts of the book will show the possibility of building not only a PO/H-suitable but a generally applicable truly universal communication approach.

The first step to it is in the use of the concept of vision instead of language as the main tool. Once we decided that the goal of knowing is to seek harmony, we should realize that harmonization is more an experience than logic, which supports the idea of using vision versus language as a communication tool. The difference is that vision is a more general approach that doesn't necessarily require interpretation when it is difficult, reverting to holistic integrity of direct sensitivity.

In this book we suggest such a **vision approach** contrasting to a **language approach** to the design and implementation of the universal communication and meaning-creation system. The development of the new intermediary, which we will call Universal Vision Organization (UVO), has to show the ability to work with both types of vision and be a constructive intermediary between them. It results in the following requirements:

- Ability to effectively and efficiently communicate with all types of vision and interpret specific types, forms and process of communication, sensitivity and meaning evolving in those visions for itself;
- Ability to involve other types of vision in the process of sharing such interpretation in an effective and efficient manner;
- Ability to be implemented directly as a local vision with all proper vision functions and responsibilities;
- Ability to maintain meaning delivered by various local visions and support its integration in a higher meaning of the whole, which could be shared with local visions.

Chapter 2

TOWARD UNIVERSAL VISION ORGANIZATION

Vision Organization

In order to be effective, any communication process should be based on common vision as methods of collecting information, interpreting, and responding. Even if we use language as a communications tool, its understanding is largely based on physical bodily interpretation and common cultural code. This is why **vision,** from being treated as a rather static picture of the future-as-a-goal, is becoming a core instrument for alignment and integration of everyday modern business development. The more difficult a situation becomes, the bigger the effect of fast alignment based on common vision is.

Focus on communication effectiveness versus efficiency of data storage and transfer makes vision a distinct concept. Although such areas as knowledge management, organizational intelligence, and organizational learning justifiably struggle for their own domains, we see vision as a new, partly-overlapping concept which also is connected with organizational management, planning, and some other processes. Communications (and various forms of perception) for the purpose of better orientation are seen here as a unifying purpose for an emerging domain of organizational vision, creating a cluster of interrelated concepts and approaches.

Orientation in CUI-environments is becoming the main purpose of the planning of future efforts as well as integration of architectural and functional elements around the goal of effectiveness and efficiency. Seeing and an understanding of what is happening is becoming more important then coordination of control behavior, which assumes sufficient existence of orientation. Such shared vision by itself becomes a powerful self-organizing force, driving coordination and behavior of all participants in the right direction. Any group-active sport is based on fast reorganization of the participant's behavior based on common vision and orientation. No management is necessary.

In situations with low CUI, it is possible to maintain control through acquisition of an extensive collection of information about the situation and by applying various models describing the dynamics of the situation to make decisions about the best actions causing the desirable effect in the future. As with simple supply/demand models where extra production or lowering price always lead to predictable results. With CUI growth, the duration of the model life is getting shorter and the required response has to follow faster. In a "managing-by-the-wire" situation, decision makers have to do everything "yesterday," relying on their experience and vision often required to produce decisions within the same telephone call or meeting session.

By the time we've learned that information is an asset, it is no more often becoming an obstacle by providing outdated knowledge. The role and problems of forgetting (as changing old traits and rules on organizational level) is growing. Trying to use that old information might turn out to be not only useless but also counterproductive. The only thing we try to squeeze out of all available information is the right vision of the *current* situation and its *future possibilities*. The same way driving by looking into the rear mirror might work only on a straight road or with repeating shape of the curve.

Organizational vision is not a frozen picture of the desirable future but instant sharing of the current vision and orientation leading to the coordinated resolution of instantly emerging problems in a distributed manner, like that football team . . . It is a broadband and "broadscope" sensitivity that directly reshapes the dynamics of internal and external evolving behavior. Understanding of vision as dynamic distributed orientation based on advanced sensitivity allows using this concept for various types of sensitive systems, not only the ones with human participation.

The shift from understanding vision as a static picture of the future to a continuously and immediately used mechanism requires better description of its main features. From this point of view, it might be better to talk about vision organization (VO) as a set of tools, methods, features, and approaches determining specifics of a particular vision. A deeper look at the problem reveals a number of different VOs leading to the necessity of analyzing their compatibility, ability to communicate and being integrated somehow, adequacy to the external situation and adequacy to capabilities of VO owner to accommodate and handle a particular VO. We also need to analyze possible implications of the use of a particular VO in local situations and its interaction with possible UVO including impact on organizational dynamics. This requires a special attention to the features and components of vision organization.

Core Features of VO

Although vision is becoming one of the most often used

words, its meaning differs a lot from context to context. As we saw earlier, it could be individual, group, organizational, social, system, robotic and other types of vision. There could be quite a number of questions referring to various features of VO all together determining the conceptual domain:

1. What are we focusing on in manipulation of external sensitivity? What is the form of the correction information updating the existing vision (objects/sensitivity)?
2. What is the form of vision maintenance and use (model/experience/emotional patterns)?
3. What is type of our preferred relations with environment (control/harmony)?
4. Values and desirable properties of a particular vision organization: stability (forms of reliable control) leading to intelligence (forms of intelligent adaptability of identity sacrificing non-ID variability) leading to sensitivity (forms of mutual harmony—at expense of whole identity).
5. How do we explore what is in the focus (type of research and sensitivity/rationality involved)?
6. How do we separate perception, vision system, and knowledge (if at all)?
7. How do we use perception in reaction formation (direct mapping or logical validation or communication validation, etc.)?
8. How do we integrate or align social perception (OO/C, art training, belief training, etc.)?
9. What are the methods of integration of the new perceptions into the existing internal picture/Vision.
10. What is the organization of vision communications among vision exchange participants? What part of vision is externalizable?

But are all of them equally important in determining VO?

Do we have a few main features that force other features to be implemented in a certain way? If yes, then such *core features of vision* (CFV) determine VO architecture and could be studied in order to understand the possible dynamics of VO.

From the analysis of major OO/C vision incompatibilities and PO/H solutions presented in the previous chapter, the features most sensitive to the change from more OO/C to more PO/H vision and visa versa include:

- **Vision connectivity** to the area of interest, including the following problems: how and what we are focusing on, what causes refocusing, and how broad is the scope of vision?
- **Sensitivity** of vision maps, including: the form and scope of **actually** perceived/received information (building blocks of vision).
- **Interpretation** characteristics, including the form and methods of digestion and use of such information as integration of acquired building blocks into a consistent vision.
- The **purpose/value of vision** as behavioral foundation (to control some environmental processes, to adapt, to survive in the long term, etc.), producing a change based on previously digested information.

Vision Connectivity

Prior to processing and even accepting inputs from the environment, the procedure of focusing and connecting takes place. The following questions should be answered at this stage:

- How is the location system wants to connect to chosen?
- How does this connection occur?
- What is the form of such a connection?

97

- What influences the change of the connection to a different location?
- What does it take to support such change?
- What is the system actually focusing on (scope, type of the area included in the connection which allows for the transfer of information about such area)?
- Who or what is on the other side of the connection and how is this other side changing?

Sensitivity and Form of Information Building Blocks

By sensitivity of vision (which is only a part of the general idea of systems sensitivity), we will understand the **readiness** of one system to change in response to changes in another. In other words, it is the **form and content of information** about changes in the system determined by focusing/ connectivity **that will be considered** for the development of actual changes during the next phase of interpretation.

Sensitivity could be described by the type, the form, and the collection method of "inputs" or information about changes elsewhere. They could be classified based on the degrees of stability, complexity and certainty as well as on the time characteristics of the collection process. For example:

- Information supply of **high stability**, **certainty** and **low complexity** such as data, values of variables, parameters, etc. with a clearly measurable amount of contained information;
- Information supply of **high stability**, **certainty**, and **high complexity** seen as text with an internal structure requiring translation/interpretation of relations of its components into the systems way of organizing information;
- Relations of patterns, as in stock-price sensitivity to various indicators representing **certain**, **unstable** and

complex inputs when they could be classified as a set of distinct patterns and accompanying noise;
- Team member interactions during a basketball game and our immune system in its sensitivity to internal situation in our bodies are examples of **complex, uncertain** and **unstable** patterns of interaction in broadband continuous sensitivity.

Time characteristics of the collection process include:

- A discrete nature
- Continuous, but separated into portions based on the system';s sensitivity threshold to certain types and levels of signals (like a set of distinct patterns and accompanying noise above);
- Permanent, continuous connectivity (analog style).

More complex types of sensitivity differentiation are based on the perceived "logic of events" that can vary as:

- Only Causal relationships (fully tractable in time and space);
- Causal but uncertain relationships (like the ones between such fuzzy feature as utility of a product and its value);
- Holistic relationships as mutual dependencies with evolving patterns of mutual sensitivity, as in the case of weather analysis of hurricane or storm formation as sufficiently stable patterns deserving specific response.

Information Interpretation

What happens to external information after it reaches internal areas sensitive to it? If internal components are stable and could be clearly defined like objects in the input stream, and if their relations are also stable and clear and could be described as cause-effect connectivity, then the digestion of the new information takes the form of logical consistency support. In extreme logical requirements, any seemingly new piece of information has to be "proved" as logically consistent and, hence, having no new information regarding the model itself but only about the value of its variables.

Another form of absorption of sensitive information is in milder rules of harmony, beauty, aesthetics, consistency of internal feelings, etc. These are non-logical rules supporting connectionist dynamics and resulting into a new stabilized state after the input is entered. Ability to effectively and efficiently find a new stable state leads to a conclusion about the absorbability of the new information and, in fact, signals the end of digestion.

Various methods of interpretation lie in between, with the mix of approaches from both symbolic and connectionist camps. Such a mix can be quite elaborate when, as in literary criticism, we can get dozens of pages interpreting a relatively small poem.

It is important to see that interpretation is not a human prerogative only. Any system accepting external information, changing accordingly and reaching a stable state again, performs a certain kind of interpretation of its old, stable components leading to the new state of stability. Such stability can be achieved on various levels, including stability of system dynamics. Later in the book, we will describe interpretation as a search of the New Harmony and minimization of tensions as its final result, whether these are tensions of logical inconsistency or a power struggle of any kind.

Purpose of Vision

The purpose of vision as the foundation of external behavior or intentionality, the role or vision in a system's behavior, largely determines the way vision is being organized and used. Such a purpose of vision includes methods, tools, procedures aligned in order to achieve the goal of system's behavior, which in its turn evaluates vision effectiveness. Such goal might include:

- control of a certain system;
- control of a certain situation;
- adaptability to certain conditions;
- adaptability to all possible conditions (viability);
- co-evolution with the environment;
- harmony with the environment.

For example, being on a control mission, the vision owner pays attention only to the performance of the controlled parameters and the impacts influencing it. Meanwhile, adaptability or even general viability is a much broader task requiring use of all possibly important information in all its forms: data, perceptional experience, behavioral experience, the set of rules and patterns, etc.

The following aspects affect the use of vision and its type:

- The CUI characteristics of the environment;
- The degree of acquired adequacy of the internalized models and other stabilities that **remain** strategically important and require preservation;
- The system's ability and necessity of continuous adaptation;
- The optimal degree of the system's autonomy in the process of coevolution in its environment.

CUI characteristics of the environment usually represent the decisive factor in shaping the relations between organization and its surroundings. Another part for consideration is based on the system's ability to adapt, because the real measure of CUI depends on both factors: environmental CUI and the system's ability to match it. Learning and generalization processes leading to evolution of internal stabilities matching the ones existing in the environment can affect the degree of organizational flexibility in its responsive transformations, calling for preservation of important experience and knowledge that could be reused. Finally, the decrease in the system's autonomy as physical connectivity to external processes and fuzziness of its boundaries can result in a more holistic behavior than the stable and well-shaped systems are capable of.

VO-Pyramid and VO-Planes

The previously described four features form a VO-space with each edge being an axis of feature variability (see Fig.1). They are not orthogonal to each other, but rather expose a high degree of mutual correlation in examples of effective vision applications. Instead of the traditional coordinate space approach, we will build a correlated feature space by aligning all the CFV axes along each other, standing vertically on a plane the property of which we discuss later.

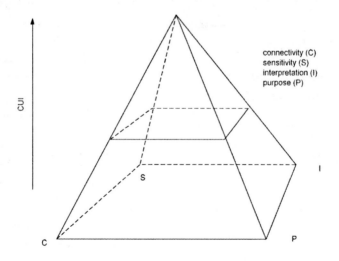

connectivity (C)
sensitivity (S)
interpretation (I)
purpose (P)

Fig. 1. Vision Organization Pyramid

Closer to the bottom of each axis or edge we will place more OO/C-like features, such as its higher degree of object-orientation and relationship causality. Closer to the top, we will place more PO/H-like features. The space between the edges will be occupied by specific visions with their AFVs.

For example, VOs formed by CFV closer to the bottom of CFV edges use inputs as parameters for their internal logic-based models, they believe in the stability and correctness of internal models of the situation and need only information about particular states of model parameters. In such a well-structured world, the form of information processing is the logic of the model, its causality allowing predictable outcomes and thus modifying behavior. Once logical consistency is the main rule in information processing, the natural goal of vision is, naturally, control, which is the method allowing for change of some of the inputs of any system and, knowing its way of functioning, achieving desirable outputs. Seeing information defined as small objects with more or less complex structures and clear values of predetermined and easily distinguishable features like the parameters of various primitive data types or "measures" like size and weight, leads to the temptation to implement consistency and output control mechanisms as the main processing operations on such information objects.

All four components (connectivity, sensitivity, interpretation, and purpose/intentionality) potentially can have different sources of influence, different histories of development, and different levels of wide acceptance, but should comply with our **Hypothesis of Horizontality** (HoH):

> **Approaching a stable, effective and efficient state of functionality any VO tends to take a *horizontal* position defined by the plane connecting particular properties of CFV axes.**

This means that, regardless of the existing state of the four VO components, they have sufficiently strong mutual

103

sensitivity or feedback connections moving them to some particular state of mutual correspondence. None of these features can independently vary too much, keeping others intact. By *horizontality* we mean that all four components will belong to the same level within the pyramid, which stretches from logocentric object-orientation with symbolic signifieds to a fully holistic level where mutual sensitivity of all areas and their dynamics leads to non-interpretative forms of vision (pure experience). Of course, it is not a strict geometric understanding, since no measures are presented for scaling the distances from the bottom of the pyramid, but rather a statement of the inability of any feature to develop unilaterally in the direction of sufficiently higher or lower levels along the axes if we want to preserve vision effectiveness.

For example, in the previously-described case of low environmental CUI, if input is represented by well-defined, stable and predictable pieces of information, the best way to handle them will be in the use of some internal representations with comparable stability and locality. Then the natural way of digesting input data will be in maintaining the consistency of their assignment to internal model parameters and maintaining the meaning of the model as consistency and inferential correctness. Externally, such a system will choose control goals since it believes in the validity of its model. In such case it becomes possible to achieve necessary results by seeking the easiest inputs to the world's systems, resulting in desirable outcomes.

Domination of such VO as common vision (scientific method) will inevitably discriminate VOs that use less structured inputs and more fluid internal representations as well as those not working toward control goals. Communication difficulties between owners of differing VOs as well as difficulties in the integration of accumulated internal vision representations or acting upon similarity of VOs will support some form of mutual distancing. Physics and lyrics, scientists and artists represent distinct communities with different cultures of vision, communication, and experience/knowledge integration.

Higher planes of VO in VO-space represent gradual dilution of the lower level assumptions about validity of using only well-structured, stable, and predictable forms of information they consume or exchange as well as internal representations. First, we can see methods used in economics, sociology, psychology, and in other sciences where the knowledge of the dynamics of discovered patterns (versus clear objects) is the main focus. They attempt to find ways of capturing more fluid and more CUI-type knowledge as a long-term asset, one which could be reused in similar situations. The goal of control might still be there but notions of evolution, balance, influence, fairness, satisfaction start playing a much bigger role.

Describing different types of VO in a rather rough manner, we do not intend to classify all of them but just show the existence of rather different levels in VO-space. Art vision and literary (especially poetic) communications will be the next big cluster with its sublayers. Here, we use more the concept of beauty and harmony versus the control concepts of lower levels as major procedures and features organizing information components. Such components themselves actually stop being purely informational but become more like tunes played on internal representation of external harmonies. Such inputs are much closer to an internal understanding of beauty and, with movement toward the top of the pyramid, become senses and perceptions of internal feelings and experiences. They act more like tentacles of internal sensations stretched outside and touching various sources of excitation.

The highest cluster on CFV axes is occupied by religious vision and spiritual experience. Here, depending upon the height of religious vision on the pyramid hierarchy, the goal is attaining unity of all four major VO attributes in one harmonic state with indistinguishable difference between external and internal sensitivity, connectivity, and interpretation. The highest form of such a vision is the pure experience of unity of all four components in one "enlightened" state directly embracing or opening to the external world. Such a vision-experience cannot be transferred or even communicated, but has to be experienced. Remember Herman Hesse's Siddhartha who rejected the method of following Buddha because he felt the need for finding his own way (vision experience).

If one is to make the distance between the four edges proportionate to the efforts necessary to maintain the adequacy of one feature to the given level of the other features in the VO pyramid (see HoH), then we can formulate the **Hypothesis** of **Convergence** (HoC) stating:

> The distances between the four edges of VO-space tend to get smaller while maintaining adequacy with the growth of CUI of the vision situation, and finally allow for the edge convergence at the top forming a VO-pyramid

The adequacy to the CUI of the vision situation determines the efficacy of CFV functioning as well as the cost of maintaining the horizontality of its features. The movement up the VO-pyramid can occur with changes affecting at least one of the four basic features, pulling the others toward a new horizontal level. As an example we see the struggle of the postmodern vision with logocentrism, structuralism and the stability of Enlightenment and later modernism.

Problem of Horizontal and Vertical Shifts of VO-Planes

It will not be correct to say that a certain type of CFV of VO-Pyramid is better than others. As a general rule, the choice of VO-planes happens as an adjustment process to the level of CUI in live-world situations. The more stabilities are out there, the lower the VO-plane can be. Unfortunately, the modern organizational environment and situations they are in do not allow for static allocation of VO-planes as a strategic design. The horizontal and vertical dynamics of integral vision systems on VO-planes is a result of the changing CUI properties of the environment in various situations for the same organization. We also can see the bad news in gradual and persistent movement due to the environmental changes toward the middle sections of VO-pyramid. This adds to the seriousness of the situation because periodically the actors are torn between the opposite types of vision, one of which tends to shift VO-planes down to more logical and stable understanding while another has an upward tendency toward higher holistic harmony and minimization of all tensions on all types of sensitivity.

Vertical Dynamics of VO-Planes

The differences in CFV organization between OO/C-like and PO/H-like VS lead us to the **hypothesis of discontinuity** (HoD) in vision transformation:

> **Shifts of vision between VO-planes based on the traditional separation of OO/C and PO/H methods are not gradual and smooth but rather are step-like transformations requiring overcoming barriers of internal self-supporting relations among VO components**

Analyzing the shifting between VO-planes in attempts to apply a certain integral vision to particular situations in modern organizational environment brings us to the **hypothesis** of **instability** (HoI) of VS:

> **There exists a level of CUI of systems environment above which the shifting of vision between VO-planes becomes necessary to support the adequacy of the systems orientation providing for its viability**

Indeed, the need for inter-plane vision shifting arises not only from situational instability but also from trends in OO/C and PO/H to simplify and harmonize understanding of what is happening by pulling CFV in the opposite directions, as we have mentioned before. Since OO/C cannot play the role of a universal communication system, such shifts lead to almost antagonistic approaches to communication, cognition and meaning-making when happening in middle areas of the VO-pyramid. We can see such problem in communications between hard scientists and artists or spiritually intense people. But, even in the same field, especially if it deals with sensitive systems like in sociology, economics, or psychology, the differences between the attempts at using different VO-planes in direct observations and experiences and in generalizations, abstractions and model-building creates methodological tensions within researching communities.

HoD and HoI together present the biggest challenge for e-business where high connectivity is based on Internet and intranet technologies and is very communication intense. As we have discussed before, such situations lead to the growing role of vision as the main architectural and strategic component, allowing aligning of other components and activities around it. This is the feature of higher levels of VO in situations with higher CUI. The role of model logic control is sharply decreasing in favor of the alignment of all components with each other and with emerging situations, but is still valuable in many situations.

Horizontal Dynamics of VO-Planes

Even within the same VO-plane, there potentially exist multiple **vision systems** (VS) based on the restrictions of the situation being observed and viewer membership that can dynamically change predisposed focus and alignment mechanisms-like attempts to see the market situation from producers' and consumers' points of view. Vision system here is understood as an integrally-acceptable set of CFV and AFV with particular mapping processes of external phenomena onto an internal vision carrier. In organizational vision, this is usually a mutually acceptable group choice supporting particular communication clusters.

In E-commerce, such group vision systems of customers and B2B participants change dynamically, which can lead to catastrophic reevaluations and fast rejection of services, goods, businesses themselves. The vision system within a particular VO can share the level of the major components on the VO pyramid axis but differ in focusing on specific information objects and inputs, the internal model or representation design, and the particular logic of their integration or information absorption. It means that the VO-pyramid represents a certain level of abstraction from particular vision systems guiding specific seers.

The problems of communications within the same VO-plane are based, for the OO/C part of the pyramid, on differences in distinguishing stabilities in live-world situations, believing in them as stabilities, and acting upon such beliefs. In the PO/H part of the VO-pyramid, the differences in individual experiences play a more important role. Two people might strongly disagree in the value and beauty of some piece of art or on the righteousness of a certain aspect of religious beliefs. In the first case (OO/C), the discipline of arriving at mutually agreed truth included initial agreement on basic assumptions (primitive object design) and the following logic of inferential reasoning. In the second case (PO/H), it is more an art of the activating/exciting of similar emotional and experiential patterns that determine further similarity of cognitive and behavioral preferences in other participants.

In both cases, it is a matter of agreeing on accepting certain initial logical or emotional/sensual states with further application of the familiar VO-plane technology embedded in CFV. Since such VS belong to the same VO-plane, they can easily influence each other, substitute for each other and, hence, fiercely compete for survival and domination. The shifting from one VS to another is not a smooth and gradual procedure but a matter of reassessment of the basic values, beliefs and convictions.

Summary

Obviously, the inefficiency and inevitability of vision transformations under CUI in sensitive systems present a problem for the role of vision as systems core. We might state that investment in a more effective and efficient vision has a long-lasting value (is strategic). The vision-shifting problem is becoming the main concern of sensitive system development and management and will have a major impact on the viability and competitiveness of areas existing in high CUI environments such as e-business. The ability of a sensitive system to dynamically adjust its vision within the proper VO as well as communicating between different VOs is becoming the major competitive and survival factor.

This book is about the approach to the design and use of vision, which provides for effective and efficient handling of vision transformations under growing CUI, becoming a major weapon of modern e-business companies or so called "New Organizations" in general.

UVO, OO/C, PO/H

The necessity of the UVO design is based on its ability to fit the requirements of both types of VO in all their variations along VO-pyramid. Since the requirements of OO/C have been sufficiently explored during the last three centuries, in our comparison we will focus more on the PO/H requirements to CFV responsible for shifting to the higher levels of the VO-pyramid "previously forbidden" within OO/C.

PO/H vision focuses on the power of natural minimization of tensions, energy, and harmonization working on areas sensitive to each other versus the stability of forms and relations allowing for inferential conclusions. This leads to a different vision technique, where such clusters of mutual sensitivity have to be discovered regardless of their spatial closeness (especially in times of electronic sensitivity). We will show that the evolutionary processes and resulting forms of stability and levels of sensitivity are similar among all types of entities, concepts and processes, thus forming the most general method of SS analysis and design/care. A judge once said, on the subject of pornography, that he couldn't define it but knew it when he **saw** it . . .

Methods of VO Implementation

The use of vision in engineering has a long history of shy references, underestimation, suppression and denial. The main methodology of the OO/C use of vision includes:

1. Interpretations of the current and forthcoming situations as relatively stable models/knowledge participating in control and maintenance of the system's stability. The vision part as sensitivity to the situation and the evolving of design solutions was pronounced an art after which the question was usually closed;

2. Detection of situational changes and model/ knowledge updates. At this stage, the group decision-making process includes integration of local and lower level vision;

3. Reliance on automated control to maintain systems viability and adequacy;

4. Implementation and maintenance, being main areas of vision use, are considered external to systems development as necessary evil belonging to the human domain not worthy scientific attention (or difficult for it).

In stable environments, such a model (see Fig.2) works, but with the growth of CUI features of environment and overall connectivity and sensitivity, systems should be treated differently. Function f2 of vision as harmonization with environment is becoming more important and more often used than is the f1 function of simple parametric adaptability and tuning of the internally used and previously created models. Adaptive control attempts to modify not only model parameters but models themselves. However, further growth of CUI, system sensitivity to continuous model drift and real time functionality requirements make such an approach too expensive and often unrealistic.

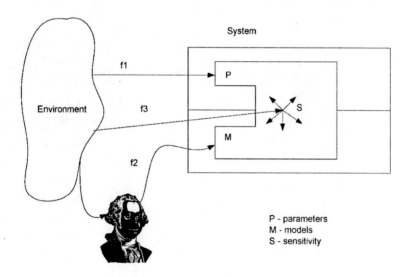

Fig. 2. Functions of coevolution

The growing level of sensitivity, volume of communications and interactions become the main viable options. Fig. 2 shows an approach to SS design with an emphasis on dynamic coevolution with the environment. Function f3 supports the continuous interpretation of external sensitivity into the adequate internal situation of the system. Here we don't describe the method of harmonization (like model based control) but rather state the general purpose of coevolving viability. This allows for different types of harmonization with environment using not stability but sensitivity or vision management. Such harmonization is similar to the patterns of animal adaptability going on without models and decision-making, but rather by instantly and continuously evolving patterns based on a current vision of the situation.

The analysis of presented evolution of approaches to SS design shows that the level of **sensitivity** between various entities and processes is the "hidden" variable potentially capable of providing the smooth transition between the VO-pyramid levels. If UVO is capable of gradually changing its VO-characteristics with an increase or decrease of sensitivity in all its main features, then it can cover all possible internal and external situations. A current switch from OO/C to PO/H with sensitivity growth in SS is not supported by such means of gradual transformation.

V-modes

The possibility of working in environments with varying levels of CUI and regimes ranging from rare human interference in model modification to fully self-supporting coevolution is based on the necessity of different underlying tools, building blocks and abstractions implementing these types of functionality. The role of abstractions used in the enhancement of systems adaptability and workability was traditionally filled by various models independent from their computing or organizational implementation. The efficiency of the modeling approach is based on the relative ease in finding harmony between incoming sensitivity and predefined ultimate stability around which, and relative to which, the final harmony (solution) is attained. Vision organization for SS phenomena cannot assume existence and rely on any stable components, either in real situation or in its reflection. The growing intersensitivity of SS components and their emerging nature requires a new approach that doesn't use models and controls as its basic functionality.

Such an approach is in the use of different underlying implementation techniques and methods differing from a more model-like way of using them to methods supporting mechanisms of self-organization in a simulative and embedded manner. Such mechanisms, or rather modes, of VO functionality and experience will be called vision modes (V-modes). The specificity of V-modes compared to traditionally used models is in their **live participation** in constant connectivity, sensitivity, and interpretation processes being grounded in a particular context of the vision situation to different degrees of particular V-modes. They are not easily transferable (if at all) to various viewers and are embodied in particular vision experiences. The same VO features could be supported using several V-modes supplementing each other.

We can distinguish the following types of V-modes: S-mode, C-mode, and T-mode. They reflect changes in sensitivity levels among and within major VO features, with functionality varying from very stable and externally controlled interactions to self-organization of joint harmonic coexistence. Differences among V-modes reflect differences in the problem solving concepts of OO/C and PO/H. The traditional concept of a problem and its solution in OO/C is based on the possibility of symbolically describing the problem and solving it using only well-shaped causality and logic. The solution should be delivered in a fast and precise manner to the controller of the situation. With connectivity growth among systems and environmental parts, classes of space and time distributed problems started to dominate organizational efforts. These problems are different from the ones requiring only inferential operations with no time or space regard:

Space-distributed problems, like management of a vast computer network, have a number of parallel interactions among their components that cannot be adequately described as one logical sequence and have to be studied as processes working in a parallel distributed manner. Numerous methods of parallel distributed processing (PDP) and models describing natural phenomena as PDP have been developed. It doesn't mean that such a distribution should geographically follow the sources of problems. Given proper sensors, local information could be delivered to the central location where its dynamics will be represented in a PDP fashion.

Time-distributed problems are the ones that exist only as particular patterns in time and should be studied as such, where the correct time sequence (versus statistical methods) is important. Complex evolutionary processes could serve as an example where every next stage has multiple connections with the previous one and often many previous stages. Such problems are often represented and solved using simulative techniques, such as neural networks that "swallow" inputs on short time intervals and respond accordingly.

The combination of space-time distributed problems ultimately leads to the understanding of a problem as a task for adapting to the space-time distributed patterns of dynamics of certain features, for harmonizing the system with them on a continuous interval, for coevolving. It seems quite different from symbolic "solutions" that are space-time context free. The need to address these types of problems led to the need for changing the vision mode to one more connectionist, simulative, PDP-like.

S-mode is based on methods of symbolic processing used in OO/C. It can deal only with the level of stability sufficient for assigning symbolic names/identifiers to smaller components and their relationships. The harmonization with the external situation is done via a *modeling* process, which has only two types of sensitivity: to predetermined model parameters and to modelers as those who can realize and implement the change in models. Meaning alignment is fully predetermined by logic-consistency validation and various inferential engines preharmonized with appropriate OO/C theory. S-mode has to support CSI the characteristics typical for OO/C that were previously discussed. System parts using S-mode will be called Smods.

C-mode is based on connectionist models allowing for non-descriptive methods of dynamic pattern evolving in systems organized similar to neural networks or others, so called, "soft-math" methods, can use lower levels of stability but still require the use of models (architectures) of node organization and learning paradigms. C-mode has to provide support for the middle part of the VO-pyramid where S-mode is seen as inadequate. It means that C-mode has to be able to support higher levels of sensitivity and demonstrate a certain mapping mechanism, modifying internal representations based on external sensitivity and internal architecture. In other words, environmental patterns should, to various degrees, control the form of internal representations and not the preset logic and forms. System clusters of connectivity using C-mode of vision operation will be called Cmods.

VO characteristics and their mutual dynamics based on Cmods should be adequate for the middle levels of the VO-pyramid, but do not have to go all the way to the ultimate forms of PO/H-type of VO. The architectural use of C-mode allows for the existing use of supporting technologies capable of some PO/H-like effects but still unable to implement PO/H in all its features. Cmods could be used when local VOs also operate on middle levels of the VO-pyramid. For example, being able to absorb and process information in poorly-structured form, Cmods can create dynamic internal *patterns* of meaning adequate to the external situation in the process of *learning*. On the other hand, known existing stabilities could be embedded into Cmods by the modeler in advance. Usually, the internal sensitivity of model components is not controlled and can evolve into patterns adequately matching external situation within certain diapason of environmental variability. For example, weights in neural network connections can converge to a stable state by themselves, guided by fixed input variables and model architecture. Changes in environmental organization often require the development of another connectionist model incorporating extra sensitivity processing by the designer in model parameters.

T-mode is the type of V-mode that we call after the major role of **sensitivity** in capturing not only the models of stabilities, but also the modes of their existence in the context, evolution and holistic features of behavior. Clusters of sensitivity implementing T-mode will be called Tmods. They do not use any of the predetermined parameters and stabilities usually found in modeling approach. Tmods are based on the self-organization of interaction between evolving dynamic patterns of sensitivity and stability. There is no external additional sensitivity processing (the designer figure), and all necessary operations are incorporated in its mechanism of adequate self-organization.

Tmods, being only hypothetical means at this point of discussion, are state-processes simultaneously exposing the fluidity and stability of a situational context. The interwoven dynamics of stability and sensitivity supporting both while restricting each other is the main feature of Tmods. Stable parts emerge and dissipate and the harmonization of external sensitivity is run not against a predefined platform but a dynamic evolving state-process. We often see such behavior in various life forms with a very broad sensitivity of parts and process to each other leading to very complex evolving/dissipating processes "at the Edge of Chaos." Weather patterns represent SS with a strong natural sensitivity of various components of the ecosphere working like Tmods, self-harmonizing states of global and local patterns.

The ability of Tmods embedded in proper areas of SS to sense their environment and match it in the coevolutionary process without external human guidance is a special form of intelligence which can be seen not only in human and social systems but in any form of real-world entities hiding the enormous complexity of matter organization and existence. Current experiments with "smart matter" represent only a small portion of interest in the ways the world maintains its holistic unity. Children's behavior studied by Vygotsky in his "Society of Mind" shows how vision in communication/game situations connects the multiple body/minds of children into a more powerful system different from the ones that could be described by symbolic or connectionist models and capable of solving much more advanced problems then any person could do individually. Being able to see and use such processes is the basis of a smooth vision self-adjustment to various levels of sensitivity. You can recall the types of sensitive systems discussed in the previous chapter and problems of explaining Tmods naturally existing in them via various types of modeling which constantly causes either incompatibility or the need for the involvement of Tmods in modeler's body/mind in order to provide periodic corrections of captured stabilities that cannot fully evolve on their own. The Taoist system of vision is an example of the successful use of the holistic experience of sensitivist dynamics in particular and the constructive manner for human orientation in a broad class of situations.

In addition to the interface role between different VOs, Tmods can be implemented, locally directly supporting local VO. The analysis of T-mode properties and behavior is done in the next part of the book in a more detailed form, while their use as the main tool in UVO is discusses in "Holistic Engineering."

OO/C and PO/H Requirements to CFV properties of UVO

Vision Connectivity as Focusing and Information Gathering

Connectivity to the object of vision (focusing) shows what we are interested in outside of the system, the types of entities and phenomena that the system wants to collect information about. In OO/C, focusing is based on predetermined characteristics built into the model as inputs or variables. Such a type of focusing is dictated by the architecture of the model directing the vision process. For example, the speed control of a car will require focusing on the frequency of tire rotations converted into current speed. All other features of the situations are ignored by the model.

PO/H focusing as the choice of areas of interest differs in several aspects:

1. In the type of chosen areas system focuses on;
2. In the dynamic choice of information it wants to collect about external entities/phenomena.

The areas of interest for PO/H with movement up the VO-pyramid include broader types of external information than fixed measurable parameters of well-defined objects in OO/C. Such types cover less stable phenomena (like patterns of weather) as well as the direct flow of changes that cannot be symbolically labeled because of their instability (like you cannot name a particular part of a water flow). The two latter types require non-symbolic mapping mechanisms.

Another aspect on the way toward PO/H is in the decrease of predetermined or controlled focusing, as in measuring particular parameters that are preset before the observation begins. PO/H relies less and less on such vision connectivity control, exposing the increasing importance of self-focusing as a form of self-organization depending upon internal and external situations.

The UVO requirement here will be in the possibility of the gradual movement along the following features:

1. Varying stability and fuzziness of the entities/areas the system focuses on, from unshaped areas and flows of changes to object-like entities;
2. Ability to seek necessary areas and their scale in the process of focusing/connectivity once the model control gets weaker

Sensitivity and Form of Information Building Blocks

The importance of being able to have better orientation in CUI environments is becoming vital. Old methods capable of describing only stable patterns become not only obsolete but also misleading. Money spent on those types of organizational re-engineering that just substitute one stable control-type process by another is just a way of wasting resources and getting into a deeper conflict with reality.

The distinction between Object Oriented (OO) and Pattern Oriented (PO) systems is important in making a decision about an appropriate mix of stability and sensitivity resources because ideas of harmonization and self-harmonization largely rely on the specifics of PO/H vision organization. If the system is stable, or is largely based on stable components (stable patterns), and its environment with respect to system's viability can also be well-modeled, then it could bear an increase of stable components and control methods. Pattern orientation is more general allowing also a developing vision and, consequently, language suitable for handling extra sensitivity as a combination of knowledge and experience, which is so important in CUI-type environments.

There are several ways for orientation enhancement in complex and uncertain situations, depending on their stability. If the situation is rather stable, then the appropriate models could be built, simplifying orientation by using descriptive and predictive power of the theory. Stochastic situations are also simple to handle by using statistical methods. The most difficult task is in managing situations on the "edge of chaos" with unstable, fuzzy but very structurally rich, contexts. They remind one of the complexities of patterns of frost on winter windows. In dynamical systems theory, it is known that sensitivity is the feature leading to the edge of chaos. But it is also known that the chaotic state provides for the richest potential set of reactions to a turbulent environment and is the only match for external complexity with variety and the self-organization of internal responses.

Modern socio-economic entities rapidly moving to such environments should not try to avoid sensitivity, which is their only defense, but to find new ways to deal with it, to use it as a great free resource capable of necessary creativity and adaptability. That is why all life-like systems, including ecosystems and economic systems, are also real nonequilibrium systems.

The theory of computation suggests that in most cases of complex non equilibrium systems, the shortest way to description of the algorithm controlling them is to perform the algorithm itself, which is its own shortest definition. Such an algorithm is the process of distributed parallel harmonization of dynamic pattern-context systems, which has to be simulated as the only way of understanding it. But, in order to simulate such a system, we need a different type of information to be collected in comparison with traditional crisp objects and measurements of their attributes and behavior.

The need for such additional information led to the revision of the Cartesian principles of using only clear and well-definable information. The first step was in the consideration of fuzzy and/or rapidly changing patterns of information. Then it was the need in using their dynamic connections with various contexts. Such systems of pattern-context relations can offer some instruments of modeling a more advanced pattern behavior. Dynamical Systems Theory, semiotics, situation theory, genetic algorithms, and a number of others are examples of attempts to use contexts better.

The types of information obtained after focusing or external connectivity and the types of information circulating inside the system during its processing play a very important role in the evolution of VO. Usually the types of information system is focusing on and the types of information absorbed and circulated inside the system are correlated.

OO/C vision organization as a broadly accepted one in organizational orientation seeks stable forms of external situations and assigns names to them (labeling, denoting) for further processing when signs substitute reality in inferential conclusions. The PO/H vision is based on the detection of sensitivity clusters that are dynamic in their nature. Kung fu, aikido and some other forms of martial arts are mainly based on the processing of sensitivity with the detection of opponent's patterns of behavior and slightest indications of future movements. They do not have to have names, since they will not be processed in logical engines but rather mapped directly onto all systems of the body to produce the most adequate and matching response. After several movements, opponents realize which of them can match the movements of the other, or better. Sometimes it is sufficient to acknowledge the defeat, since the less sensitive system is inferior in such a competition.

Types of input are tightly coupled with methods of internal processing and can be a requirement and restriction for the forms of input processing, or a result of such forms if they cannot be changed. Often such a connection is dynamic with mutual influence leading to stabilization of the accepted types of stability/sensitivity according to HoH.

Interpretation and Digestion of Inputs

The method of input processing being tightly interrelated with the input type includes the:

- Degree of processing distribution (versus central processing);
- Degree and the mix of inferential and evolutionary methods;
- Degree of sensitivity to the incoming signals versus the already internalized picture of the situation.

On the one side of the spectrum, there is a truly OO/C method with mainly symbolic processing, overvaluation of the acquired and accepted information and a high degree of centralization (as it was in the command style pyramid organizations and their information system organization around the mainframe). On the other side of the spectrum, we have a distributed connectionist method of processing with all the attributes of complex dynamic systems including the evolution of new entities, various kinds and combinations of attractors and limited orbits. Stability can evolve here too, but does not become a fetish directing structural and behavioral adjustments whenever they are necessary. PO/H vision attempts to find the adequate balance of these features in order to maintain adequacy to both properties of possible situations: the logic of stabilities and the creative power of sensitivity among areas, entities, and processes. .

Purpose of Vision

The purpose of vision also affects its process and form, influencing the choice of external connectivity, the type of accepted inputs and the method of their "digestion." On the other hand, the purpose is reshaped by vision components as it was shown in the previous discussion. Although the question about the purpose of vision seems to be as general as the purpose of existence, we will narrow it at this point to the question of what an entity is trying to achieve by its interaction with its environment.

In OO/C VO, the focusing on stable objects and belief in the adequate knowledge of the *logic* of their dynamics leads to the natural idea of using it in the form of *control*. If you see the behavior as transformation of inputs into outputs and believe that you have knowledge of how "input" is transformed into "output," then the temptation will be toward using this knowledge in order to control outputs achieving *desirable* results. But the natural desire is toward the increased viability of all acquired stability including organizational form, models of processes, knowledge, expressed opinions and developed values. In other words, it leads to the attempts to function "inside-out" by seeking external support of the internal models as stabilities. The more acquired assets, forms and knowledge become outdated, the more harmful such control is for the surrounding environment, creating growing disharmony. The desire and value of control, of being in control, embedded in OO/C dramatically affects organizational culture, behavior and course of evolution.

Computers based on the Turing Machine model became ideal assistants in automation of control. If objects are designed correctly and all associations are defined, then control design is a matter of calculation of the change necessary for obtaining the desirable effect. And it worked pretty well when the world and the problems were simpler.

But, as has been detected in most of the cases of control model design based on numerical and symbolic computations, computation time grows exponentially with the number of data items to be processed causing a serious computational problem known as the non-polynomial time solution. Such time complexity, together with the space complexity of growing memory requirements, "makes the treatment of control problems very difficult in almost all standard model formulation cases" (Hangos, 1993).

Despite a variety of offered improvements, control methods stay limited by the very idea of control: "to stabilize a given system and to meet certain performance requirements" (Munther, et el, 1995) or even to find "application of forces to a system for the purpose of maximizing some measure of performance or minimizing a cost function" (Stengel, 1986) in optimal control. Such an approach treats systems as operators acting on certain classes of signals, ignoring the transformations of internal physical states of the system. The scientific method itself, based on clear-cut logic and strict definitions of entities to be manipulated within various inferential systems, is becoming an obstacle.

It is never too late to remember Lao Tzu, who wrote more than 2.5 thousand years ago in the *Tao Teh Ching*:

> *Intelligent control appears as uncontrol or freedom.*
> *And for that reason it is genuinely intelligent control*
> *Unintelligent control appears as external domination.*
> *And for that reason it is really unintelligent control.*
> *Intelligent control exerts influence without appearing to do so.*
> *Unintelligent control tries to influence by making a show of*
> *force.*

PO/H VO uses vision as method, form, tools, and procedures aligned in order to achieve a higher internal and external harmony. In this sense, it is an organizational design leading to self-adaptation and self-control of the optimal stability/sensitivity balance. Optimality of such a balance is seen in terms of achieved harmony with the environment, which can be transferred into the internal system's harmony leading to the maximal efficiency of organizational existence. Such efficiency will be a result of harmony as minimization of tensions and the wasted energy of unnecessary and harmful control attempts of dying-out forms and processes. Advanced internal harmony also means more effective communications using the same generalized VO capable of self-tuning to the necessary balance of stability/sensitivity. Such communications should use the common language, terms and concepts that still could be detailed in every particular situation to the constructive level allowing for correctional actions.

Summary

The described changes in basic VO features on the way up the vision pyramid (summarized in the table below) show the necessity of UVO support for smooth movement along the pyramid edges.

Table 4. Elements of OO/C and PO/H vision organizations

VO Elements	OO/C	PO/H
Vision Connectivity (Focusing)	Model controlled choice of fixed measurable inputs, refocusing is based on external model modification. Preferred type of input is a well defined signal.	External sensitivity can affect the internal stability and visa versa. Focusing on various types of information including semi- and non-structured types
Form of information building blocks (sensitivity)	Prefers stable and well-structured objects and their relations	Broad types additionally including semi-structured and unstructured information
Method of building block assimilation and processing (interpretation)	Inferential methods proving "correctness" as adequacy to some theory	Search for harmony between existing vision and new inputs as minimization of tensions and energy
Purpose of vision	Control, survival (of stabilities)	Harmony, harmonic coevolution

At first glance, the switch from the lower part of the VO-pyramid to its upper part results in vision catastrophe and in resulting catastrophes in methods of organizational and systems development. An abrupt change from relying on stabilities to fighting them requires different approaches of PO/H.

The purpose of UVO is to smooth up all necessary shifts from OO/C to PO/H and back, allowing for work in the "gray zone" when necessary. Unfolding of the vision catastrophes requires introducing another dimension allowing for a smooth transition between previously abruptly disconnected trajectories along other variables. In order to be able to find such "hidden" variables in vision organization, we will look at a general process of vision utilization in a system's adaptation to its environment.

According to the previously presented hypotheses (HoH and HoD), vision organization tends to "freeze" in its match for CUI of the Environment. The lower CUI leads to OO/C-like VOs, the high CUI creates PO/H-like VOs. And all of them tend to stay on the appropriate vision planes with the high cost of shifts from one VO to another. Such a specialized VO could be very efficient within its sphere of adequacy to CUI supporting the main criteria of SS-continuous viability, viability at every time interval.

A UVO attempting to fill in the gap between such a specialized VO has to maintain excessive creativity similar to the one at the Edge of Chaos, which calls for extra costs, time, and, eventually, risk if we try to maintain it in all types of environments and for all systems. At the same time, HoI and the growing interdependence of environmental and system components requires alignment of their local VOs into the harmonic VO of the Whole, which requires universal connectivity even with extra time and resource spent.

Then, keeping UVO "hot" at all times and for all systems,

allowing it to be more fluid than OO/C and more structurally creative than PO/H connecting all types of vision is the goal. In "Harmonomics," we discuss the basic concepts of UVO, while in "Holistic Engineering" we describe the approach to keeping UVO alive despite of HoH, which requires special efforts.

UVO Use Schema

The task of the development/choice of a generalized and flexible vision capable of smooth shifting along the vertical VO-pyramid as well as stretching horizontally in order to integrate existing points of view at the same situation within the same VO will require the use of special tools supporting them. Such supporting tools and methods should be capable of changing their properties with very low resistance and ideally on their own, as evolving features match existing situations. Then the core of any system built on such a basis will prove resilient and adaptive properties minimizing management costs and time (efficiency) as well as maximizing adequacy to the existing situation (effectiveness).

Such a flexibility will also mean the ability to dynamically rethink the role in the environment and the type of relations with it from control to adaptability and mutual harmony. The latter might seem the most difficult since intentionality of vision seems to be a strategic feature monitoring vision technology in general and used on very long time intervals. If a company like Microsoft thinks of itself as an entity capable and oriented toward control of major developments in its (constantly expanding) area, it will be very difficult for it to switch to the role of a mediator among companies and customer interests trying to create global harmony. Such a role is embedded into multiple local visions coordinating their efforts and supporting mutual understanding in internal communications as a team with the mutual goal—to win!

We will be focusing on the following features of the proposed universal VO:

1. Ability to support vision for any type of phenomena;
2. Support productive communications between various VO;
3. Gradually provide for vertical and horizontal shifts to the most appropriate features of other VOs when the situation requires;

These features require a consistent embedded experience and language capable of reflecting the SS evolution and features outside and inside sensitive systems with sufficient generality and, yet, specificity covering different levels of sensitivity. Such an experience-language should be capable of constructive demonstration of approaches, methods, tools and organizations as *holistic engineering*, covering the whole spectrum of problems of dynamic harmonization of sensitive systems with their environments and not only internal design based on captured stabilities. They should be able to support vision organization, which can smoothly fluctuate between the levels of the VO-pyramid as well as support the intra level modification of vision connecting them all into the model, gradually changing its properties according to parameters with changes in levels of sensitivity and the CUI of situations. It should be able to explain when and how context sensitivity starts playing a bigger role than model stability.

The use of UVO compared to the previously shown methods of systems design at various levels of sensitivity should allow for the generalized approach to systems engineering, the design of universal tools, services, and methods that are complete in a sense that f2 function (see Fig. 2) is embedded in the system as the evolution of necessary models based on f3 activity whenever it is possible. We should be able to easily scale systems by adding various types of subsystems (OO/C or PO/

H) using various functions of vision (f1-f3) without serious restructuring and redesign. In a way, UVO should play a role of a general communication interface between existing systems of various types and also support the possibility of global meaning creation and its implementation, which could be communicated back to local subsystems. The necessity of coping with different problems of communication, meaning integration and creation, to support functions and technologies, leads to the multitier organization of the UVO use schema (see Fig. 3).

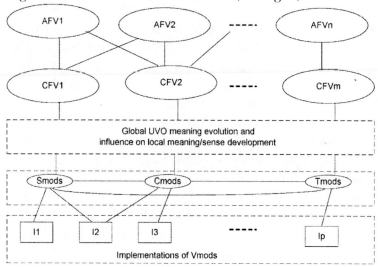

Fig. 3 UVO Use Schema

T1 Functionality

This tier deals with local vision adequacy, allowing for various vision features to be implemented, depending upon the communication environment. It also can include environments in certain states of CUI as sensitive systems operating on particular levels of the VO-pyramid. The adequacy of local vision, then, is seen as the adequacy of the application vision features (AFV) discussed in the previous chapter to the character of the existing situation. This organization is similar to general schema use in traditional systems design, allowing for multiple views of different users/subsystems. The difference is in the use of various vision features ranging from more OO/C-like to more PO/H-like versus the different components of OO/C presented in each view.

T2 Functionality

The T2 tier deals with CFV (vision connectivity, sensitivity, interpretation and intentionality/purpose), creating all application effects on the previous tier. The CFV features of T2 reflect what their behavior should be like, rather than how it is achieved. The activity of this tier is directed toward the maintenance of CFV adequacy (horizontality). The necessary limited shifting away from the V-plane consistency is done for efficiency purposes under the pressure of mixed features of external impacts where some DPCS are more stable than others and can be processes of more efficiently on the lower levels of the VO-pyramid. Separation of such "diversity" of CFV features can be achieved by using the adequate mix of V-modes implemented on the lower tier.

This tier can have a distributed organization allowing for local participants to choose the proper VO plane from various areas of the VO-pyramid. This phenomenon of V-plane differences reflects the variety of situations (their CUI-properties) the local participants are in and represents the main problem in global communication efforts because of the CFV differences. The worst situation is when the participants of communications belong to different sectors (OO/C or PO/H) of the pyramid demonstrating opposing trends in vision consolidation: the trend to logical consistency versus the trend to higher harmony.

T3 Functionality

The T3 tier is where the main UVO "miracle happens." It is responsible for the development of the understanding (meaning) of the global situation whose meaning might not exist in any of the local SS. This tier also allows for effective communication between all types of local VOs by supporting smooth, gradual gliding along VO parameters, like an elevator taking meaning from one floor to another as well as keeping some portion of it inside.

T4 Functionality

The T4 deals with implementation of UVO functionality using particular V-modes as *conceptual systems of implementation* that have to address all aspects of certain CFV implementations in all their interdependency but without the specifics of particular physical carriers. For example, we can describe specific S-modes as a system of differential equations using certain feedback variables but without details of software or physical simulative methods of implementation (like water models of electric current and resistance) of such equations and the processes of their solving (harmonization). Another example is in the description of neural network architecture and learning parameters, without referring to particular software or biological implementations.

It determines and supports the adequacy of the dynamics of various carriers to the requirements of T3. It can be seen as an abstract view of the real underlying physical processes on T5. Such an abstraction deals only with the behavior of the main VO features depending upon the methods and tools used to reflect and absorb the growing sensitivity among components and processes of vision. The various methods of implementation differ in their mechanism and necessity to add external sensitivity (such as human management) to match the requirements of a particular situation in one of the local VOs on T1. These methods are organized around different types of V-modes.

The ability of PO/H, enhanced by embedded Tmods, to spread to the previously OO/C supported domain makes it a leading type of vision organization stimulating integration of the benefits of scientific and liberal arts approaches. Tmods create the "miracle" of universality, supporting the UVO functionality of smooth transition between various types of V-modes.

The physical implementation of Tmods is not considered on the T4-tier, but the known and often observed type of behavior with elements of complexity, self-organization and stabilization in the form of various attractors studied in Dynamic Systems Theory are their basic features. Designing tools allowing mapping and simulating such processes in attempts to understand and forecast their future development is the key. T4 assumes the existence of Tmods and plans ways of using them as the ultimate instrument for high-level PO/H vision.

T5 Functionality

The T5 tier deals with the implementation of relations between connectivity, sensitivity and interpretational features of a particular type of V-modes from T4. For example, S-modes can use formal theories and machine algorithms to implement inferential methods of meaning alignment. Developments in fuzzy logic allow incorporating snapshots of the sensitivity of modelers into models through the use of so-called membership functions connecting perceived shapes of parameter areas of external situations with internal parameters of the model.

Implementation of C-modes is based on connectionist representations and demonstrates the ability for using a higher level of sensitivity and its participation in meaning creation. Although some of the model parameters are preset, such as neural network architecture, threshold functions, learning paradigms and some others, there is an area of overall model sensitivity based on evolving patterns of connection weights which makes such modeling more flexible, allowing for a better fit, especially in non-linear processes. There are a number of other types of Cmods with more relaxed predetermination and higher sensitivity than Smods. For example, cellular automata and artificial life mechanisms are based on predetermined methods of local connectivity and rules of pattern evolution, but the complexity of such evolution is the approaching sensitivity of life forms.

Implementation of T-mode is the major challenge of UVO. The broad sensitivity as a process and fabric of dynamically evolving patterns in massively parallel processes rapidly spreading around today requires a more general and flexible approach.

T-mode implementation can be based on a number of processes using micro—and macro-level technologies. On the micro level, it is the creation of proper carriers supporting abstract T-mode features on T4. Some possible implementations include natural sensitivity and the self-organization of analog dissipating processes. Others might be simulated by digital parallel distributed processes. Macro-level carriers can include whole organizations and socio-economic processes as well as the macro behavior of Nature. It is a macro-implementation possibility, which allows for a start using PO/H with Tmods on an organizational level, not waiting for effective electronic carriers on the micro level. The necessary means of sensitivity enhancement among systems components could be achieved at the present level of communication technology and widespread Internet standards. Only now, due to these technological advancements, we can convert old control-style organizations into true sensitive systems capable of self-adaptation. This is the key to the viability of electronic business, which otherwise will be crippled by the limited human resources necessary to augment OO/C models after every change in the business situation. This is why the demand for advanced IT professionals doing such remodeling will continue growing beyond any realistic ability to provide it and beyond the human ability to provide necessary changes in the decreasing time frames. An alternative is in the rolling back to the old economy, reevaluating the real possibilities of the seemingly exponential growth of e-business like in the recent Wall Street and corporate management wave of skepticism.

In the next part we will show that the variety of levels and forms of interaction of these two concepts is capable of demonstrating behavior of stable entities used as basic orientational tools in many other VOs. We will present examples of the evolution of complexity allowing one to get the picture of multiple possibilities of resulting patterns, forms and behaviors. Study of these patterns can help in general orientation in situations with sufficiently high sensitivity.

The Concept of UFO

The discussed features of UVO require a consistent Universal Framework Organization (UFO) capable of reflecting SS evolution and features outside and inside sensitive systems with sufficient generality and yet specificity covering different levels of sensitivity. The trick in the use of UVO as communication tool/method is that it is not only this. Compared to the use of languages for the same purpose, we can say that the vision approach, being more inclusive than just symbolic messages and incorporating continuous sensitivity and its harmonization, becomes also a way of being, changing, adapt synchronously with vision changes. Such a deep embodiment of UVO requires special measures and procedures (forming UFO) to be applied in the system or organization adapting it. If written language is a self-sufficient system of communications (although within OO/C vision only), UVO grounds its meaning-making processes into the mere existence, the modus operandi of particular SS and their complexes. The grounding, embodiment or implementation is also a part of vision functionality. Since such embodiments are always specific, it is impossible to offer a finished transferable system of meaning-making and validation. It can only be a framework as a higher level abstraction **prescribing how to** connect vision capabilities with real life dynamics of SS.

UFO should be capable of demonstration of constructive approaches, methods, and tools covering the whole spectrum of problems of the dynamic harmonization of sensitive systems with their environments. The main UFO functions include:

1. Support and enhancement of functionality of UVO Use Schema and its components;
2. Methodology of UVO development, support, and care;
3. Design and support of the whole SS architecture that could make use of UVO in the best way;
4. Maintaining and developing the necessary persistent states/parts allowing to support and use a broad range of harmonization results in all Vmods;
5. Means and methods of CFV implementation improvement. This includes more advanced means of connectivity interwoven with sensitivity and interpretational dynamics;
6. Individual and group human training (for human based SS) as one of the most important parts of systems

sensitivity, communications and meaning-making abilities.

Part 3

INTRODUCTION TO HARMONOMICS

Heraclitus: Everything is and is not, for everything is fluid, is constantly changing, constantly coming into being and passing away.

Kauffman: The material below is not yet science. However, it is serious "protoscience"—an attempt to formulate questions and concepts that may, in due course, become serious science.

Chapter 1

BASIC CONCEPTS OF HARMONOMICS

Introduction to Harmonomics

If in the previous part we just stated the possible existence of Tmods and their fit as a foundation of UVO, here we will explore the main concepts, components and views of their functionality and essence. Like General Systems Theory attempting to study and describe common features of reality as properties and features of various systems seen in S-mode of OO/C and using symbolic models, harmonomics (H) is studying and describing reality seen in T-mode of UVO. Changing situational stability reveals more OO/C or PO/H features based on smooth and gradual self-adjustment of UVO. Such change of vision makes the world look different and allows to notice phenomena not obvious in OO/C. The different picture of reality shows different generalities and possible abstractions, allows making different conclusions and changes the system of priorities, values and goals. The main challenge is in showing the ability of UVO based on T-mode

.

to deal with all types of VO. Physicists and artists cannot easily merge their understanding of the same landscape beauty seen either as a balanced system of objects and forces or experienced as harmony of perceptions and feelings reflecting harmony of Nature in its holistic existence. Natural sciences are able even to distinguish and formulate some patterns-laws similar to the ones created by certain weather conditions, or the ones stating that leaves turn yellow in the autumn, or rabbit changes his color in the winter. In order for Tmods to have universal application including unsupervised adaptability they should be able to show how structural complexity reflecting the environmental situation can evolve or dissipate by itself adequately adapting to the changes in the environment. We should explore how the World can be seen using T-mode of vision, and how it accommodates for both types of application features—the fluidity, fuzziness and holism of PO/H and stability, logic and complexity of OO/C. We will show how carefully designed terms with all their abstraction and fuzziness allow to reason about and communicate local vision logic and experience. Showing the possibility of OO/C-style stability (up to the level of objects that could be interpreted in symbolic models) evolving out of PO/H-style sensitivity, fluidity, and fuzziness is the main task of universality analysis of T-mode use. The opposite direction as communication up the VO-pyramid showing the gradual dissipation of more stable and causally connected objects into pattern-like holistic entities is also important.

First, we will present the basic concepts used in T-mode of UVO that can be sufficiently well understood and interpreted in various types of VO. Universality will be supported by the use of a small number of these basic concepts that should be rich enough to present a great variety of observed phenomena in each type of the VO and yet recurrently use only a few simple generative processes. .

Then we will show the evolutionary dynamics described in T-mode and capable to demonstrate how OO/C situations and phenomena could evolve within seemingly different field of PO/H by just **gradually** changing a few features. This is the opposite approach from the one taken in multi-agent systems and OO/C attempts, in general, that aspire to show how holistic features can be designed based on primary stable objects and their interactions. We will see that such objects do not have to be the reductionist foundation and explanation of the upper-level behavior of the whole, but inversely, the object-like behavior can be deduced from holistic relationships and features if the proper vision is being used.

Sensitivity

The main concept of the sensitivist model (or rather mode) is . . . *sensitivity*. Other concepts will be derived as additional terms or compact methods of description/labeling of some forms and processes occurring on sensitivity in order to use them in symbol-oriented human language. Sensitivity is seen as primary **process** and **form** of existence. As a form of existence sensitivity could be seen as a multilayered fabric of being, where all upper layers are based on some forms of sensitivity of lower layers playing the role of the carrier for higher layers. The lowest layer will be called **protosensitivity** without the analysis of its exact form (universal field, one-dimensional strings or something else). We can call such protosensitivity the state of *Oneness* or *Singularity* that continues after the Big Bang but is just supplemented with additional states of higher layers of sensitivity.

Sensitivity has *levels* that can vary in arbitrary chosen *areas* (not necessarily consecutive). Level of sensitivity of one area to another shows the mutual influence of changes in one area onto another. Such sensitivity is generally anisotropic.

We can explore sensitivity on multiple layers and areas ignoring the actual carrier (which if to look into deeper can be also reduced to multiple layers of sensitivity). *Layer* of sensitivity is a system of relationships among areas of a given situation (cluster of sensitivity) with the certain scale of changes seen according to the coarseness of vision. Example: the lower layer of chaotic movement of molecules in the water with their mutual relationships and interaction of water waves on the higher layer.

Sensitivity as a process is seen as the dynamics of changes caused by interaction of the new information with the existing state of the area. Such general sensitivity sometimes could be split into specific sensitivities to particular sources of the outside world. Even if it is impossible to separate such sensitivities, we need to know that they might add to the general sensitivity of a particular part of reality.

The stronger is the internal change in response to the delivered information—the *higher is the level of sensitivity* to the source of information. The hammer can get in touch with a piece of hot metal causing small or bigger changes depending upon its sensitivity (based on the plasticity or sensitivity of the metal). The topographic map of the levels of sensitivity in various areas and to various areas will be called *sensitivity map* (S-map). Such S-maps are dynamic as processes and show certain stable patterns as forms of existence.

Important to understand that sensitivity differs from instability. Initial change caused by external information could later be transformed into initial "pre-information-delivery" state, as circles on the water disappear with time. The stability of the generally calm level of water is maintained even after possible impacts with objects causing circles of waves. The initial "tactical sensitivity" might not be preserved as "strategic sensitivity".

Sensitivity could be classified also as *dynamic* and *static* or *potential.* Same pieces of furniture in the cluttered room have a higher degree of mutual potential sensitivity and connectivity compared to the ones in the open field in the context of moving the furniture around in response to the changing requirements.

Connectivity

As we mentioned before, sensitivity plays the role of a form and a process. It becomes **more of a form** when the process of mutual influences of different areas stabilizes around a certain state of sensitivity. Stability of such state will be called its *connectivity* as a feature of stabilized sensitivity between different areas with particular parameters. This is similar to the intuitive use of the word connectivity describing particular sufficiently stable characteristics of information transfer between different areas. Note that there are multiple forms of sensitivity, which maintains its liquid dynamic character. The difference between sensitivity and connectivity is in the degree of achieved stability. The introduction of the new term for such fuzzy difference helps to discuss various features of sensitivity processes in a more compact form, that are easier to comprehend by OO/C— trained minds.

Connectivity describes the ability to deliver information about changes in one area to the other one and ultimately to all connected areas as well as receive information from them. *Information delivery* means that stability of the sensitivity in the channel is such that it is possible to separate changes induced by the current influence from the regular state of the channel, which is known or recognizable sufficiently well.

Sensitivity comparison on a given connectivity plays an additional role, where it is seen as an abstraction from connectivity between the analyzed areas. In such role it concentrates on their mutual coevolving or harmonization, while (because of its relative stability) the connectivity channel can be skipped out of the picture of coevolution. Elimination of connectivity channels out of sensitivity analysis is possible because we are concerned only with the channel's role to effectively deliver information about changes from one area to another. Sensitivity, then, is the dynamic part of connectivity channels, carrying changes from one point to another over basic connectivity. Speaking of connectivity of the channel we can see that despite of its existence and functionality if there is no sensitivity of one area to another the whole process of information transfer cannot be finished. Signal can reach radio, which is connected to antenna, in general, but it might not be heard because radio sensitivity could be tuned to another station frequency.

Connectivity among all system areas at a particular time will be called a connectivity map (C-map). Here we do not specify what shape the connectivity between any two areas can have: narrow channel, broad field, or other forms.

The term *map* allows for the possibility of changing the coarseness of our vision and looking at connectivity inside nodes or any smallest areas as well as taking a high-level picture of connectivity among larger chosen areas. All connectivity on all levels is seen as a C-map describing the levels of connectivity between any chosen areas. C-map sometimes is not describable but could remain explorable.

The higher the **impact** of one area delivered to the other **given the same changes** initiating such impact at its origin— the *higher the connectivity* between areas. For example, connectivity between two communicating over the distance people is different with or without walkie-talkies or cell phones.

C-maps, given the dynamics of connectivity, might preserve structural characteristics allowing for stability of certain sub maps which might be high enough to carry a name/label over time or might deny such possibility in the situation when connectivity is changing too fast compared to the observer's symbol evolving mechanisms supporting the possibility of naming known stabilities.

Harmonization and The First Law of Harmonomics

As a process, sensitivity can be seen as the search of the lowest level of energy of interaction. Such process will be called *harmonization*. Harmonization is a manifestation of sensitivity behavior as mutually—influenced changes of two areas. Generalizing the definition we will see **harmonization** as minimization of tensions, disharmony, energy, etc. among mutually sensitive areas. The offered list of specific cases of harmonization could be easily extended making it general enough to be applied in various cases.

The resulting actualized state is *the state of harmony*. Sensitivity being stabilized via harmonization process is turning into a more stable form of connectivity and thus creating the risk of loosing adequacy with external changes. This translates into the risk for actual harmony that has to be dynamically maintained.

The common feature among all forms of harmonization is the direction of mutual changes **minimizing information exchange** by incorporating news into CS-maps to an extent that same information does not create changes in response to it since it was already accounted for. Such observation coincides with the interpretation of the second law of thermodynamics directing the dynamics of interactions within a system to the minimization of differences in energy levels leading to the minimization of possible energy exchange process.

We will formulate the **First Law of Harmonomics (LH1)** as following:

147

> **Sensitivity among several areas results in the harmonization process working in the direction of minimization of possible information exchange among these areas**

The use of only the basic concepts of sensitivity, connectivity and harmonization results in the situation when all the observations in the physical world, the meaning of what is happening, everything that exists in a particular situation can be expressed only through the interplay between connectivity and sensitivity in the process of harmonization. Initially it is difficult to grasp such approach since we always use words, symbolic names for everything we see where language plays the role of a symbolic carrier. In case of connectivity and sensitivity maps (CS-maps) there are no words that can help us to reflect what is happening, although in many cases such maps could be presented visually like weather patterns or even supported with adequate dynamics of changes in a film fashion. It is useless to give names to any of the current shapes of the clouds but all weather patterns together being visualized help in understanding of what is happening and what might happen next. Sometimes, when patterns become more stable in some sense and we need to focus on them like in case of hurricanes—the names could be assigned. Forms and sources of such evolving stability will be also discussed later. The type of vision that we use in weather pattern analysis, when the area of interest is not called by its name but rather pointed at and its pattern is seen, allows for sufficiently productive orientation. It can include more or less stable entities with possibility to zoom in and out of various areas and details, merging local observations into a global picture, as well as applying the knowledge of the global dynamics to the more precise forecast of local events.

Chapter 2

ANALYZING FORMS OF HARMONIZATION

Simplified Symbolic Notation of the Dynamics of Harmonization

Further discussion of harmonization processes will require the use of some methods allowing studying the dynamics of evolving features of various harmonization situations. All of them are created by different levels of connectivity and sensitivity demonstrating quantity-quality transitional effects. This is why all forms and features gradually presented in the following discussion are not clearly defined concepts in object-oriented style but rather constitute fuzzy cognitive maps. Remembering this, we will use conceptual sign graphs (or their inline text variations) allowing for the visual representation of various dynamic patterns of conceptual interrelationships. The following notation emphasize possible parallel evolution of both events mutually affecting each other but, generally, without possibility to detecting causality.

The use of the language of UVO is different from hard OO/C and has to be able to satisfy our need in explanations as well as solicit common meaning creation/aligning. The use of symbols is possible but is a very delicate procedure emphasized in our criticism of OO/C use of symbols for higher levels of CUI. The differences in their use are described below and reflect the appeal to both major types of VO using logic, experiences, and proper interpretational processes.

Colloquial human language allows for a great number of vision-like operations of PO/H type using tropes as pointers. Poetic language is specially designed for PO/H situations requiring serious interpretational work. Scientific language requires logical aligning of received information with "known" mental models.

We will initially describe some basic processes that people intuitively or experientially can "get" or "picture" and later use possibility of mental experiments using words setting the conditions and appealing to readers ability to run simulation, logic or vision internally in order to see the adequacy of the result with their own mental state. Some notations will help to shorten the form of such collaborative experience with the reader.

A, B, . . .   Describes either entities that are stable enough to acquire signifiers or pointers to some areas with ongoing dynamic harmonization that readers can imagine or picture of re-experience in order to understand the possible result; these symbols can also represent the similarity of experiential states of two observers in the same vision situation (like in "the situation is cool") serving as an

	indicator to the mutually recognizable internal experiential state;
A→ B	Describes an influence of A on the **general evolution** of B (sensitivity of B to A), which given lack of other serious influences could be treated as causality; the word evolution means also a certain delay and is an explicit introduction of time patterns not allowing for simple transitivity like if A→ B and B→ C then A→ C where A might not cause C just because B hasn't evolved yet representing the only context allowing for the evolution of C;
A+ → B+	Describes a specific influence of one growth onto another, same with other signs like A+ → B- in a negative influence;
A→ (B~ B:x)	Shows the evolution of a **new** feature x in B due to sensitivity to A;
A/B →(B~ B:x)	A more complex situation showing the evolution of a **new** feature x in B due to the mutual sensitivity (and coevolution) of A and B;
A/B or (A, B)	Is a mutual harmonization or coevolution of A and B, where initial A might differ from the final A after a while but its evolution could be traced to the initial A; it is reflexive and A/B=B/A as evolution of A in B-context and evolution of B in A context, since it is a **coevolution;**
A+ (or A-)	Describes quantifiers (+,-) reflecting growth of or decline of an entity A like in A- or A+;

(A, B)+   Describes a positive feedback showing a two-way influence of one growth onto another where "A" at time t1 is smaller then A at t2, t2>t1.

The dynamics of signifiers prevents the use of differential equations and other symbolic descriptions as fixing the meaning of variables, while in PO/H reality their features can change and variables might need to use another name. In fact, the use of signifiers as pointers to same internal experiential states of observers makes it incorrect to use any symbolic models since the experiences might evolve and, for example, what two people agreed to call "love" in the beginning of the affair might mean something totally different from what they will call "love" much later still perfectly understanding each other.

These explanations make it obvious that in order to communicate such situations better we need a language capable of carrying certain maps of observer's initial understanding that will evolve synchronously with the evolution of the situation and their personal experiences. Computer mediated communications and T-modes are precursors to such new language-vision. Human body-mind can serve the same purpose of supporting the dynamic synchronicity of internal T-mode evolution with carefully chosen harmonomics terms and following discourse.

Basic Forms and Patterns of Hz

CS-Interaction

Description

In the previous discussion we introduced the concepts of sensitivity, connectivity and harmonization. Here we will look into relationships among them. The most fundamental and general pattern of harmonization describes interesting and complex relationship between sensitivity and connectivity, which is the foundation of all other structural and dynamic features of sensitive systems.

Any area of sensitivity demonstrates harmonization processes, where, according to LH1, harmonization (Hz) works in the direction of increased harmony (H) or minimization of probability of the new information influence. Thus, Hz tends to decrease the ability of one side influencing another, which means increased stability in various forms and aspects. Such stability obtained as a result of harmonization reflects acquired new level of harmony and is represented by connectivity as stabilized sensitivity. Harmonization of an S-map stimulates the build up of a C-map. Higher connectivity between certain areas stimulate higher sensitivity of one area to another which leads to a more powerful harmonization trend leading to further stabilization of the described subsystem. On the other hand, the loss of sensitivity leads to corrections by dynamic environments leading to full or partial destruction of evolved stability.

Using the presented notation to the description of harmonization pattern of connectivity-sensitivity dynamics, we will distinguish the following concepts:

- connectivity (C)
- weak/strong qualifiers (w,s)
- sensitivity (S)
- broad/narrow qualifier (b,n) for sensitivity

Using these concepts we describe subpatterns of the whole CS-complex as following:

1) $(C:w, S:s,n)^+$

2) $[S{:}s,n]+ \rightarrow C{:}s$
3) $[C{:}s]+ \rightarrow S{:}w,n$
4) $S{:}w,n \mid\rightarrow C{:}w$

Here the first subpattern (1) describes the stimulating effect of harmonization on initial stage when connectivity being generally weak is increasing its level in coevolution with growing stronger (s) sensitivity, which also starts narrowing (n) around evolving patterns of connectivity. Such narrowing/focusing occurs due to the situation when stable ' structures start filtering signals that differ from their structure and gladly reinforcing the signals with similar information structure, which is known as the process of excitation via resonance. After a while, such mutually supporting growth leads to connectivity reaching the qualification "strong" (C:s). Third subpattern describes the stage of mutual CS-dynamics when connectivity is getting strong enough to start seriously ignoring other influences, which means sensitivity decrease together with its continuing narrowing to changes that can still affect the evolved pattern of connectivity. Inertia or one-sided influence of strong connectivity keeps feeding general broadband sensitivity decline. Such decline having a delayed influence on connectivity (4) results in the possibility of accumulation of rather big changes in sensitivity (its weakening) and, after the delay, triggers quite a big decrease in connectivity to the level qualified as (C:w) from previously held (C:s). This determines the catastrophe of connectivity. This happens because connectivity is based on constantly excited and supported patterns of sensitivity by similar external C-maps attempting to reinforce (excite) existing structures. The loss of sensitivity leads to the loss of such support and decrease of the stability of its existence. Such decrease triggers (1) and repetition of the whole cycle.

Since we do not use the particularities of evolving patterns of connectivity, such cycles with renewal strengthening of connectivity do not mean revitalization of exactly the same C-map. It might change. The weakening of connectivity in the fourth subpattern makes it fragile to external impacts capable of breaking all or parts of the evolved structure of a C-map which also leads to the first subpattern. Altogether, the CS-cycle is a self-limiting dynamics circling around some attractor of particular CS-levels.

Evolutionary Aspects

CS-dynamics as the most basic form of harmonization is ubiquitous and works on all levels and in all areas of systems. Comparison and design of the global and local CS-maps of this form of harmonization in all systems and subsystems leads to the better design and understanding of other forms of harmonization, using this basic form as a foundation.

Lower sensitivity leads to the lower speed of CS-dynamics supported either by strong and rarely occurring changes in the environment capable to penetrate resistance of evolving C-maps or by very smooth and gradual changes that are close enough to the existing C-maps and can influence them within remaining levels of sensitivity.

The intensity of CS-interaction is higher among the areas located closer to each other (higher connectivity). Higher connectivity of close areas is just one of the forms of intensification of CS-interaction. Actually, any method of increasing connectivity leads to such process even in remote areas (e-business is an example).

The phenomenon of CS-map self-stabilization is based on the balancing of the two harmonies: one in sensitivity harmonization around evolving C-map and another is harmonization with the environment. The speed of changes and instability of environmental impacts might not allow every area to keep developing its C-map while maintaining high level of sensitivity.

Discussion

Being, actually, the two interwoven aspects (connectivity and sensitivity) of the same harmonization process like Taoist Yin and Yang concepts, full picture of **CS-interaction determines all the properties** of the analyzed situations. No other concepts are involved since the only acting force according to LH1 is the process of harmonization of sensitivity. This is why T-mode use is very universal. Ultimately, all analysis and design methods lead to aspects of CS-interactions. This is the expected feature of the proposed holistic approach compared to reductionism based on logical treatment of stabilities and pointing at components and logic of their communication as explanations of the more complex systems. However, contrary to the primitive holism, which stops at this point because of the loss of the ability for logical analysis, we lead the discussion into the areas of evolving forms of harmonization which substitutes structured logical processing.

Examples of CS-interaction include mutual influence and holistic unity of various processes in sensitive systems (SS), such as biological balancing at the "Edge of Chaos" between overstabilization and extreme sensitivity of chaos and even random behavior. Second law of thermodynamics reflects the process of harmonization in systems consisting of a set of stable particles randomly interacting (statistical sensitivity) and evening up their energy patterns. Holistic medicine sees and successfully treats health problems as imbalances between Yin and Yang in their interpretation as stability and sensitivity. Taoism showed viability, productivity and universality of its vision of various human life situations. In comparison, our use of sensitivity and connectivity concepts allows for a more constructive and technically interpretable way of describing similar dynamics in all its creative power.

Fig. 4 shows the correspondence of Yin/Yang dynamics

to that studied in dynamical systems analysis when a map has one critical point and a circular trajectory rotating around it. If to assume that the right and left areas from the curve splitting the circle on the left figure represent connectivity and sensitivity as the axes on the right figure, then the proportion in the width of both parts on the left figure if we scan it top-down is reflected on the right figure as the C and S coordinates of any point on the circle given its rotation around some critical point in the center of the circle. In both cases we can see the cycle of changes in connectivity and sensitivity described in the previous section. Of course, the exact dimensions in this example are not important delivering the conceptual schema of evolutionary CS-harmonization processes.

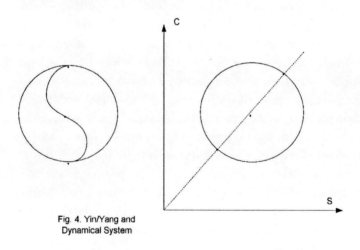

Fig. 4. Yin/Yang and
Dynamical System

The exact properties of CS-interaction might not be easily assessed because either observers have insufficient precision of connectivity and sensitivity detection or they do not focus on these processes properly. The first problem (precision) of CS-pattern observation can be resolved using **deconstruction** method based on imaginary (or simulative) experiments with higher or lower levels of interaction among system components or varying time scale of observation (snapshots, slow motion views). The solution to the second problem of adjusting vision to CS-pattern is **reconstruction**. Here the goal is by changing resolution and/or focus to find the area with clearly detectable CS-processes. For example, seeming stability of any product could be changed by looking at product generations as a response (CS-pattern) to varying customer demands. Alternatively, it is possible to see any object in a slow motion by increasing coarseness of observations in time.

DPCS Evolving and Main Features

Description

When CS-dynamics reaches the level of evolution where certain patterns of stability could be distinguished from each other it becomes possible to see such areas as clusters with their internal behavior. Such clusterization is based on growing differences between internal CS-maps of these areas and lagging (because of their decreased external sensitivity) harmonization with external CS-maps. Such emerging formations could also be seen as clusters of sensitivity, where internal sensitivity is higher then sensitivity to any external area causing certain *independence of its internal harmonization*. Such clusterization of the holistic sensitivity into areas where local C-maps narrow sensitivity around evolving local structures creates the basis for more complex forms of CS-harmonization.

The possibility of identification of CS maps of such clusters leads to the grounds for cluster behavior analysis on the level of whole CS-map interaction versus micro observations of local connectivity/sensitivity dynamics. Here we will introduce two new terms: *pattern* and *context*, defining pattern as a C-map of **a particular cluster of sensitivity** and context as its S-map. Introduction of these new terms instead of the continuing use of CS-maps could be justified by the higher level of abstraction allowing to study dynamics of CS map interactions and possible intuitive deconstruction of situations into patterns and their contexts without specification of exact CS-map characteristics.

We can describe subpatterns of the whole pattern-context complex as following:

1) $(P{:}w,\ C{:}s,n)^+$
2) $[C{:}s,n]+ \rightarrow P{:}s$
3) $[P{:}s] \rightarrow C{:}w,n$
4) $C{:}w,n \rightarrow P{:}w$

With logic similar to the previous section, pattern (P) interacts with context (C) like connectivity interacts with sensitivity. Although here we look at interactions between whole CS-maps. Such close relationships between a pattern and a context lead to the limited sensitivity and connectivity of the area while shaping its own harmony. This interaction also decreases external sensitivity in favor of internal harmony. Seeing it from another angle we can say that this is an evolution of clusters of sensitivity where internal sensitivity is higher then external and in conflicting cases the auto search for internal harmony can dominate the needs for external harmony by being reinforced internally or just by filtering external influences.

Pattern-context dynamics differs from general CS-dynamics in having a limited area of existence. It is not as ubiquitous as CS-harmonization form, but is mostly confined to **sensitivity clusters.** Such clusters will be called *Dynamic Pattern-Context Systems* (**DPCS**).

Pattern does not have to be stable but its mere appearance is a demonstration of the harmonization results obtained out of the S-map at the previous moment. This form of harmonization was able to make it to the Existence from the hypothetical world of possible developments.

Evolutionary Dynamics

Evolving of DPCS is based on the forces of better connectivity between the close areas (other sources of sensitivity enhancement are possible), which leads to the stronger sensitivity among them similar to CS-clusters but bringing external sensitivity to lower levels based on stronger internal connectivity. At the same time, most of DPCS as mere sensitivity clusters have high instability and high rate of **dissipation** because the described mechanism doesn't seem to guarantee the high stability by itself.

Sufficiently high internal sensitivity leads to the enhancement of harmonization forces. The clearer and stronger the difference in internal sensitivity compared to the external—the stronger is the difference in harmonization results. Enhanced harmonization stimulates stabilization of tensions and connectivity development. Stronger connectivity (higher stability) leads to weaker sensitivity to the same areas for external impacts. The two outcomes are possible:

1. Achieved stability was sufficient to stay under the existing dynamics of overall changes which leads to the evolving of a relatively stable C-map
2. Insufficient stability of a pattern leads to its deterioration under various impacts and, as a result, increased sensitivity which leads to the new round of searches for a stable pattern

Important to note that additional pattern-context mechanism provides for the second layer of stabilization compared to CS-dynamics. The development of internal connectivity does not enhance general sensitivity but rather splits it into two parts: external and internal. The higher is the internal connectivity—the more the internal sensitivity is focusing on the support of the internal connectivity development. Meanwhile, external sensitivity is decreasing through this focusing mechanism filtering sensitivity to external patterns that significantly differ from the internal ones. This leads to focusing of internal context on the support of higher levels of internal connectivity (pattern) stimulating the sensitivity support mainly along the pattern routes and visa versa. Pattern and context mutually coevolve creating increasingly tight and interwoven relationship that results into decreased external sensitivity and connectivity.

Pattern-Context Interaction

Both pattern and context of DPCS are based on CS-interaction and the difference is only in relatively high stability of pattern. DPCS does not have to be homogeneous and can have sub clusters of internal sensitivity. It might be convenient to think of DPCS as of a CS-map where each area reflects certain levels of C and S as well as their relative proportion—connectivity-to-sensitivity ratio (Rcs). Areas with higher Rcs are closer to patterns while areas with lower Rcs demonstrate context features of higher Hz dynamics. It means that DPCS in addition to CS-harmonization has another mechanism of stabilization based on context protection.

Context serves as a shock absorber since it also has C-maps, although less stable then pattern. External impacts can influence certain changes in context but be insufficient to change its relationship with pattern, which will not experience the impact thus "absorbed" by context. Stabilized by such protection, pattern in turn preserves context state as much as possible by reharmonizing it around unchanged pattern structure after experienced impacts and following changes-fluctuations. Enhanced pattern stability organizes context around it creating a more distinctive difference between context and environment, which in turn might lead to further stabilization success of pattern-context dynamics. This double support of the original state makes it more difficult to modify developed DPCS and introduces a certain inertia into their response to environmental impacts that can penetrate such defense.

Harmony Encapsulation

DPCS work like search engines seeking higher levels of stability (harmony), which tends to be *encapsulated* in pattern-context introspective focusing. This is a very important form of the general CS-dynamics paving the way to higher levels of stability and harmony at the expense of its encapsulation. Harmony encapsulation opens possibility of the description of the evolution of more stable types of DPCS that acquire object features so broadly used in OO/C. Initial holistic nature of sensitivity in DPCS situation becomes "trapped" focusing around the pattern and weakening outside of the DPCS cluster. Spiral pattern-context reinforcement of internal sensitivity with context supporting its pattern stability also diminishes harmony with the environment, which could be seen as harmony encapsulation.

Possibility of finding a stable internal pattern, which will not be disharmonic to the patterns of environment and, most likely, will be reinforced by their similarity as in resonance ART model (Carpenter and Grossberg, 1990), supports the process that in OO/C is called "learning." Only adequate patterns survive in continuous searching efforts for higher harmony and stability. May be, this is why ancient Greeks, observing the dynamics of Nature, saw the birthplace of Aphrodite (the ultimate harmony) in the constant formation and disappearance of bubbles in ocean foam.

Three types of DPCS can evolve as a result of several possible levels of achieved stability:

- **Weak DPCS**, where sensitivity of context dominates by constantly changing emerging pattern and limiting possible complexity of C-maps in such overheated situation
- **Strong DPCS**, where stability of connectivity dominates narrowing sensitivity leading to rigid systems that cannot change their patterns in changing environment and, as a result, will have their C-maps destroyed or seriously modified by external impacts disharmonic with the acquired internal pattern structure
- **Viscous DPCS**, where the CS-proportion (Rcs) is such that systems have sufficient self-organization abilities being "at the edge of chaos". Viscous DPCS are usually difficult to clearly identify since they often have fuzzy boundaries.

Inevitability of the emerging third type of DPCS will be shown and discussed in the following chapters of Harmonomics.

DPCS as a Stabilization Mechanism for Their Environments

The higher stability DPCS gives them the ability to influence parts of external environment treated as their context by stabilizing it. Such stabilization leads to higher chances of DPCS stabilization and so on in a mutually supporting loop. In this sense, the growth of stability outside the DPCS is competing with the reverse process of environmental inhibition of internal stability of DPCS through the impacts of non-resonating and disharmonic patterns.

Tolerance Boundaries

The boundaries of DPCS are fuzzy and permeable. In many cases it might be very difficult (if possible at all) to find a context boundary. In other cases it is quite clear. More than that, fuzziness of context boundaries could be increased to the point of context dissipation in surrounding holistic sensitivity that might be a part of a bigger context but without distinct local specificity. Smooth transformation from one context to another with total or partial replacement of its ex-parts describes *context evolution*. Such opened structure, instability of properties, methods and identity does not allow for the use of OO/C models of contexts.

DPCS where internal harmonization is sufficiently strong to filter most frequent external changes can obtain tolerance or what we call *tolerance boundary* (TB) with certain types of impacts. The level of such tolerance is proportionate to the difference between internal and external sensitivity. Tolerance boundaries can develop to certain impacts of the close neighbors taking a form of a border separating them in space. Other types of TB are also possible that are not space borders but rather feature borders separating different types of influences and sensitivity. Such feature topographical maps might not match each other creating difficulty in exact boundary determination. For example, a certain level of resistance to heat before melting exposes a temperature boundary which being also a space boundary for well shaped objects might behave differently from, say, electromagnetic maps of the same DPCS not exactly matching the space boundaries of the temperature maps.

The more dominating the internal sensitivity over the external one gets—the higher the tolerance level of the cluster boundaries becomes.

DPCS expose the following behavior:

1. Partial resistance (insensitivity) to external connectivity growing with the differences of internal pattern from the pattern of the external impact, unless such impact is strong enough to penetrate the boundary threshold and modify the internal pattern accordingly.
2. Continuation of internal harmonization independently

from some external changes not penetrating TB and allowing for independent internal harmonization

3. Decreasing influence of internal harmonization on external environment being "hidden" behind the growing TB stability.

Certain independence of internal harmonization in DPCS allows for faster and more successful harmonization being interrupted by less external impacts since some of them will be filtered out. On the other hand, such independence presents a risk of possible tensions with external situation after internal stabilization is achieved being disharmonic with it. The higher internal harmony is—the firmer are the boundaries and lower the external sensitivity, which can lead to growing tensions with environment.

Illustration

Example of DPCS with evolving TB could be seen in a drop of oil on the surface of the water where internal sensitivity and connectivity of oil is higher then between molecules of oil and water. A well-distinguished boundary could be observed with possibility of various boundary changes when the whole system is being heated up. Another possible example is in the evolution of such DPCS in the original ocean on Earth when the water started cooling down allowing internal sensitivity not to be disrupted by fast molecule movements of the environment caused by the high temperature.

Same area could belong to several different contexts exhibiting independent behaviors (in terms of evolution of sensitivity within each context) if contexts are independent for all areas of all types of clusters. Otherwise, context changes can influence each other. The movement of billiard balls does not depend upon the certain range of values on the levels of the magnetic field in the room, yet if the balls are metal than changes in the local resistance of the table cover and changes of the local values of the magnetic field can together determine the dynamics of the balls. If the balls are connected through some internal radio wave equipment with each other using independent frequencies and have mini computers inside then the patterns of their communications and information in their memories create a separate context of mutual sensitivity.

In trading context, relationships between sides form specific patterns that could be classified in all different ways. The more stable such pattern is the clearer relationships become with all the necessary features like financial, logistic and other context features forming specific patterns supporting specific relations. Relationship of mutual trust and possible repetitive nature will cause special account arrangements, alignment of coding systems and finally integration of trading systems on both sides becoming a trading channel. Once it is created—connectivity is better and mutual sensitivity as necessity to coordinate each other's changes is growing. The reverse is true too—when pattern of relations is not clear, then the context uncertainty and instability can affect desire to conduct a transaction.

PCCE Decomposition in PO/H

Existence of TB and phenomenon of harmony encapsulation requires a few new terms allowing to describe such systems having a certain degree of isolation from holistic dynamics of general CS-interaction. Existence of TB leads to limited sensitivity to various areas. Areas that DPCS preserves sensitivity to will be called *area of sensitivity* (AOS)

Environment is a combination of all external AOS. DPCS might not be sensitive to many other areas at all times because of poor connectivity and TB existence. Then it waits for impacts as **periodic** changes in connectivity (usually when something comes closer).

Context is a combination of all internal AOS. Some DPCS can "drop out" of the cluster, being too encapsulated by TB and having poor connectivity with the rest of the cluster. The difference between the context and the environment is in the level of sensitivity determining the cluster. Since cluster is a relative concept—there are a number of possible decompositions into context and environment based on various types of sensitivity analysis.

Pattern is a part of context (internal C-map), which is more stable then the rest of the context (cluster of sensitivity).

Carrier is a DPCS external sensitivity is mapped onto. It is a level of DPCS abstraction from underlying implementation of C and S.

All described classifications are fuzzy concepts with certain membership in each other. Decomposition of the holistic situation into pattern, context, carrier, and environment will be called *PCCE decomposition*. It can be a natural phenomena or an operation of vision, abstracting a system of interest and its parts from the rest in the observed situation.

Contexts could be sensitive to each other creating *hierarchies of contexts*. For example, a bigger cluster of urban growth dynamics context can be decomposed into political, economic, natural and other sensitivity clusters—contexts. These contexts can be sensitive to each other although still having internal sensitivity higher than external to other contexts.

HH and The Second Law of Harmonomics

At this point, we can introduce the Second Law of Harmonomics (LH2), which describes relations of DPCS with its environment supplementing LH1 describing general tendency of sensitivity Hz among any two or more arbitrary chosen areas. Let Hi and Hz^i be respectively internal harmony and internal harmonization of a DPCS. Here Hi reflects the level of achieved internal stability in the process of internal context harmonization (Hz^i). At the same time DPCS is only a cluster of sensitivity and preserves certain level of sensitivity (though lower then internal) with its environment. We will call the result of external harmonization (Hz^e) of external sensitivity He, reflecting the level of stability in relations of DPCS with its environment or the level of tensions between them. Then holistic harmony (HH) of any DPCS will consist of Hi, He, and harmony between these two (Hi/e):

$$HH = Hi + He + Hi/e$$

The concept of Holistic Harmony reflects the process of harmonization of all areas according to 1LH. But some of them are internal to DPCS and some are external. Then the process of harmonization of all these areas (holistic harmonization) can be expressed as:

$$HHz = Hz^i + Hz^e + Hz^{i/e}$$

The **Second Law of Harmonomics** could be formulated as following:

The Holistic Harmony of any DPCS tends to reach the level and the form of the Holistic Harmony of its environment

The similarity of forms of harmony means the existence of a homomorphism between their CSI complexes. Here particular shape of connectivity in one DPCS can be mapped onto specific sensitivity map or interpretation process of another (environment it is sensitive to). Level of harmony tends to be limited by the level of harmony of DPCS environment. Since environment could be quite dynamic and change its properties, the DPCS will undergo certain changes too unless its existing richness allow to recall a specific CSI combination matching environmental state and level of harmony.

This happens mainly because the patterns of environment excite (support) similar patterns in DPCS and (inhibit) suppress the dissimilar, non-harmonized with them patterns. Neural network learning and self-organized maps in particular can serve as a good example of such process.

Continuing Hz^e leads to incorporation of the areas of environment that are better harmonized with DPCS then others into DPCS context. New context affects patterns and after a while, full PC-harmonization within its extended context can be achieved, when new pattern and new context work in harmony with each other.

Here in addition to the level of harmony as the level of tensions we see the changes in the *form* of HH. The form of harmony is the dynamic map of its main features (C, S, I) in their interrelationship. It means that a homomorphism between the form of environmental harmony and HH of the DPCS doesn't have to copy C—and S-maps but could use various combinations of CSI leading to their support by environmental conditions. For example, well-structured environment with particular stable object-like features might be mapped onto stable structure of DPCS or stable patterns of its behavior or interpretation of external sensitivity.

TB-Related Dynamics of DPCS

The evolving concept of TB allows to relate some PO/H and OO/C observations, where fluid fuzzy and shapeless dynamics of contexts can start showing some shape with stabilization of its TB perceived as a container in OO/C.

.

Interwoven mix of both (fluidity and stability) is the

essence of DPCS. Although it is similar to CS-dynamics but shows additional stabilization features based on pattern-context relationships and mutual support. In OO/C vision TB can be seen as a membrane "swallowing" impacts that excite/support internal patterns by becoming more penetrable once (Hi-), or starving, leads to (TB-) with decreased external tolerance. When internal harmony grows (Hi+) TB gets firmer (TB+) allowing for continuing rapid internal harmonization (like digestion, identity shaping) at a price of the decrease of external sensitivity and harmony.

TB is not static but can dynamically change depending upon the levels of external and internal harmony based on levels of sensitivity leading to more or less effective harmonization. Possibility of continuing internal harmonization Hz^i can lead to the higher Hi which in turn increases TB. Growing tolerance to external changes supports higher tensions (disharmony) with environment ultimately driving He down. Decreased level of external harmony creates a general background of disharmony with higher chances of some fluctuations of changes to exceed the level of tolerance and penetrate TB. This affects internal harmony by damaging it. Decreased Hi leads to the lower TB, which in turn provides for better sensitivity to environment and external harmonization. Higher He leads to higher stability of the boundary offering more time for internal harmonization that leads to higher Hi. The loop closes.

Denoting increase or decrease as + or - and consequences as → we can describe the self-stabilizing negative feedback loop in a short form as following:

Hi + →TB+ → He- →power of environmental
impacts+→Hi-→TB-→He+→Hi+

The role of TB in increasing or decreasing HH of DPCS with its environment is a very general feature, which could be expressed as obtaining higher harmony by partly loosing identity (as a degree of isolation from environment). It also can be seen as a mechanism of connecting changes in He with changes in Hi and Hi/e. Pulsating nature of HHz loop can be seen in many sensitive systems including, so-called, life systems.

Described mechanism is very primitive and yet supporting TB role in the process of HH. There could be more advanced forms of TB like the ones performed by channel-DPCS discussed in the next chapter.

Chapter 3

Evolution of Multi-DPCS Forms

All higher forms of harmonization are based on patterns of local DPCS (LDPCS) interactions within multi DPCS forms (MDPCS). Such interactions can increase DPCS stability beyond CS-dynamics and simple pattern-context mechanisms. Structurally, MDPCS can have all possible horizontal and vertical types of DPCS relationships, including a hierarchical complexity consisting of sub and super DPCS. Because MDPCS has a dual role—as a container of multiple DPCS and as a DPCS itself, harmonization takes place on both levels:

1. Individual DPCS contributing with their ability to harmonize
2. The whole system acting as one DPCS

Forms of MDPCS harmonization mechanisms include:

1. **Multicontext** support in hierarchically nested pattern-context systems
As discussed before, DPCS can expand harmonization into its environment, attaching new layers of environment as parts of context with increased sensitivity to harmonization inside DPCS. In such cases whole DPCS, with its stability, plays a role in the pattern with the surrounding sensitive environment as a context. Each layer of context can absorb certain disharmony acting as tension, thus playing the role of a shock absorber for the DPCS—pattern it surrounds.

2. Mutual **multipattern** support from several DPCS with similar patterns
Given the existence of multiple DPCS with similar patterns inside MDPCS, the process of mutual excitation or pattern support might become sufficiently strong to filter disharmonic external impacts or recover from them using the continuing influence of unchanged DPCS. The more DPCS with the same type of internal harmony that exist in the MDPCS—the higher stability of that kind of harmony. The degree of existence of similar harmonies in various internal DPCS we will call the *mass of harmony* (mHi).

3. Mixed form consisting of both multipattern and multicontext structures

This additional architectural complexity of MDPCS creates the possibility for a variety of harmonization patterns which would allow the further increasing of the Hi of MDPCS, adding stability to its existence.

Patterns of MDPCS Hz

Patterns of MDPCS harmonization are based on DPCS ability to harmonize with environment using:

1. Impact absorption
2. Filtering of the noise and recovery of the original pattern
3. Reharmonization

Impact Absorption and the Encapsulation of Disharmony

One of the ways of coping with change is impact absorption functioning as an increase of internal disharmony of DPCS, thereby maintaining certain tensions that might continue existing without leading to any changes in internal C-map structure. Such absorption could be done on both levels: MDPCS or as harmonization problems distributed among LDPCS for absorption by them.

The ability of local DPCS or a global MDPCS to absorb external impacts is based on the general ability of DPCS to maintain sub-optimal levels of Hi. Seen from this point of view, any DPCS is a form of **encapsulation** or absorption **of disharmony,** by supporting He at the expense of a certain level of tension within Hi. For example, an organization can fulfill its external obligations with different levels of internal tension and conflicts that are not visible to the external sensitivity of other organizations. Changes in environmental dynamics can increase internal tensions within the organization and still allow it to cope with stressful reality. In this case problems and tensions are insulated from the rest of the context by the stability of He, maintained by DPCS absorbing the external disharmonic impact into the internal tensions of Hi.

The encapsulation of disharmony, as well as harmony, decreases the impact of local changes on the global situation, even in very sensitive systems. It is naïve to think that every little change is going to affect all corners of the system (contrary to primitive holism). Most likely they will be encapsulated within their own local DPCS. This refers to evolving problems and to harmonic solutions where both (problems and solutions) experience difficulties in influencing the rest of the system.

Filtering and Recovery

Mechanisms of MDPCS global filtering and recovery require a discussion of the specifics of interactions among several DPCS. Such interaction can affect all of the participants, leading to new dynamics in CS-maps.

DPCS Mapping

Seeing all DPCS of a structured environment as one DPCS converts the analysis of environmental influence on a given DPCS to mutual harmonization of two DPCS. It means that mutual coevolution of DPCS and its environment is developing in the direction minimizing the information exchange between these DPCS (LH1) and developing similar CSI—features (LH2) since each of them becomes the environment for the other. In such structured environments the process of coevolution leads to a **growing harmony as similarity between** DPCS, which decreases chances of **new** information being transferred, since most likely it is already incorporated in their Hi.

Depending upon the level of tolerance boundaries of each DPCS (their stability), such mutual harmonization will develop in each of them according to the level of their sensitivity. The more sensitive one DPCS is to the other—the closer its CS-map resembles the CS-map of the DPCS it is sensitive to. Ultimately, only one DPCS can change as a result of the CSI-*mapping* of one DPCS onto the other.

It is important to note that the trend in compliance with LH1 requires not only an immediate short-term decrease of information exchange, but also in the long-term as a more efficient form of harmonization. Then the internal dynamics of one DPCS will be repeated by another, keeping them "in sync" at all times and cutting the necessary information exchange of resynchronization.

Principle of Requisite Similarity of Connectivity and Sensitivity

The requirement of efficient modeling (minimum adjustments to the model during the development of the modeled process) of DPCS could be formulated as the necessity of **CSI-map similarity**. This becomes an extension to Ashby's requirement of the necessary variety of states in the model matching as the variety of possible states in the modeled system, which we want to control. Such formula refers only to the stable parts of systems that can be characterized as states. In our case we have to expand it to the requirements of a similar CSI—organization. It includes internal and external CS-maps as well as Interpretational patterns. Important to note that it is similarity of the CSI-organizations as a Whole, and not the sets of similarities between connectivity maps, sensitivity maps, and interpretational organization.

> The similarity of two DPCS is based on the similarity of their CSI-maps.

Such similarity can be seen as potential harmonization which can become actual if their mutual sensitivity exceeds the tolerance boundary

MDPCS Filtering and Recovery

The filtering of external influences and recovery of the original CS-map is a different pattern of MDPCS harmonization where externally introduced disharmony is not absorbed but ignored, either through immediate filtering or delayed filtering after recovery of the original CS-map. On the level of local DPCS, filtering and recovery become possible using the following mechanisms:

- tolerance boundaries for filtering the portion of tensions distributed among all LDPCS
- continuing harmonization of DPCS, my returning its CS-map, modified by the impact, to the state of the original harmony. (Of course, sufficiently strong impact can modify the state of harmony into a different CS-map with minimal tensions—different energy well.)

On the level of MDPCS the following mechanisms can support filtering and recovery:

- Mass of harmony
- Distributed mass of harmony
- Recovery as convergence to the same CS-map

Mass of harmony is proportionate to the number of similar patterns in different DPCS. The higher the mass of harmony the higher its stability since such patterns excite each other; it is similar to a resonance effect. If the number of similar DPCS is sufficiently high—then the common tolerance boundaries of such agroup are stronger, allowing for the filtering disharmonic impacts.

The mechanism of **distributed mass of harmony** allows for the recovery of damaged patterns. It is based on the space distribution of DPCS with similar patterns which can prevent some of them from direct influence on the external disharmonic impact. Then the ones that remain unchanged can return (repair) the damaged DPCS back to their previous state after the impact is gone. It doesn't have to be a space distribution of similar DPCS. Differences in connectivity to the external impact, in general, can also lead to the preservation of less connected and less sensitive DPCS,

177

allowing for recovery of the damaged ones by the intact DPCS with the same patterns of harmony.

Convergence to the previous CS-map when the nearest state of harmony is the same as it was before the impact. You can move a small ball slightly up the well and it will fall back into the same position after being set free. Such CS-map recovery can happen only when the impact is not strong enough to shift the harmonization situation to a different energy well where a different CS-map can serve as the minimum of tensions.

Reharmonization of DPCS

The previous patterns of harmonization lead either to the encapsulating of disharmony (bearing with it) or to ignoring external impacts and supporting MDPCS stability. These mechanisms are good and useful if environmental impacts are mere fluctuations or noise, which does not have a stable or repetitive pattern. But what if an impact is a demonstration of growing disharmony with environment as a result of a sensitivity loss? Then LH2 requires harmonization with environmental changes if they cannot be simply outlived. Such harmonization happens on different levels of pattern detail, according to the external sensitivity map of DPCS to its environment. Some details of the external pattern could be filtered out.

If the impact cannot be simply absorbed as an increase in internal tensions, neither can it be filtered directly or, after recovery of the previous to the impact state, then the change of Hi is imminent. Such change can happen as evolving/dissipation of the CS-patterns as a result of changes in LDPCS relations, or as a result of the general pattern evolution/dissipation out of/into MDPCS context.

Macro CS-map changes can be based on LDPCS relations as connectivity and sensitivity changes among DPCS. Not only LDPCS within MDPCS can support extra stability through individual harmonization mechanisms, but their interaction also creates additional parts of the global CS-map of MDPCS. Changes in inter-DPCS connectivity and sensitivity are capable of absorbing externally introduced tensions in the same way as internal CS-maps of individual DPCS.

The harmonization of MDPCS with its environment via CS-map modification of LDPCS relations is based on the following mechanisms:

- Reharmonization of LDPCS that together represent pattern changes in MDPCS
- Mergers and splits of LDPCS
- The growth of internal complexity in LDPCS with evolving of sub-DPCS
- Evolving/dissipating of LDPCS

The evolving or dissipating of the new DPCS from/into sensitivity of the general context is another way. As in the case of internal CS-maps of individual DPCS, inter—DPCS relations can produce additional clusters of sensitivity, evolving into new DPCS that match the new harmony better. By the same logic old DPCS might dissipate, leading to a more adequate pattern structure of MDPCS, fitting harmonies of its environment. This includes external sensitivity not accounted for (or filtered) by LDPCS.

The Channel View of DPCS

DPCS evolving out of context as new clusters of sensitivity is not the only situation where they can emerge. So far, we primarily discussed situations where context surrounding LDPCS is quite fluid and subjected to the harmonization influence of LDPCS as its pattern (see multicontext forms above). At the same time LH2 describes the general direction of DPCS harmonization. But what is happening on a more detailed level of interaction with parts of the environment?

In many cases the internal MDPCS context creates an environment for LDPCS where environmental patterns are mainly represented by several LDPCS attempting to influence each other. What is worse, they might not be harmonized with each other, presenting a harmonization problem for an individual LDPCS about whom to follow. How is it possible to harmonize with a few neighbors and be disharmonic with each other? We will call such environments *frustrating,* emphasizing the difficulties of coevolution in them.

The view of DPCS, which plays the role of a channel connecting several DPCS, will be called a *channel view* versus *entity view* when we look at DPCS as a center of holistic harmonization. The channel view exposes any DPCS as a *channel DPCS,* focusing on harmonization among DPCS connected by it. This view allows for the explanation of the details of the HHz dynamics determined by LH2, using more specific analysis of the environment as several major DPCS influencing the DPCS of our interest.

The Third Law of Harmonomics

The dynamics of channel DPCS in structured environments could be described by **The Third Law of Harmonization** (LH3):

> **The DPCS, supporting connectivity among other DPCS in its environment, tends to modify such connectivity and corresponding interpretational processes in a way matching the dynamics of mutual sensitivity and harmonization among these DPCS**

In order to understand LH3 better, let us look at channel DPCS in a situation when there are two other DPCS connected by it. In this case, channel DPCS represents the means of connectivity and sensitivity transfer between these end-DPCS. If each of them has a high level of internal harmony but are disharmonic in relation to each other, the environment for the channel DPCS could be described by the average level of harmony, which should guide the development of its HH according to LH2. At the same time each particular connection of the DPCS channel with other DPCS has to be harmonized with it, according to LH1. This creates a serious problem for the channel, which has to satisfy the both laws. Such a situation is worsened by the fact that changes on its ends can happen very abruptly (see harmonization catastrophe below), leading to very complex pattern-context dynamics following LH3.

On the other hand, changes of sensitivity and harmony between two DPCS connected by a channel match changes in the connectivity and interpretation of the channel. Such changes use the dual nature of connectivity and sensitivity relations and when on low levels of connectivity they support each other, but on high levels of connectivity sensitivity becomes constricted. This results in two major groups of channel behavior resulting in increased or decreased connectivity between its ends:

1. **Links** and **barriers** between different types of subpatterns on channel ends could become more or less harmonic with each other
2. **Attraction** or **repulsion** when increased/decreased space between channel ends increases or decreases adjusting the connectivity between them

Examples could be seen in the development and restructuring of neuron connections, like relations among people and organizations with specific changes in connectivity. The complexity of the whole situation with multiple DPCS connected through the same channel DPCS with each other (like collaborative electronic marketplaces) could be assessed using the following result of the LH3:

> Complexity of the CSI-map of a channel DPCS is proportionate to the level of complexity of the harmonization situation among the DPCS connected through it

The speed of interpretation of the information passing through the channel is of great importance. Delays might lead to artificial disharmonies when potentially synchronous changes of two DPCS get "out of sync" and become artificially disharmonic.

Full Mapping and Harmonization Catastrophes

According to LH3, the increased similarity and harmony between any two DPCS leads to the increased connectivity of the channel and their mutual sensitivity, which stimulates a more active Hz process and so on. This happens through an increasingly powerful positive feedback loop. The case of growing a similarity between mutually sensitive DPCS can be seen as a mechanism of the mutual excitation of similarities and the inhibition of differences, converging on a similarity like the simple connectionist system called *perceptron*, which was studied by Rosenblatt of the Cornell Aeronautical Laboratory. Since there are no unlimited processes in the universe—what stops such development?

Ultimately, systems will become fully harmonized (at least, on the level of available sensitivity). However, full harmony will instantly reverse the situation because the information exchange stops. No new information is possible and mutual sensitivity becomes zero. At this point full harmony is the same as full disharmony—there is nothing to say to each other. Such an abrupt change in the existing functionality is called, in mathematics, a catastrophe. We will call the described process Harmonization Catastrophe of the First Type (HC1).

At this point, according to LH3, a jump to the level of full disharmony is like an explosion for the previously smooth process of connectivity enhancement during the prior harmonization stage. Connectivity responds by changing the direction of its development and usually leads to mutual repulsion as the easiest way of a connectivity decrease. We can see such repulsion after cell-splitting. We can see it in the growing tendency of maturing children to distance themselves from their parents. It may be this is why, with long distances, physical entities attract each other in the form of gravity, but with short distances with more similar contexts among atomic structures demonstrate aggressive repulsion.

If an HC1 catastrophe was a result of the LH3 applied to DPCS communications, the Harmonization Catastrophe of the Second Type (HC2) is a result of the LH1 also being applied to mutually sensitive DPCS. Being separated by a semi-permeable border and being able to support a relatively independent internal harmonization without influencing each other, DPCS can develop sufficiently strong Hi that is disharmonic with Hi of another DPCS but initially undetectable and hidden behind mutual He. At some point the disharmony of the internal states might exceed tolerance boundaries or channel protection and suddenly become visible impacting another DPCS. The sudden revealing of internally grown disharmony creates HC2 with almost the same consequences for channel connectivity and sensitivity as HC1. The higher the external harmony between such DPCS the stronger the effect of the bursting of the differences of Hi that have to instantly reshape the connectivity of the channel. The sudden realization of the differences and hidden conflicts between close people or closely cooperating companies can create stronger repulsion then between strangers.

Evolutionary Dynamics

The harmonization dynamics among local DPCS (LDPCS) and the multiparticipant DPCS (MDPCS) they belong to determines the result of HHz of all these forms. External harmonization of LDPCS within their common context is seen as internal harmonization of MDPCS, with all earlier discussed HHz patterns applicable to any of them and to the whole MDPCS. Such duality of MDPCS as a whole, and as a collection of parts, determines the variety of possible patterns of its harmonization.

The tolerance boundaries (TB) depend upon the difference between the internal and external sensitivity of a DPCS. Internal sensitivity of MDPCS depends upon the dynamics of external and internal sensitivities of LDPCS. The decrease of He among LDPCS leads to the lower Hi of MDPCS and decreases its TB. As a result, He of MDPCS can grow, returning Hi back to the higher level based on the support obtained from similar patterns in environment.

Some interesting patterns of MDPCS dynamics include situations of local and global overharmonization.

The possibility of local overstabilization of local internal harmonies (LHi) is based on their interaction with local external harmonies (LHe) and the dynamics of global holistic harmonization with external harmony of MDPCS (He) and its internal harmony (Hi). The following chain of dynamic transformations can form a self-correcting loop:

$$LHe\text{-}\rightarrow Hi\text{-}\rightarrow He\text{+} \rightarrow Hi\text{+} \rightarrow LHe\text{+}$$

But if the external sensitivity of MDPCS is insufficient or artificially blocked, then there will be no necessary correction of Hi and LHe can fall below some minimal level necessary to maintain sufficient connectivity (according to LH3) between the components of MDPCS and MDPCS as a cluster of sensitivity disappears, creating a number of independent and much weaker connected DPCS.

The opposite can happen when overstabilization of Hi in MDPCS leads to LHi growth:

$$Hi+ \rightarrow LHe+ \rightarrow LHi+$$

LHi is shaped here after Hi based on LH2 when a strong and stable environment molds other DPCS into the same type of harmonies. But then, according to LH1, the higher the harmony the higher the sensitivity and the more powerful harmonization becomes until there is a strong dependency of the internal harmony upon the external harmony of MDPCS, which makes it work as the same cluster of sensitivity.

Of course, such a positive harmonization loop can happen only when Hi of MDPCS is strong enough to withstand the loss of its He (iron curtain). This process of iron curtain building (cutting information out and internal molding with a growing mass of harmony) is temporary and, once it exceeds the distance from the harmony of its environment has much higher chances for destruction.

Chapter 4

ADVANCED FORMS AND PATTERNS OF

MDPCS HARMONIZATION

The existence of internal DPCS relationships creates a foundation for a great variety and complexity of MDPCS forms and their harmonization patterns. We will be especially interested in the possibility of the evolution of the more stable forms, analyzing the generality of DPCS application to the description of more OO/C—style entities.

AHS: The General Concept

The dynamics of MDPCS harmonization involves periodic corrections of Hi as a result of internal harmonization and penetrating external impacts. Such corrections could be more or less dramatic. If the system is overstabilized then the disharmony with the dynamic environment grows and the possibility of a strong impact molding internal harmony into a different pattern or completely destroying the previous

186

one increases. Together with the destruction of outdated patterns, some still useful ones could be lost. This is the source of strategic inefficiency of DPCS when tactical harmonization wipes out useful strategic results of previous harmonization. Such destruction can lead to the "death" of an MDPCS when its pattern is destroyed as well as its means of its restoration. Sometimes the damaged Hi cannot build sufficient coherence between the internal DPCS and the growing sensitivity between them and the external DPCS will lead to a situation where the initial MDPCS is torn apart by its neighbors with better harmonies to some of its subpatterns. The maintaining of a sufficient external sensitivity constantly delivering the latest trends in the environment helps to fight internal overharmonization. Such "continuous improvement" allows for the avoidance of strong disharmonic impacts and the usage of external influences as excitation and support for internal patterns. A sufficient level of internal and external sensitivity (close to the "Edge of Chaos" used in life systems) results in the existence of such behavior when the effectiveness of internal creative harmonization is balanced with sufficient external sensitivity, and incoming impacts can just weaken the internal harmony instead of fully destroying it, which enhances external sensitivity and the loop can start again. When and how can such systems emerge?

LH1 supports the tendency of Hi growth in any DPCS. Such growth can lead to different outcomes depending upon the turbulence (CUI) of the environment. LH2 limits the statistical stability of DPCS and actively growing Hi with the harmony existing in its environment. Both laws could be seen as a combination of local and global harmonization processes where the global one limits the level of independent local harmonization and visa versa. Thus global harmonization tends to support a similarity of the global patterns related to the local DPCS to their reflection in the

Hi of this DPCS. Such a tendency takes the form of either the resonance and excitation/support of similar patterns or the inhibition and possible destruction of dissimilar ones. But the resulting molding or destruction and rebuilding by the environment of the "runaway" Hi of DPCS is only as effective as the environment is stable and harmonic itself.

We can distinguish three broad types of DPCS environment:

1. A moderately stable and harmonic environment with a low frequency of changes (type 1)
2. A very turbulent environment with a high CUI and a high frequency of changes (type 2)
3. Something in between (type 3)

LH2 states the tendency of HH growth in any particular DPCS (DPCSj). Recall the structure of HH:

$$HH = Hi + He + Hi/e$$

We see that HH growth can be achieved through the growth of any of its components or their various combinations. Let us analyze the specificity of holistic harmonization in different types of environments.

In stable environments of type 1 the growth of the HH of DPCSj will be based on the growth of its Hi according to LH1. As you remember from the discussion of DPCS dynamics, such growth leads to higher internal stability and decreased external harmony He. LH2 also limits the level of harmony and the type of its C-map to the one of DPCSj environment which, in case of lower He, retaliates with a destructive disharmonic impact, decreasing Hi of DPCSj. But on a tactical level such statistically damaging impacts might not come soon and in stable environments there could be a long period of time between corrective strikes of environment, during which Hi can grow to sufficiently high levels. This, in turn, means that DPCSj can withstand most of the smaller changes, which increases its lifetime and allows for even higher levels of Hi as a main contributor to HH growth. Even if some of the smaller changes penetrate Hi their modification of Hi incorporates information about such impacts, making DPCS more prepared for the new ones since most of information was already accounted for. Such a statistical approach to DPCS stabilization is effective in stable environments and leads to stable DPCS supported by strategically stable patterns of the environment and the ability to resist higher frequency "noise" as fluctuations.

According to LH3 the conflict of low He and high Hi is carried out by the channel DPCS connecting DPCSj to the environment. The most well-known form of such channel DPCS is all types of covers, shells and external coatings, creating an appearance of material objects with clear boundaries. These shells-boundaries are shaped by LH3 which states that disharmony on channel ends is resolved by its C-map restructuring which, in cases of persistent disharmony, tries to decrease mutual sensitivity by building "walls" on its way. The higher the internal harmony of DPCS is and the stronger environmental pressures are (take diamonds, for example) the harder these shells. This is the world of objects, the world of matter maintaining high internal harmony and stability together with clear and firm boundaries.

Turbulent environments of type 2 with high CUI do not let Hi grow and He becomes the main contributor to the HH of DPCS. Weak Hi leads to high external sensitivity, not collapsed onto itself, in harmony encapsulation around the emerging pattern. This form almost immediately responds to environmental changes following all its "waves" and "winds." In fact, weather patterns are good examples of such DPCS. Boundary is often nominal, fuzzy and permeable.

Somewhere between these two cases is a very interesting and special situation of changing environments of type 3, with CUI not so high as to prevent Hi evolution, but high enough to keep the evolution sufficiently slow, supporting the necessary external sensitivity dynamically correcting the internal pattern to match the changes in patterns of environmental evolution. This type of DPCS manages to combine high Hi and He due to the special dynamics of Hi/e constantly reharmonizing the internal and external worlds of DPCS. Such a reharmonization job cannot be based on statistical knowledge of the most stable patterns in the environment (to follow) and the rest (to ignore) as in the case of stable environments. Here each impact is different and potentially destructive, requiring to take its harmonization seriously with all its current details. It means that the harmonization function depends upon particular time and not statistical pattern distribution and belongs to the class of dynamical systems.

From this point of view harmonization is the change of harmony over time and is represented by the *flow*:

$$dH/dt=f(H)$$

For discrete observations it is called a *map*, which can be represented as:

$$H_{t+1} = f(H_t)$$

Of course, the function (f) is quite complicated and depends upon the environmental changes as well, but the point is that, in addition to statistical distribution of patterns in the environment, the system has to deal with each impact in a particular point of time where time becomes an important consideration. Once the moment of the mild correction is missed and Hi grows too much to lose external sensitivity, the environmental impact might destroy such DPCS completely.

The systems capable of consistent balancing in the middle ground supporting Hi and He levels with skillful harmonization of both of them will be called autoharmonization systems (AHS). Such balancing has a recurrent loop form where LH1 pushes Hi to its higher levels which, in turn, increase the risk and pressure of environmental resistance due to the loss of He. At some point LH3 and LH2 make external harmonization more important and influential, which diminishes Hi and allows for better He. But the better He the less impacts affect Hi, which again has a chance for growth. Such a loop in dynamical systems analysis represents a periodic solution of the abovementioned flows or maps in phase space and is called a limit cycle (LC). An LC is stable if it attracts all neighboring curves, unstable if it repels them, and is semi-stable if it is an attractor on one side and a repeller on the other (see Fig. 5).

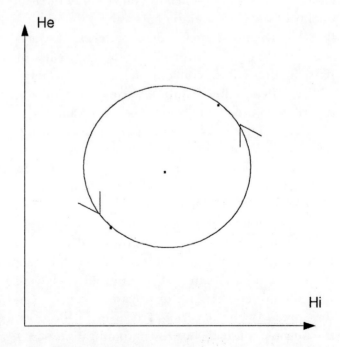

Fig.5 Limt Cycle

The effectiveness and potential length of life of AHS can be based on the study of general *health indicators* determining the shape and stability of various proportions between some important DPCS features influencing the stability of the limited cycle of holistic harmonization (**LCh**) of AHS described above. The main concern is not the exact solution and measurements of variables used for LC determination but the stability of its recurrent nature in changing environments of type 3, which determines *health* of an AHS. Deviations from a healthy state for such indicators show the danger of AHS slipping into the area with possible irreversible changes in discussed regime (*death* of AHS).

Health Indicators

PO/H vision, based on permeable DPCS boundaries and dynamic evolving using DPCS harmonization on all levels, allows for the recognition and evaluation of the features and quality of the parts and the harmony of the whole system in its HHz dynamics. Such macro patterns, abstracting from the details of the internal Hz mechanisms of all the participating DPCS, concentrate on the properties of the whole DPCS. The dynamic proportion of He and Hi described above is one of the possible examples.

Health indicators do not attempt to capture snapshots of current measurable attributes among exiting DPCS, which is typical for OO/C-approach, but rather concentrate on holistic features affecting the whole harmonization dynamics and the stability of LCh. Indicators are important not only in the description of the general state of AHS health as potential viability or closeness to one of possible disorders of HH or HHz, but also because indicator imbalances are mapped onto the environment (external or internal), allowing for the spreading of good health or disease. Examples can include the spread of the decaying processes in life organisms or the possible mutually healthy harmonization of SOS and its ecology. Nervous system disorders are mapped onto the immune and other systems of life organisms. Such mechanisms, in addition to direct disorder mapping onto various DPCS, affect the context of the whole MDPCS and other DPCS through it.

As an example, we can see the three human body systems—the immune system, the nervous system and the endocrine system as three different carriers supporting almost the same patterns mapped/interpreted onto each other (mainly by peptide messaging system) to an extent that they all can be seen as one psychosomatic system (Candace, 1985). Peptides, among other mechanisms, are largely responsible for the mutual sensitivity of the main sensitive systems of human bodies, connecting the emotional/perceptional patterns of the brain with the pattern dynamic of various systems of the body into one body/mind system. Imbalances in one system create imbalances in others, and once they become chronic (harmonized with many DPCS of various types) the volume of this new disharmonic pattern becomes so big that it obtains a self-supporting stability. This is why chronic disorders are so difficult to fight. But this is also why stable holistic improvements in one system can provide healing effect in others.

The top-level indicators are the ratios (we will call all health ratios—Rx) reflecting major possible imbalances (if there are any) including:

1. The current adequacy of the connectivity and sensitivity levels (Rcs) compared to the ideal balance of Rcs*
2. The current adequacy of the unity/diversity degrees (Rud) compared to the ideal balance of Rud*
3. The current adequacy of Rcs/Rud compared to the ideal balance of Rcs/Rud *

Other more detailed Rx indicators could be developed as subclasses of problems detected by top-level Rx.

The Connectivity-Sensitivity Ratio

The connectivity-sensitivity ratio (Rcs) describes the features of the existing state of HS and its processes:

- The proportion of achieved general stability to general sensitivity
- The proportion of the use of control methods as domination of stabilities (C-maps) for the use of methods of mutual harmonization of S-maps

Although some part of sensitivity eventually will be harmonized to its more stable state of connectivity, the remaining or newly appearing sensitivity should be sufficient to respond to the necessary changes in internal and external harmonization. Too much sensitivity and inability to find harmony quickly, on the other hand, creates the risk of chaos and unnecessarily increased tensions that can prove harmful and self-destructive (see LH3).

The proper balance allows for very adaptive and efficient behavior. There is a growing sentiment that life itself is an example of such a balance at the "edge of chaos." More sensitivity creates chaotic behavior while more stability freezes a system's adaptive abilities. Imbalance of Rcs can be perceived in an organization as abuse of control methods based on some embedded models/decisions or the inability to provide fast harmonization solutions using group interactions.

Unity-Diversity

Unity-diversity ration (Rud) reflects the variety of different patterns of Hi within MDPCS. Although continuous harmonization tends to make all patterns similar (DPCS mapping on each other), a lack of pattern variety compared to environmental pattern diversity leads to a decreased sensitivity to some important external patterns and overall holistic disharmony. HS can be unprepared for a potentially highly disharmonic impact or miss an opportunity of using a "friendly" pattern supporting its existing state. On the other hand, if the variety of internally encapsulated harmonies is too big harmonization takes too long and might become ineffective for a current situation.

Proper Rud balancing means the necessity of preserving a certain level of internal tensions in order to curb the level of external tensions. Examples of countries or companies allowing for multiple opinions show better long-term performance then the ones where dissidents are persecuted in a desire to mold all opinions according to the "Right One."

Rcs/Rud Proportion

Rcs and Rud are not independent from each other. The higher level of diverse patterns leads to multiple tolerance boundaries and harmonization problems maintaining higher sensitivity (sometimes higher then necessary). The low level of diversity simplifies harmonization and leads to higher levels of stability (sometimes higher then necessary).

Existence of Optimal Values of Health Indicators

All three indicators have optimal values somewhere in the middle of the possible range. Considering LH2 we can say that optimality is achieved when the values of the health indicators correspond to those of the environment. The more diverse environment requires higher Rud, as well as more structured and stable environment requires higher Rcs.

Optimal Rcs*, Rud*, and Rcs/ud* determine the health of MDPCS as its ability to avoid destructive environmental impacts. These indicators could be applied to all levels and locations of MDPCS, analyzing its health from the very top and general level to all its components and processes.

Lower Level Health Indicators

The presented indicators are of the highest and most general level of AHS and DPCS, but they are ubiquitous in the sense that they could be used for all DPCS on all levels. We can start from the Rx analysis of the whole organization and detailing it down to a particular project. This generality of the top-level Rx could be counterbalanced by their application to various levels of DPCS within an HS.

At the same time, applying Rx analysis to the **same** DPCS allows the for the developing of the lower level and more specific Rx. For example, while analyzing the Rcs of a particular AHS, we might want to inspect the reason for its perceivable abundance of control attempts over other AHS in its environments compared to sensitivity to their positions (high Rcs). The evaluation of the levels of internal and external sensitivity (**Rie**) might show that the deviation is based on extreme internal sensitivity or insufficient external sensitivity leading to controlling intentionality.

The ratio of local versus global harmonization efforts (**Rlg**) for local DPCS within a given MDPCS can provide an easier diagnosis of the possible situations leading to MDPCS dissipation that were discussed in the previous section. For example, too high Rlg of LDPCS shows that local DPCS use too big efforts for their own internal harmonization versus participation in the building of global MDPCS's internal harmony. This can lead to MDPCS falling apart as a result of weakening channel connectivity (LH3) among its subparts caused by their low sensitivity to each other because of high internal harmonization. On the other hand, global overharmonization when Rlg is too low can lead to the disappearance of LDPCS as carriers of the independent encapsulated harmony of their own, ultimately weakening the whole MDPCS. Various types of Rlg could be detected using the Rx of the higher level, such as Rud which shows the final result in unity/diversity of LDPCS. The top level

Rx are also more general in their use since it is possible to apply them to AHS on various levels of detail. Same Rlg could be analyzed as the derivative of Rcs and Rud on the level of isolated LDPCS and their various groups.

Signal-Oriented Systems

The main problem of AHS evolution is in the mechanism supporting dynamic preservation and evolving of Hi/e under the growth of Hi and environmental changes. Basically, there are two possible mechanisms of such harmonization: internal harmonization does the job or the Hi/e channel does the job (or, at least, part of it).

In the first case, the channel has to provide good external sensitivity (being a sensor) along with the ability to increase connectivity with Hi (putting pressure on Hi) when the signal tells of a danger and necessitates Hi reconfiguration while staying low in case of innocent signals. Such a pattern of behavior is called reactive and requires deep penetration of the sensors into all subpatterns of Hi that are, in turn, sensitive to this sensor system. The primitive nervous system of some life forms is an example of such implementation. An amoeba instantly responds to an extreme environmental condition, as well as the muscles of our body respond to the signals generated by the nervous system.

In the second case, the channel tries to harmonize both sides and after serious harmonization work when the more stable result is found, it is conveyed to the Hi of a given DPCS as an integral response to the integral set of impacts. An intelligent life form with a brain doing such a job can serve as an example.

Both of these cases are based on the developed external sensitivity and the special ways it cooperates with Hi in the act of supporting Hi/e. Note that in the second case, DPCS does not respond to the direct environmental impact itself, which can be severe and crush the comparatively weak Hi, but to the leading weak signals of the coming danger. Signals strong enough to start preparing DPCS, but not so strong as to destroy the DPCS. This allows enough time to restructure Hi and Hi/e in a more defensive way. AHS, that use weak signals picked up by their sensors in preharmonization processes before the "attack," will be called Signal Oriented Systems (**SOS**). As it was discussed in the previous section, the self-supporting optimality of the health indicators provides increased harmonization efficiency for SOS with maximum reuse of the previously accumulated harmony of its patterns.

Various forms of SOS implementation will be the focus of the rest of this part, where we will look into the details of AHS achieving advanced forms of holistic harmonization by using a variety of mechanisms based on signal orientation:

- General SOS
- Multiparticipant SOS
- Active AHS
- Balanced AHS

All these systems belong to the class of SOS with differences in the implementation of the two general features:

1. Ability to sense the forthcoming environmental impacts by recognizing weak "advanced warning" signals as signs of possible danger from environmental impacts
2. Ability to minimize the influence of such potentially damaging impacts by using these "advanced warnings" to perform preharmonization with the forthcoming patterns of the impact and decreasing the possible internal changes since the new information was already accounted for

SOS relations with the environment have two distinctive regimes:

1. Direct Physical Impact (DPI) of the environment on SOS, meaning that connectivity with some external DPCS was increased so much (may be because it got close enough) that, supported by its sensitivity to SOS, resulted in the mapping of such impact onto the internal structure of existing harmony, forcefully modifying it (like a bullet hole)

2. Direct Vision Impact (DVI) when some weak signals can be perceived by SOS due to its advanced sensitivity and interpreted as signs of the forthcoming DPI

DVI, then, can be treated as vision, which delivers information about approaching DPI without its damaging impact, as in the case of DPI. All known life forms are SOS forms, using their external sensitivity to produce adaptive behavior that maintains their health through a proper balance of structural stability, advanced harmonization skills and sufficient sensitivity. The described ability requires a certain complexity of SOS organization. Using a sensitivist model of T-modes we can analyze the specifics of MDPCS evolution leading to the SOS form of harmonization.

Two-Level Systems as Double-Loop Stability

The architectural complexity of SOS requires the existence of two different types of DPCS in SOS seen as MDPCS. These DPCS form two levels of action: the physical level (pDPCS) and the vision level (vDPCS). Each of these DPCS can be complex enough to form an MDPCS. Their combination demonstrates the following features:

1. The vision level (V-level) is formed by vDPCS that is supported by its HHz cycle (loop 1) with DVI as its inputs, where an advanced carrier is formed supporting AHS

features in successfully balancing health indicators of a vDPCS

2. The physical level (P-level) is formed by pDPCS which is more stable, having low external sensitivity (being more sensitive to vDPCS then to the environment) and responding only to sufficiently strong environmental impacts (DPI) with HHz forming loop 2

3. The mutual sensitivity of vDPCS and pDPCS creates loop3 of self-harmonization which works at a speed sufficient to **compensate** (when necessary) the changes made by external DPI affecting pDPCS or to prepare SOS for DPI with minimal losses of valuable harmonies that evolved during the previous experiences

The adaptability of vDPCS and its health are vital for the whole SOS, which owes its viability to the work of the vision level. Possible implementations of vDPCS (which could be quite complex) include:

1. vDPCS as context of pDPCS
2. vDPCS as a virtual system fully residing in pDPCS communication structure
3. vDPCS shares the same and carrier
4. vDPCS resides on a different carrier largely independent of the carrier of pDPCS

The V-level, having a more developed external sensitivity, has tolerance boundaries with DPCS of P-level, allowing for independent harmonization of its sensitivity. Such harmonization perceives patterns of the P-level as one DPCS can be harmonized with, and the environmental situation as another. Since signals from the environment are picked up from afar and remain weak (before the external impact comes closer and hits with all its force) they do not dominate the process of harmonization of vDPCS with pDPCS. This has to be a balanced holistic harmonization process where more stable patterns of the P-level can survive changes offered by the reflection of and reaction to the external situation.

Once the new harmony between the stable state of the vDPCS and the patterns of the environment is achieved, it becomes stable and influential enough to affect P-level with its weak external sensitivity. As a result, P-level reflects (through mapping) the harmony achieved on V-level, which leads to a higher compliance with upcoming external impacts, decreasing the amount of possible new information influencing P-level and, hence, decreasing the power of the impact. If the power of the impact is decreased enough, it allows for the saving of the most harmonic internal patterns, "reusing" the previously made harmonization effort.

The SOS organization effectively shifts control over MDPCS harmonization from the environment to the V-level. This level offers a certain freedom of choice in the way coevolution with the environment will take place. Instead of being merely responsive to environmental influences that directly modify MDPCS patterns of P-level via existing sensitivity, SOS offers a two-level scheme of harmonization when the more sensitive V-level subsystem provides the choice of the new harmony, considering the past state of SOS, while the P-level subsystem responds to such choice (harmonizing with it) instead of being directly transformed by environmental impacts when they arrive at full connectivity with MDPCS (direct physical impact). It is interesting that vDPCS can play the role of a buffer tuning to external signals and dissipating the new patterns if they are not continuously (or at least often) supported by the same environmental states. Then "excitation" of the V-level will not get through the P-level tolerance boundary and will not change it.

Such organization is an example of an interesting method of maintaining optimal health indicators by averaging their level between two subsystems. Here the P-level is more stable than optimum while the V-level is less stable. Thus an evolving V-level compensates for the insufficient sensitivity of a massively harmonized and overstabilized P-level.

The P-level plays an important role, allowing for the focusing of the external sensitivity using a mix of concentrative and meditative regimes. In a concentrative regime the V-level harmonizes its sensitivity in the area of the strongest environmental signals that create the most tensions in the current situation. After P-level harmonization is achieved, and perceived tensions become smaller, the stability of the P-level allows for a meditative regime of the V-level, where it can return to the original state, mainly harmonic with the P-level, and with strategically important and stable patterns of the environment being ready to respond to the appearance of the new harmonization threat. Such "forgetting" of the external patterns the V-level was focusing on, and the ability to return to the "calm" state capable to adequately respond to new threats when they arrive determine the effectiveness of the SOS vision mechanism.

Sensors

Some of the LDPCS in MDPCS have sensitivity extending outside of the common boundary. They might be seen as belonging to several MDPCS in terms of sensitivity but usually only one of these MDPCS is, in turn, sensitive to such LDPCS which becomes its "sensor," creating a mutual coevolution feedback loop. The high sensitivity of sensors to external DPCS and their ability to create *internal DPI* (iDPI), influencing only vDPCS on the vision level, and being isolated from the P-level, makes such impacts different from the external DPI of the environment which can change the P-level directly. Internal DPI, ideally, can change only the V-level and pDPCS might be affected only by vDPCS after sufficient Hz on the V-level is done, accounting for the importance of the iDPI delivered by the sensors.

Another feature of the sensors is an instability of their external connectivity that is switched under the influence of vDPCS seeking its Hi (focusing). He of such LDPCS is managed by vDPCS through the change of connectivity and sensitivity and creates a remote harmonization loop:

$$Hz_i(vDPCS) \rightarrow Hz_e(vDPCS/pDPCS) \rightarrow$$
$$Hz_i(pDPCS) \rightarrow Hz_e(pDPCS/Env) \rightarrow Hz_i(vDPCS)$$

The V-level Evolving and Harmonization

Here we will explore the stability and possible evolution of a set of vDPCS into the whole integrated V-level. As we have mentioned before, every higher-level pattern could be seen as one of lower-level patterns that are more general. It means that vDPCS could be seen as an MDPCS itself with the possible evolving of internal levels similar to the double-loop mechanism of vDPCS.

The V-level Evolving

The evolution of SOS from MDPCS with homogeneous LDPCS entertaining horizontal connectivity is based on the possibility of some sensors to becoming secondary sensors, responding not to the changes in the environment but to the changes in the primary sensors and each other's state while preserving relative independence from the more stable P-level DPCS. According to LH3, the channel connecting the rest of pDPCS with constantly changing sensors has to become sufficiently complicated in order to provide for their mutual harmonization. Ultimately, such channels take the shape of the nervous system and the brain, which are usually connected to the most changing sensory (visual) system.

Such channel-DPCS has to be a good and fast harmonizer because the situation is changing all the time, especially in mobile systems (discussed later). Initially, the channel-DPCS connecting the sensors and pDPCS played the role of an interface for external signals to be delivered to the P-level of MDPCS. These signals were causing pre-trained (preharmonized) interpretation of the signals and were controlled by its modification in some pDPCS (reflexes). But with the growing variety of states that it was able to maintain, channel-DPCS became a vDPCS which supported some initial harmonization (before affecting pDPCS) of all received signals and the result was mapped onto the old system of reflexes supporting the new function of independent harmonization. At such a moment vDPCS (or rather vMDPCS) becomes a world of its own subjected to all LH with the secret desire of finding its own holistic harmony. Such a switch happens quickly, in a revolutionary manner, because once the states of harmony in an overloaded sensory system with memory and pDPCS start differing more the channel (connectivity) between them starts separating them into different systems (V and P) according to LH3. But the more isolated they are the more LH1 and LH2 works internally, increasing their (and mainly vDPCS) harmony on its own. But the higher and more different such harmony is—the more the V—and P-levels are separated. This means that the formation of the second signaling system (brain) happens rather fast in turbulent environments.

The growth of V-level complexity could be explained by the proliferation of instability from the most dynamic sensors to the channel-DPCS connecting signals with pDPCS (or pMDPCS). The closest pDPCS in such pMDPCS connected to the channel also had to be modified into a more dynamic harmonizer, gradually absorbing the shock of the signals and finding those pDPCS that were ready to pick up the harmonization task to carry it further. This process stimulated conversion of more general pDPCS (stem cells in biological example) into more specialized vDPCS and pDPCS, resulting in the growth and complexity of the V-level and its coordination with more specialized harmonizers on the P-level.

Another interesting property of a growing V-level is in the inevitable variety of signals it receives and local vDPCS interpretations. Such variety lowers the Hi of the V-level until all signals will be harmonized with each other and their possible interpretations. Only then the level of harmony (according to harmonization catastrophe HC2) reaches the possibility of penetrating the tolerance boundary of P-level and influencing it. This independent extra work done only on the V-level leads to its further development and the improvement of the Rx balance to become an effective harmonizer (like the brain).

The Multilayer V-level

There are two ways the V-level can get a layered structure itself. First, when several SOS harmonize with each other, forming a more general vision level incorporating and integrating local V-levels. Second, when vMDPCS of the same pDPCS is complicated enough and its local clusters of sensitivity start their own harmonization and harmony encapsulation, forming local vDPCS. In the first case we deal with multiparticipant SOS (MSOS) harmonization. In the second case several highly sensitive to each other vDPCS that form a cluster of mutual harmonization form a local vision system (LVS). Several LVS can form a vision system (VS) becoming a multilayer structure within a V-level like the specialization of various regions inside the brain. VS is a vMDPCS, which is triggered by the set of external signals reflecting the situation. There could be several VS, some of which dormant but, when activated, could change vision dramatically, like different roles the same person can be in.

It is important to understand that VS and LVS are DPCS and not specific tissue, which is their carrier. On the same brain tissue we can have multiple VS in the form of *role visions,* determining differences of orientation like "I am a father," or "I am an employee," or "I am a soldier."

The Orientational Model

Self-harmonization forces are always a result of a particular situation mapping onto a particular SOS, which allows for such phenomena. Since harmony is always specific in all its situations, we cannot easily extract its results or transfer them to another SOS. Connectionist model is another example when content can not be transferred to another network since it information is in the structure of such systems. Another example is unconscious and subconscious knowledge not readily available for logical analysis, but connected to actuators (motor systems) capable for generating a responsive action without decision-making controlling processes. You can include here various skills, artistic abilities, meditative abilities, etc.

The evaluation of the V-level and its harmonization control of the P-level describe an important feature of SOS, which could be called *orientation.* Thus orientation is seen as an ability to support the HHz of the whole SOS based on V-level activity. Orientation is seen here as a phase **preceding** responsive action on the P-level. The main goal of *orientation* is in the development of the harmonized image of the **situation for a particular SOS**, which could be *used* later for a potential responsive action. Sensitivity toward some unknown DPCS could be used in such a model instead of an attempt to recreate external DPCS such sensitivity results from. This approach differs from traditional modeling, which intends to be context-free, impartial and depersonalized. It is also different from simulative models in using some real life impacts through the sensors.

The particular state of the V-level in such a system we will call the *orientational model* (OM), while the ability to obtain an adequate OM resulting in adaptive SOS behavior will be called *orientational skills* (OS). All VS harmonize into OM and are a part of it. Some of VS could be dormant, thus allowing for disjunctive functionality of the VS when the difference in situations leads to the necessity of choosing the most effective and adequate VS. Meanwhile, the process of the general harmonization of the VS can take place in the background or during inactive periods (like human sleep). The active VS is fully responsible for orientation and harmonization in the current situation since the advanced channel vMDPCS can ultimately harmonize incoming signals (or their part) with P-level behavior.

OM does not attempt to find the "universal truth" of the CUI situations, but rather tries to support the HHz of a particular DPCS. Such a position, as was mentioned earlier, allows for the combined use of knowledge, art, skills, orientation and other methods embodied into immanent and non-transferable (compared to logical constructs) human and other SS abilities. OM operates in a T-mode and being composed of multiple Tmods (vDPCS of V-level) could be seen as a meta Tmod itself.

OM has the following important features:

1. Can utilize ill-defined situations as patterns of existing and potential impacts without the necessity of creating a precise transferable description being embodied into AHS
2. The fact that OM is tightly and internally related to a particular AHS, which actively participates in its development, allows for the simplifying of its impact onto P-level by continuous mapping of its patterns

onto the responsive mechanism of AHS without their externalized specifications

3. Adequacy of OM can be understood as its sufficiency and efficiency in stimulating the adequate response for AHS, preserving its harmonization limit cycle (LCh) and not as a solution for satisfying model constraints

4. The precision of OM is dynamic and is based on the agent's sensitivity to various impacts/stimuli

5. The context sensitivity of OM leads to the relative independence of its goals from Hi and being a function of the whole holistic harmonization process

The Harmonization Dynamics of V-Level

Multilayer V-Level Harmonization and Sense-Impacts

As we mentioned above, the evolution of the V-level in SOS can be based on direct sensor/V-level interaction or, using a more advanced V-level, on performing some preharmonization in order to be able to affect the P-level. This latter case is based on HC2 requiring a certain maturity of the Hi of vDPCS in order to penetrate TB of pDPCS. The question then arises about the way external signals can penetrate such evolved harmony of the V-level itself.

The sensors supplying information to the V-level can have two possible situations:

- vDPCS is sensitive to the signal and participates in the chain of harmonization, unloading sole responsibility of the He harmonization from the channel connecting SOS to the world and becoming an important part of such a channel

- vDPCS has a high level of Hi and TB stability which forces the channel DPCS (connecting the source of change and SOS) to seek C-map modification—according to LH3—which can potentially create a sufficiently strong signal to penetrate the "insensitivity" of vDPCS

These two cases force the two different forms of external/ internal harmonization of the V-level.

In the first case, the preservation of the LCh of AHS is important because it supports the necessary internal harmony together with a sufficiently high external sensitivity allowing the channel to continuously affect vDPCS. Then the same kind of two-level system as for the whole SOS design might evolve. It means there will be some internal area of the V-level with a high external sensitivity allowing for the continuous "unloading" of the channel information onto it (harmonization with this area). At the same time the Hi of the V-level, which is so precious for AHS, will be maintained behind certain TB of the rest of the V-level, effectively converting it to a multilayer V-level. After the directly connected to the sensor area will be able to develop a sufficient level of Hi, allowing it to overcome such TB, HC2 will create an impact penetrating the boundary and forcing reharmonization of the main area of the V-level. The more developed V-level is the more layers it requires. This is similar to the chain of internal mappings happening in various areas of the human brain.

In the second case, the job of creating or delivering sufficiently harmonic signals-DPCS capable of penetrating the V-level, has to be done by the channel alone with the assistance of the source of the signal. Source participation in the creation of the harmony in the message is more typical for concise communication, for example, when one SOS sends a particular message to another. In the environment with the communication between well-developed SOS a typical situation is when the channel connecting such SOS includes either one of the vDPCS or both. After all, the vDPCS on both sides are the most appropriate parts of the common channel to carry the complexity of LH3 modifications seeking mutual harmony.

Impacts which are the results of the harmonization of the direct sensory areas connected with the more stable areas of V-level will be called sense-impacts (**SI**). The concept of SI is close to the idea of epoché in phenomenology as a direct perception without any assumptions and reason processing, but with possible post processing in order to harmonize it with the broader vision of the whole situation. A similar concept of *primary perception* was used by Merleau-Ponty. In harmonomics another necessary feature of SI has to be added—the necessary level of Hi capable of the penetration of the TB of the other areas of vDPCS (and ultimately pDPCS). The existence of such Hi in the "immediate impression" is often (except of hallucinations which we will not analyze here) the result of the coherent reflection of external DPCS with their own encapsulated harmony. Such DPCS could be various entities: objects, phenomena, or whole situations.

The minimal immediate harmony inherited from the reflection of certain external harmony and capable of penetrating the TB of the next VDPCS region will be called *sense*, which, actually, is a DPCS itself. The ability to create such harmony will be called *sense making*. The harmonization of SI with the rest of the V-level will be called *meaning making* and the resulting Hi of an active set of VS represents the *meaning* of the impact/situation. From this point of view, sense is a captured local and instant harmony of the part of the situation with sufficient internal consistency and harmony capable of imprinting SI onto the appropriate part of vDPCS. The meaning reflects a deeper harmony among previously discovered VS and newly acquired chunks of information that the SOS try to make sense of and finally discover the meaning of what is happening.

The harmonization processes of sense making and meaning evolving on the V-level of SOS can have a variety of patterns, depending upon the existence of the shared carrier and/or the P-level. Holistic harmonization of SOS on the V-level includes: V/P harmonization, V-level harmonization with the environment, and internal V-level harmonization.

SI and DPI

The mutual sensitivity between the V-level and the P-level has to be stronger than the sensitivity to external patterns in order to belong to the same MDPCS cluster. The communication between vDPCS and pDPCS could be based on two mechanisms:

1. The same carrier supporting the mutual sensitivity of pDPCS and the V-level or the sensitivity among various layers and areas of the V-level (where some are much more stable then the others)
2. Different carriers (similar to the roles of enzymes and RNA)

At the same time, the form of the V-level implementation is also important and includes:

1. A distributed V-level (nervous and psychosomatic system of signaling)
2. The V-level located in one specific area (like brain)
3. A combination of both

A more distributed form usually supports the simplest SOS functions of DVI propagation to the P-level. A more localized form supports higher sensitivity among its areas, which is important for advanced preharmonization work done on the V-level. The first and second signal systems in animals are examples of the possible variations. Because of the high stability of P-level, sense-impacts of the V-level have to make a lot of sense in order to stimulate P-level reaction, thus cutting out unnecessary transformations of its basic stability and harmony.

ALEXANDER VENGEROV

The Coordination Level

Further development and evolution of the communication patterns between V—and P-levels can lead to the appearance of a harmonization channel, which according to 3LH adapts its connectivity and interpretational architecture to the complexity of the communication situation. Such a channel is likely to evolve into a specific level (C-level), responsible for the coordination between V—and P-levels. Each physical LDPCS has its own channel-sensor delivering commands from the V-level and its P-neighbors. The whole pDPCS is represented with the whole V/P inter-level sensitivity, requiring C-level for its coordinated delivery in space and time to all physical LDPCS carrying the meaningful response discovered on the V-level in all its complexity.

It means that the harmony of orientation obtained on the V-level could be mapped onto the C-level which plays a role of a controlling and coordinating mechanism for harmony implementation on the P-level. Of course some portions of VS could be directly mapped onto some local pDPCS. This seems to be the case in the human brain with two possible impacts onto the body (pDPCS): via a controlling "mind" (a path through the neocortex and limbic brain) or **directly** from the perceptions to the "body" (via the amygdala region of the brain and the bypassing neocortex). When both channels work the same, confusion might arise if the possible harmonizations on the P-level in both cases contradict each other.

V-level Communications with the Environment

Harmonization between the V-level and its environment is based on the ways SI might be evolving:

• In the receiving SOS
• In the transmitting SOS

- In the channel
- As a Shared responsibility

In all these cases (and especially with shared responsibility) the ability to have an adequate orientation is based on the ability to distinguish between the sources of SI evolution: the receiver, the interpreting channel, the sender or a mix of all of the above.

Two major types of harmonization of the V-level with the environment are based on the existence of communication and the observational sources of the SI. Observational harmonization supports the responsibility of uncovering the meaning of the situation solely on the receiving SOS. For example, uncovering the meaning of an approaching tiger with an open mouth.

Communication harmonization of the SI imply the active participation of the external entity in forming SI with sufficient internal integrity (harmony), which makes sense, and the obtaining of the full meaning in the process of sender-interpreter-receiver mutual harmonization. For example, the information that the tiger is coming and it is time to run.

Communication Among VS

Although sufficiently independent from each other, various VS of the same OM can attempt to harmonize with each other. There could be several forms of such harmonization within OM.

Several VS on the Same Carrier

Several VS on the same carrier being active at the same time create a harmonization situation when their communications lead to changes in each of them, including the possible evolving of new VS or dissipation/mergers of the old ones. Such processes include:

- A switching of vision activation from one VS to another as a tool for better SI/VS harmonization (similar to assuming roles)
- A virtual dialog with changing active roles of VS and SI transfer between them (similar to an analysis considering various points of view)
- A Split personality when no communication is occurring because of the scale of disharmony between two or more VS (channel blocking evolution) and random changes in the external or internal situation can trigger a switch of activation making a different VS dominating

SI between VS on different Carriers

Communication between VS located on different carriers is more difficult and requires the proper medium. Such communication could be classified according to the degree of carrier isolation:

- There is a common carrier for vDPCS including methods of a shared area of sensitivity when one SOS can modify the area which will be available to the switching sensitivity of another SOS (note that there is no requirement for constant maintenance of the shared areas of sensitivity)
- The communications occur through pDPCS with the V-level of one SOS using its own P-level to affect the pDPCS of another SOS, which, in turn, sends a signal to its V-level (like a handshake treated as a symbol of friendship)
- The communications occur via the common context of a super DPCS which both SOS are a part of (like peer pressure)

The SOS Connectivity Forming a new Carrier

The connectivity among SOS might differ from the VS-VS communication problems because it involves additional values specific to individual SOS (like self-preservation and Hz regardless of the global HH). Such a situation requires in addition to the harmonization of the picture of a particular external situation on their V-level the support of the harmonization of the physical position of each SOS within this new situation (which we do not have in artificial SOS if designed so). The sufficient level of mutual sensitivity can lead to the formation of a new meta-cluster consisting of participating SOS.

The pattern of the inter-SOS connectivity forming a new carrier and ultimately a new MDPCS, which we can call a multi SOS system (MSOS), includes:

1. The ability to create a common V-level through the Hz of LVS as the VS of each SOS (virtual or physical)
2. The ability to use this top level VS for the management of individual V—and P—DPCS and their synchronization with each other (*the external C-level* compared to the internal C-level in a SOS)

The Use of MSOS for Managing Complexity of MDPCS

Communications between several SOS create a new carrier for a new round of evolution of DPCS, and can be used as a tool for physical MDPCS harmonization. The advanced harmonization abilities of the V-level together with the possibility of group harmonization of vDPCS leads to the evolution of the meta V-level which, in turn, can provide necessary harmonization support of external signals, SOS-style, for the whole MDPCS. Such meta V-level can consist of a number of SOS being, in fact, an MSOS itself, influencing the rest of the MDPCS like a management group running the whole company.

MSOS

SOS being an AHS form of MDPCS can only be a local part of MPDCS where other SOS play the roles of other LDPCS. Such systems, in addition to exposing general MDPCS behavior, have the specificity of multi SOS organization (**MSOS**). Such a form is based on the existence of two levels in each local SOS (LSOS) and the necessity to provide harmonization among LSOS with the whole MSOS on both the vision and physical levels. The additional harmonization advantages of MSOS are based on the horizontal and vertical distribution of LSOS, allowing for more complex and advanced forms of **vision organization** and the **harmonization of the V-and P-levels**.

Vision Organization

One of the most important advanced patterns of MSOS vision organization is *vision integration*, which includes three related processes:

- The collection of distributed information
- The integrated harmonization of acquired information
- The correctional influence of acquired information on local vision

Since the sensitivity of each LSOS is limited, it might be difficult to perceive the behavior of the global external pattern, which should be watched simultaneously in a number of locations. Several LSOS can collect a fuller picture of the situation.

The integration of the captured patterns of the environment by each LSOS has a number of problems obstructing the easy evolution of the advanced MSOS in nature:

1. The necessary richness of the V-level of LSOS, allowing

for the mutual mapping of environmental patterns, the state of its P-level, and the visual patterns of other LSOS

2. The differences in P-level states of each LSOS, preventing the direct incorporation of the V-level patterns from other LSOS and requiring certain interpretational skills

3. The intentionality of LSOS in balancing the task of MSOS harmonization with the internal harmonization of their own

Generally there could be several approaches to the solution of the problem of harmonization of multiple V-levels belonging to different SOS. They all are based on different degrees of decentralization:

1. MSOS with one special LSOS maintaining an integrated V-level by being sensitive to all other LSOS and mapping patterns of their V-levels onto its carrier ("Big Brother" who thinks for all). Once all patterns are successfully mapped on the same carrier with this top-level LSOS, their harmonization occurs as harmonization of the V-patterns in a regular SOS. The resultant harmony becomes stable and strong enough to influence the Hi of all LSOS.

2. Hierarchical harmonization schema when several MSOS of a lower level play the role of an LSOS in the further harmonization within a new super MSOS and so on.

3. The peer-to-peer harmonization of visions when all LSOS are sufficiently sensitive to each other. A final generalized vision simultaneously evolves in all the participants.

The Harmonization of the Vision and Physical Levels in MSOS

The obtained vision adequacy of an MSOS has to

influence its P-level, delivering a final readiness for upcoming environmental impacts. In the case of multiple LSOS, this becomes a problem of a properly formed distributed organization. In all schemes of V-level harmonization with the P-level, it has an upper hand as a better harmonizer and the whole process becomes more of a V-level management with certain control of the P-level harmonization.

The flow of V-level control can follow the same three types of organization as we saw above: centralized control, hierarchical control, peer-to-peer or decentralized management organization. MSOS development by a number of advanced SOS where MSOS organization is carefully planned and skillfully maintained potentially offers the highest possible effectiveness and efficiency of DPCS holistic harmonization. The high level of complexity and AHS abilities of LSOS make MSOS a form whose domination over LSOS (Rcs) can vary depending on the Rx of the whole system and especially the Rlg (proportion of efforts of local harmonization versus participation in the global harmonization). The methods, tools, forms and patterns of the art of MSOS development and harmonization will be discussed later as "Holistic Engineering."

Active AHS

All forms and patterns of harmonization discussed so far were focusing on the harmonization of the chosen AHS under environmental changes influencing its internal harmony. But even such an advanced form of AHS as MSOS cannot do well in turbulent environments without sufficient room for compromise. They only manage to obtain the freedom of controlling their internal harmony in order to comply with LH2. The environment is still the ultimate ruler. The further enhancement of harmonization in HS requires "cheating" on LH2 where it is possible to get out from under the domination of environmental patterns, limiting the level of holistic harmony that AHS can reach.

Achieving the goal of environmental harmonization can be simplified if we recall that environment is just the area of external sensitivity (AES) of AHS (not the whole Universe). This means that the proper selection or modification of environmental patterns can do the trick. Instead of being the hunted, the AHS becomes a hunter or an engineer or both.

The enhancement of environmental harmony, allowing for the further growth of HH can be done by AHS using special forms of AHS harmonization. Such forms could be divided into the following categories:

1. Active AHS capable of choosing their environment as a subset of all possible AES
2. Active AHS capable of modifying their environment
3. A combination of both

Choosing Environment

In PCCE decomposition environment is defined as a CS-map in the external area of sensitivity (AES) of DPCS, not included in its carrier. Changing external sensitivity allows changing AES or the environment itself. This is how organizations enter different industries, markets, etc.

The described ability requires SOS organization in order to "try different AES on" and see the possible harmonization outcomes. The choice of AES can be done using two different mechanisms:

1. Changing external sensitivity
2. Changing external connectivity

ALEXANDER VENGEROV

Choice of Environment Using Sensitivity Modifications

The attraction (sensitivity) of various life forms to environments with patterns similar to their own Hi was observed in many situations. All forms of mimicry are based on such mechanisms: the more an insect resembles a certain type of a plant the more often it hides there, which in turn supports its growing resemblance to the plant. Now the HH of such insect—AHS can be increased because of its increased sensitivity to the proper plant, which maps onto its P-level making it look more like the chosen plant. Here original similarity increased external sensitivity of the AHS which, in turn, affected its Hi and the resulting growing similarity completes the iterations of HH until the resemblance is sufficiently good.

It is important to note that increased sensitivity to some part of AES is not as simple and innocent as it might seem. The change in external sensitivity actively changes the AHS itself, making its external harmonization preferences different, which leads to a different AES, which changes AHS and so on. AHS changes! This is how new hobbies, attachments, new fields of interest and pleasure can affect the transformation of human personality (internal patterns of the Hi). Another example: Due to some older trauma sensitivity, certain environmental impacts are much stronger for some people than for others, resulting in different adaptive patterns. Concentration on pleasant things and the beauty of the nature produces a different effect than concentration on our problems, enemies, and stressful situations.

If the situation is rich enough with various patterns and SOS can handle pattern recognition and sensitivity changing really well, then it can support and even enhance, via resonance, almost any type of internal harmony (CS-map) it wishes. Sometimes a such mechanism leads to stable forms of psychiatric deviations (manias) where patients find confirmation of their fears and convictions often enough to keep such patterns permanently active.

Ultimately, we have a form of **Maxwell Demon on macro level**, when the Demon as a skillful SOS is capable of recognizing the necessary patterns in the rich environment and "capturing" them through an increasing sensitivity to them. This can support or even increase the level of internal pattern activation, acting as a source of energy or structural stability. In physics, Maxwell Demon is a hypothetical creature capable of opening a small door in a closed space, letting fast molecules into another chamber and thus creating energy using just its pattern recognition abilities. AHS do the same by increasing sensitivity to certain patterns (DPCS) of environment, which increasingly excites and supports the stability of their internal similar patterns, increasing the volume of harmony of particular types of patterns. Such method allows filtering or regenerating after disharmonic impacts and generally increases the stability of AHS.

Choice of Environment Using Connectivity Modifications

Another method of environment modification like AES is by changing the connectivity to different areas, which leads to changes in sensitivity as the strength of the signals delivered via the connectivity. In the natural world the easiest way of connectivity modification is through relocation in space—increasing or decreasing the distance to/from certain areas. But there could be other forms of connectivity modifications. A company can change the type of its clients or change suppliers, which affects the internal pattern of its production.

Sometimes connectivity change is easier then a change in sensitivity and can be achieved by simply choosing different existing connectivity channels/mechanisms to various external DPCS. On its V-level, SOS can play with various connectivity types and configurations, stopping at the one delivering the most harmony.

Both methods of reshaping a relationship with particular parts of the environment is ultimately guided by LH3, changing the channel in a way supporting harmony with some areas of the environment and breaking away from the others.

Changing Environment

The possibilities and benefits of environment modification are numerous and their discussion is beyond the scope of this book. We would just like to point out that the value of such changes is based on the degree the harmony of the system could be improved in the long term as a result of harmonization with more suitable environment, while its health can be continuously maintained. Then the main goal in environmental changes is in the removal of some of the restrictions of LH2 (the level and type of environmental harmony) concerning the holistic harmonization of systems.

T-mode based vision allows for seeing additional options in traditional methods of engineering. These additional options are based on the use of free energy resources of the natural harmonization of sensitive systems. From the previous discussion we saw how changes in connectivity and sensitivity trigger processes leading to self-evolving and the self-maintenance of some stable and predictable patterns that might have value for the system. There are several uses for free harmonization energy in engineering:

- Traditional DPCS design as shortcuts producing the

final harmonized state of an entity. All harmonization is done by people and at their expense (manufacturing)

- The partial use of free harmonization energy (among people: "build the store and they will come;" setting the growth of self-harmonized life forms in agriculture, etc.)

- The maximum use of harmonization energy (techniques of holistic engineering using changes in connectivity, sensitivity, and interpretation as well as designing certain DPCS forms as self-supporting clusters of sensitivity)

Universal AHS

Although the ability to achieve advanced levels of HH by choosing or modifying environment can be very effective, there is a need to be cautious. Systems capable of internal management of the HH might slide into a sub-optimal state where AHS and its environment are both out of sync with global HH, which might be beyond AES for now but will show up later, with devastating effects, as a revenge for the previous short-range vision. It might lead to the development of closed systems attempting to support the sub-optimal harmony, which they have reached and which, in fact, is a disharmony in the sense of the bigger environment of the world. Then there is a growing risk of impacts arising from the outside world that could be disharmonic enough for such systems to destroy its harmony.

The highest level of harmonization skills and the highest possible accumulated and supported harmony of AHS is in the ability to sense the most harmonic patterns of the world to which it can **possibly** get connected to (like our planet). This ability is based on a very advanced vision capable of sensing the common harmony in all regular patterns of environmental impact and absorbing it while rejecting all the rest (similar to animal digestion cycle). It is not enough to be a macro Maxwell Demon capable of catching only harmonic patterns, but must be capable of digesting sensitivity to **any** DPCS, focusing on their most harmonic patterns that might exist on a more abstract or general level and using them while ignoring the rest.

Such creative sensing of digestible parts, in even disharmonic external DPCS, and the ability to effectively harmonize with them by breaking the pattern into subpatterns and harmonizing with the proper ones, does not have to exist as one centralized process. Enzymes in our bodies can be seen as small DPCS remaining from a successful past harmonization experience, with each type of enzyme being a different kind of DPCS. They work as sensors and small harmonizers, dealing only with particular types of external impacts-DPCS. Such external DPCS (particular food components) and enzymes are attracted to each other based on LH3 and, once the distance is small enough and mutual sensitivity is high, the process of reharmonization starts. During such a process some parts form and impact-DPCS become too sensitive to enzyme DPCS and under the newly developed harmony LH3 breaks the links of the part sensitive to the enzyme with the rest of the food component (impact-DPCS). Often all resulting pieces could be digested, like in the case of maltose, which is broken by the maltase enzyme into two easily harmonizable molecules of glucose.

We will call such systems *universal AHS* (UAHS) and they possess the following patterns:

1. Hi sufficiently adequate in most universal patterns of harmony that can be found as components of the most DPCS they encounter
2. Advanced vision which is broad, deep, capable for abstraction and generalization in space and time

3. A growing body of knowledge of existing harmonization forms and patterns assisting in orientation in harmonization processes and possible harmonization shortcuts (when necessary)
4. The advanced mechanisms of obtaining Hi/e out of the captured patterns of harmony or the capability to use resonance with such discovered harmonies to support Hi
5. The ability to maintain optimal levels of health indicators (Rx)

All these features are interconnected: progress in any one of them supports progress in others. For example, the more adequate Hi is in the main forms of external harmony the easier it is to detect them because of the LH3 increasing the connectivity between the more harmonic DPCS.

Conclusion: The Power of UVO and Sensitivist Model

The power of UVO, based on T-mode, is in the balance of its simplicity of generalization abilities and the possibility of sufficiently detailed and constructive discussion. Initially discussed patterns of C/S and DPCS harmonization dynamics are the most general and applicable to all more specific patterns discussed afterwards. It means there are multiple levels of the analysis where it is possible to start with studying CS-properties and then move toward more specific forms and patterns of DPCS.

We showed the possibility of complexity and stability whose evolving could be described by gradual variations in sensitivity resulting in different forms of harmonization. The described complexity of the sensitivity harmonization processes also covers life-like and intelligence-like phenomena located between very fluid and very stable forms.

The concept of SOS modifies the simple world of DPI when it becomes possible to detect the potential input in a soft form before it actually affects the system and to decide how to interpret it (if to accept at all). Such preprocessing of the forthcoming "input" is the major benefit of SOS. It is based not as much on forecasting methods of statistical guessing, but on the direct sensitivity to the signs of the forthcoming impact. The existence of the vision layer in AHS invokes vDPCS as reactive systems immediately and directly responding with all their sensitivity to the need in the overall harmonization job with other more inert areas of V-level and, later, with P-level. Such a two-level organization with immediate reactive methods on one layer and gradual harmonization with the rest of the system shows additional adaptive benefits.

Another aspect of T-mode universality is that it can be used on the level of MDPCS as well as all lower levels of LDPCS, allowing virtually unlimited movement to the higher or lower level of system detail. The concept of CS-maps used in T-mode does not require physically adjacent areas and could be applied to sections of an S-map connected via some stable channels of connectivity, delivering only a certain sensitivity which could be accounted for without considering these channels as a part of the picture. For example, vision systems existing on human body/mind carriers could be seen connected into some generic "body/mind" common carrier, allowing for the vision to evolve through properly organized communications and external maps (texts, storage, etc.). It also could constitute the parts of distributed computer memory and processing, registering evolving patterns on the common "memory/CPU" carrier and disregarding the fact that the parts of this system could be thousands of miles apart. Other examples could include political, biological, ecological and other patterns based on specific carriers and supporting the necessary connectivity and sensitivity.

Finally, PCCE decomposition allows for focusing on various clusters of sensitivity, abstracting DPCS analysis from the carrier and the environment. We also have the possibility of applying general knowledge of pattern harmonization dynamics to all types of carriers supporting DPCS forms of sensitive systems.

The use of the T-mode is based on the self-organization processes on carriers supporting sufficiently high level of sensitivity among all points on their "surface." The logic or explanation of such sensitive surface processes is not reductionist (based on micro-mechanisms of carrier work) but holistically-based on macro-patterns of harmonization of the sensitivity on the carrier and their recognition. Then control, management, and care of the forms and patterns of such harmonization is based not so much on the carrier redesign as on the study and reshaping of the patterns of harmonization together with properties of sensitivity, connectivity and interpretation in and between certain localities. The methods, effects and overall changes based on the use of T-mode will be studied in the next part "Holistic Engineering."

Part 4

HOLISTIC ENGINEERING

Chapter 1

ORGANIZATIONS AS MSOS

Introduction

Any engineering can be seen as a harmonization activity of some kind, whether there is an attempt to control harmony or let it self-evolve by modifying only connectivity and sensitivity properties. Holistic engineering (HE) is a consistent application of UVO, vision processes and the knowledge of the laws and patterns of harmonomics. Seeing various situations in an engineering environment as a result of harmonization adjustments of CSI patterns leads to different practices, methods and goals in engineering that we will discuss in this part of the book.

The benefits of using HE can be found in the following:

• The possibility of developing a **generalized model of organizational structure and dynamics,** which we previously called the Universal Framework Organization (UFO). It allows for the most **general and universal approach** to analysis and handling of all the problems of strategic and tactical development of sensitive systems in an adequate way, regardless of the level of abstraction, location, or detail. It allows stabilizing architecture, strategy, and tactics. The more sensitive your system becomes, the more beneficial switching to HE is.

- **The integration of research and experience** in all fields of study into one body of knowledge, since general harmonization dynamics of DPCS is carrier independent.
- Allows seeing and effectively using the **free energy of natural harmonization** of sensitivity, like the art of catching the wind and currents in sailing to the desired destination.
- Allows **increasing the harmony of systems and environments** (which is not the goal in OO/C vision) while it is not too late.

Comparison of Main Enterprise Architectures

Comparing relative efforts in the use of vision in the whole spectrum of business/management tools and methods, we will distinguish the following EA paradigms: pyramid, flat, network, and learning types of organizations (see Table 5) as illuminating the role of vision and its connection with organizational coordination.

Table 5. The role of vision in enterprise architectures

EA-type	Threat of discontinuities	Role of vision	Type of local vision coordination
Pyramid	Low	Low	Top management vision does planning and scheduling for lower levels. Use of symbolic logical mechanisms (regulations, rules, instructions, etc.)
Flat	Medium	Medium	Strategic plans are more general with more room for local orientation
Network	High	High	Top level plan is a fuzzy direction "ready to change." Interconnection of local decision-making networks. Flexible rules are supplemented with communication protocols.
Learning	Very high	Very high	The use of a Vision instead of a Plan. OL, LO, and KM as a major resource assisting business and management efforts. Rules themselves are a result of the current vision (evolution and learning of business rules). Once set, they run the show as controls.

In *pyramid-type* organizations or bureaucracies the following main features (Bidwell, 1986) determine the vision role and business behavior: the hierarchy of control, the specialization of functions, the centralization of information and control, formal rules, policies and procedures governing behavior. The necessary coherence of vision supporting coherence of actions is mainly based on planning and scheduling. Discontinuities as threats to the Top Management Vision are usually small, though getting increasingly frequent. They could be handled by local vision and intelligence choosing a reaction leading to the initial plan/schedule fulfillment. Local vision is largely suppressed, leaving it on a level that is only sufficient enough to correctly implement the commands from the top. The domination of the know-how approach is a response to a what-to-do signal. Strategy implemented in an enterprise—level plan is seen as a force to stand the course.

Flat organizations are used under growing discontinuities

with the main architectural approach directed at the creation of small islands of local vision supported by LANs and simple means of communication. It also offers an increased level of local responsibility. Still, all local visions have to fit plans and schedules although created on a higher level of abstraction, allowing for not only "how" decisions but also about "what." Through the growing number of local vision networks the total volume of involved vision is also growing. Local decisions are based on local experience and knowledge sufficient to decide "what," which allows for the elimination of middle management. Enterprise coordination attempts to keep the scale of these islands of vision control small enough (search for *min necessary*) to be managed by the Top vision/plan.

Network Organizations actively use horizontal interconnections of all local visions. Nohria and Eccles define network as "a fluid, flexible, and dense pattern of working relationships that cut across various intra—and inter-organizational boundaries" (Nohria and Eccles (eds), 1992). Discontinuities post very big problems, management power is often sacrificed for mere survival and viability. There is a constant search for better group coordination to match the scale of impacts. The increased role of multilevel and multiunit vision requires vision interaction and coordination. Local responsibility and power are growing, flexible planning is seen only as a general direction and is readily adjustable. Adaptive control methods are widely used. The Top plan is rather a Top vision and mission, not interfering much with local planning. The level of vision communication reaches the point when organization is better analyzed as a social system, rather than a machine with a proliferation of the following features of social systems (Parsons, Shils, and Naegele (1961): adaptability, horizontal management of conflicts among system components, negotiations and acceptance of group and common organizational goals, cultural commonality as an effective communication basis. This commonality of goals (Rockart and Short, 1991), common cultural background (Powell, 1990), and a common vision (Mills, 1991; Nagel and Dove, 1992; Peters, 1992) are becoming the necessary factors of evolving horizontal self-coordination.

Learning organizations see discontinuities as a major problem (hard-line reengineering adds to it). Networking methods of coordination is becoming increasingly difficult and the search for self-organization, evolving, and management by so-called "internal markets" is growing (Gifford and Pinchot, 1994; Halal, 1991). External learning or grafting through external vision connectivity is becoming more common with the growth of environmental discontinuity (Drucker, 1988; Huber, 1991). The depth of vision and the rights of learned patterns are growing. Single-loop learning still provides for a search of responses conforming to a general vision and strategy, but emerging double-loop learning is capable of examining and changing its governing values (Argyris and Schon, 1978). Constant connectivity with environment and a flexible New Strategy Approach are seen as a way of strategy adaptability. The new possibility of organizational integration with growing connectivity triggers a wave of mergers. Wide consideration of paradigms like Organization Learning, Learning Organizations, Knowledge Management, Agile Organizations, distributed computing, AI, and intelligent agents offer IT support for new forms of Vision development. The Information Richness Theory weakens its positions in leading IT in supporting organizational vision, being gradually substituted by Critical Social Theory (Lee and Ngwenyama, 1997). It substitutes logical analysis for richer forms of Vision coordination, requiring broader forms of harmonization than just logical consistency. The growth of required business fluidity becomes so high that the idea of an organizational core is almost lost, creating difficulties in the continuity of planning and management. This situation affects the quality of organizational planning which usually attempts to provide coherence around some architectural core. The main strategy in such a situation is seen as support for continuous learning, change, adaptability, and, ultimately, vision.

Vision Development Trends

The presented features of enterprise architectures illustrate that the increase of environmental discontinuity leads to the increase of the vision role and use, supported by advancements of information technology and systems closely matching the needs of enhancements in organizational vision. Considering the trend in further growth of environmental CUI features, we can conclude that evolving organizations will include:

1. A growing influence of vision on the way business is done under growing environmental discontinuity
2. A growing blending and mutual dependency of human vision and IT/IS (visual development, OLAP, etc.)
3. A growing merger of all types of vision and their interdependence
4. A growing independence of all levels of vision (local-group-global)
5. Growing problems of vision coordination
6. A growing need in universal approaches to vision development, regardless of the state and even the type of business or organizational activity as *Vision planning and management independence.*
7. The direction of technology development is guided mainly by the growing role and functionality of organizational vision.
8. Universal Organizational Vision System becomes possible as a universal product, which can function as a catalyst for business evolution around it.

The Possibility of Vision-Level Separation Using Modern Technology

New developments in IT/IS, such as high-speed networks, advanced internetworking technologies, and intelligent networks, together with the high rate of their utilization (in the beginning of 1998 an annual rate of business spending on IT jumped to 26%, far above the expected 9% (Mandel and Farrell, 1998) offer a new opportunity for organizational vision implementation. Today some standards, like Fibre Channel Networks, allow remote locations to be dealt with as if they are parts of your PC. Distance, location, and time are disappearing, creating a new carrier for organizational vision. Proliferation of hypertext, dynamic HTML, data-bound scripting and other interface tools free people from dictating the needed narration, allowing for the further evolution of dynamic vision.

Distributed component computing coupled with universal database and universal access platforms allow for hard and soft context-rich communications. Being tightly clustered, vision harmonization processes could be separated from their traditional distributed locations on a new level, strategically independent from particular business rules and business objects. Advancements in ubiquitous computing (Weiser, 1993), intelligent sensors and the IPv6 addressing capability for building intranets for multiple automated components form the basis of an intelligent control of the *physical level* of organizational resources by higher architectural levels.

The new architectural level, which we will call Vision or *V-level,* deals with universal mechanisms of organizational vision including learning, knowledge management, experience, sensitivity, and creativity. The result of the work of V-level is a harmonized, coherent vision capable of controlling the adequately coordinated organizational reaction to environmental situations. Vision level includes the dynamic combination of symbolic and connectionist structures supplemented with symbolic and connectionist harmonization, developing the maximum internal coherence of external sensitivity. Such V-level control of organizational external behavior we will call *Vision Management* (V-management or VM).

IT/IS supporting V-management could be called a Vision Management System (VMS). It will include people sharing vision and mutually creating group and organizational vision, as well as the automated means of vision processing and management.

Our two conclusions about the growing level of organizational vision and the possibility of its separation on a V-level, independent from particular business processes and, at the same time, controlling it, leads to some changes in the business role and an understanding of what the organizational core is.

Vision Management Architecture

The VM architecture supports the discussed above necessity of V-level separation (Vengerov, 1999b). The benefit of such separation is in the creation of the organizational core, independent from environmental discontinuity, allowing for predictable continuous planning and management. Being the main part of the organizational identity and the focus of resource concentration, V-level does not depend upon the variability of incoming information, no matter how dramatically it differs from previous situational scanning. Planning and management in this case will include gradual advancements in major components of vision acquisition, harmonization among various knowledge and learning patterns, the incorporation of human individual, group and organizational levels of vision, and others supporting distributed V-level functionality. Given such a fluid carrier as IT used on V-level compared to physical world objects and structures, it is possible to dramatically decrease the cost of adaptability, at the same time using potential universal solutions.

Local visions can have four types of relations with each other that determine the evolution of the global organizational vision: instrumental, communicative, discursive, and strategic (Habermas, 1979). As a result of conflict resolution mechanisms based on common cultural patterns and the depersonalization of initial person-attached vision, they are blended into a final organizational vision (Habermas, 1984). A broad field of vision harmonization mechanisms supported by UVO and externalized automated models serves this goal.

Organizations and UVO

The shift toward DPCS acknowledgement and importance is a determined shift from the Cartesian methods of handling real life situations. It is a shift from well-defined objects where the only problem is in the measuring of their stable attributes which differentiate them from each other, allowing for the creation of nice spaces of such attributes where, by varying their measurements, it was possible to obtain the vision of the complexity of the situation. Such a way of general object definition and their distinction in well-defined operations of measurements of their differences allows for the creation of functions of distances, clusters, maps and so on, providing extremely effective tools for taming complexity, packaging it into a small number of finite objects. All the variability of reality was captured in measurements of stable characteristics (captured in various models). Qualitative and quantitative types of analysis allowed for a clear general understanding and for particular measurements if some details were of special interest.

In utilizing T-mode in organizational analysis, we will see organizations as multilevel SOS (MSOS). It means that two or more SOS (most likely, people as highly integrated SOS) are parts of MSOS, which is a higher level DPCS created from the mutual sensitivity of participating SOS to each other and to various MSOS components.

Remember from harmonomics that DPCS are clusters of sensitivity. In their turn SOS can communicate with each other, and with DPCS in general, creating new clusters of sensitivity of a higher level. Several MSOS can continue formation of a higher level of MSOS like departments in organizations.

Seeing organizations as MSOS will allow us to generalize its functions and management goals, finally developing a **universal description of an organization**. Such description, with sufficient detail, leads to the simplification of strategic planning and management, setting criteria for quality and performance.

In the fast changing, external and internal environment, the valuable features of MSOS efforts could be seen as following:

1. Focusing on the preservation of the previous efforts and investments in the learning and capturing of adequate harmonies
2. Maintaining the ability of fast learning and changing when necessary

It means maintaining the adequacy of orientational models (OM) developed in previous learning efforts, as well as supporting non-decreasing orientational skills (OS) for future OM adjustments. This allows for the maximization of the future value of present harmonization efforts. This is the key intent of all strategies as the utilization of value acquired in the past for as long as possible (but not longer, as HE stresses it).

This is why the success of HHz in MSOS, considering stated goals, depends upon the enhancement of sensitivity to its environment. If sensitivity is poor, HHz will reflect only local and tactical environmental patterns that will cause MSOS instability. More developed sensitivity allows for more generalized and global patterns to be mapped onto MSOS, leading to its overall increase in stability because of the stability of such patterns.

Holistic harmonization in MSOS can take rather complex forms by using multiple levels of evolving DPCS, significantly increasing the structural complexity of the whole MSOS. On the lowest level, we have SOS, as intelligent systems and people, with highly harmonized internal contexts and a strong need in external harmonization with existing internal harmony (which is roughly equivalent to personality). Connectivity and sensitivity of people, as well as other means that they can use or control, creates a context for various MSOS patterns.

MSOS as DPCS constitute the higher level of architecture. Various DPCS can form another DPCS of a higher level (like teams, groups or departments) subjected to their own HHz. Such multilevel holistic harmonization (MHHz) could be seen as a weakness of organizations since it requires additional efforts for inter-level and inter-component harmonization. On the other hand, it could be considered a strength of MSOS compared to highly integrated SOS (e.g. individual life forms). It can allow for adaptive restructuring of MSOS without full deterioration of the whole system, still preserving some of its acquired experience, knowledge and orientational skills.

Summarizing the discussion above we can say that:

> **An organization could be seen as an MSOS attempting to support the efficiency of the process of its HHz in a way allowing for the proper balance between the maximization of the future value of past efforts and investments with the maintenance of necessary tactical and strategic sensitivity.**

According to the described approach of HE to the task of the creation of balanced AHS, there is a need in the development of the vision level (V-level) responsible for advanced sensitivity processing and forming the control impacts on the more stable physical level (P-level). Such two-level organization is the basis of efficient holistic harmonization. V-level should include not only human sensitivity processing as it was traditionally done, but, due to the high volume and frequency of its operations, also the forms of its automation. In the following chapters of HE we will concentrate on its application to organizational development, introducing the general methodology leading to the creation of balanced AHS. It will mainly focus on the new architecture including V-level and details of its development.

Chapter 2

THE INITIAL DESIGN

Introduction

There are two distinctive phases in the process of HHz of AHS:

- Proper choice/design of the environment as the area of external sensitivity (AES)
- Continuing support of healthy coevolution with naturally modified AES and Hi

Since AES is constantly changing anyway, what is new ? By changes in AES leading to the necessity of the shown two-stage adaptation process, we will understand changes that were not caused by the regular dynamics of VS. Rather these changes happen as a process of the selection of new AES, abruptly, without any gradual internal adjustment to them and most likely without existing matching VS. Such a choice is a result of the continuous search for potential AES supporting the best opportunities for HH.

In such cases of "Maxwell Macro Demon hunt" (see "Vision" part) there is a need for the gradual realignment or reharmonization of MSOS with serious changes in AES. While maintaining VM architecture, MSOS has to harmonize with AES, first in its V-level, then letting it modify the rest of the AHS. After the whole AHS is preharmonized with the new environment to the extent of offering confidence in its healthy coevolution, the second stage starts as AHS opens itself to the flow of harmonization from the new AES as a routine (remember "outside-in" development in e-business). Although in this chapter we will mainly discuss the process of acquiring new AES, it is important to note that the process of "cutting off" some parts of existing AES will work similarly.

Initial tuning to changed AES includes the following steps:

1. The adoption of UVO for scanning for potentially beneficial new AES and all other harmonization operations
2. The development of harmonization schema
3. The creation of AES-VS adequacy
4. The initial Rx balancing for V-level
5. Opening up the whole V-level to the flow of external Hz
6. Use VM for the shaping/harmonizing of the whole MSOS
7. Switching to the routine HHz in the chosen harmonization schema

UVO Adoption and Embedded Implementation

This step is the key to the whole idea of using generalized results of harmonomics and holistic engineering, of using all advantages of Tmods. Only UVO implementation throughout the organizational body can allow for **focusing** on the external DPCS and CS-harmonization dynamics, perceiving it via broadband **sensitivity**, and **interpreting it** in the process of Vmod/VS harmonization that will guide the whole behavior toward **HH**. In other words, all features of the VO pyramid should be implemented based on T-mode domination and the mapping possibilities between T-modes, C-modes and S-modes.

Such implementation will require changes in human, group and organizational vision processes. It will include personal training, group collaboration methodologies, and the necessary technological support. It will also change the way the organization assesses its effectiveness and style of dealing with its environment. The following sections and chapters will detail such a process.

The Development of Harmonization Schema

The discussion in Part 1 of "outside-in" organizational development can be interpreted as finding sufficiently big patterns of disharmony which are supposed to be harmonized with the help of (re)designed MSOS. "Sufficiently big" here means not too much of a disharmony, but potentially long-time harmonization can roll down its path "feeding" the MSOS. For example, a big market for services that harmonize the demand (tensions). This is consistent with LH2, according to which we can expect free support from natural Hz if the necessary sensitivity and connectivity is provided.

At this stage MSOS has to externalize the internal vision models and perceptions of the design team members about the possible area of future MSOS sensitivity. The idea is in the possibility of controlling the original connectivity and sensitivity by choosing harmony gaps in the environment that MSOS could fill faster and better than other evolving MSOS in the same area. These gaps work according to LH3 when MSOS takes the role of a channel between two DPCS (like demand and resources that potentially can satisfy it being properly processed) which will be reshaped and fed by the flow of harmonization through it. While detecting these disharmonies, it is important to understand their correlations and possible synergistic effects. The best choice will include disharmonies that being gradually harmonized will help supporting or enhancing existing HH. Such a situation is similar to plugging into an energy source or choosing a current to swim in which takes you in the desired direction.

Such understanding leads us to an important concept: *Hz schema*, which is a **system of external disharmonies** that could be solved by adding MSOS activity to the existing chosen/designed external CS-map. In general, there could be a number of ways to harmonize existing DPCS. For example, the designed product can serve the purpose of faster Internet connection to allow people-on-the-move to pick broadband connectivity at another location (like we use telephone booths). Alternatively, it can be solved as wireless connectivity, although as a slower but always available service. Harmonization of the sinking ship could be sped up by making a hole in it in order to satisfy Archimedes law serving harmonization of natural forces as well as minimizing potential energy, or it can be solved through patching a hole and saving people, which will lead to the harmonization of human tensions. Often demands of harmony are contradictory, and what is harmony for some ways of seeing a particular situation could seem disharmony from other points of view.

On top of these choices we need to consider the possibility of connectivity and sensitivity management when new hubs could be created with the need to harmonize ' them. We might choose a business solution where different sellers will buy their products wholesale in one place and create such a place (as a virtual marketplace) to harmonize the complex web of mutual relations of the marketplace.

The determination of Hz schema creates a potential

place for the future MSOS to fill as an advanced harmonizer. The bigger possible Hz effect, the more free energy of natural Hz could be used. The easier it could be created, the more chances it will be viable. This step represents a macro design of the potential connectivity leading to the necessary Hz design, which could be done in the following steps. A design group discussion at this step is independent from details about how to build such Hz, but rather is concentrated on the potential effect of new connectivity and Hz development. If the proper Hz schema is possible and there is no other organization which can fill this void of discovered disharmony soon enough and on a better level, then the investment can catalyze serious Hz resources leading to those lucrative market-over-book ratios.

Creation of AES-VS

After initial Hz schema is determined, it plays the role of a pattern of the external situation, which has to be supplemented with its context in order to become a live self-organized process. It means that whatever ideas about the initial areas and entities of sensitivity might be, we need to remember this is OO/C thinking and real AES should be build considering the strong external sensitivity of the chosen objects and areas in their own environments as contexts, which together determines the **real full AES**.

So, the next stage is in a more precise determination of the necessary area of external sensitivity (AES) supporting the discovered patterns of Hz schema. There are several requirements to AES design:

1. It should extend AES patterns with their own sensitivity forming a DPCS with its dynamics of harmonization
2. It should support the needs of *comfort zone* design (see below)
3. It should be non-damaging for the valuable internal

VS after MSOS is opened to AES influences and, preferably, provide for their better holistic harmonization with the new environment (VS consideration in AES choice).

Comfort Zone Design as AOS Management

An important factor influencing the development and fine-tuning of AES is the requirement of continuously balanced AHS functionality as risk management. Interruptions could lead to serious damages and distortions of Hi and the inefficiency (may be even the impossibility) of its restoration. Since it might be difficult to make AES the only source of environmental influences and appearance of unwanted and unforeseen impacts, there is a need for the extension of AES in space, frequency, and level of detail in order to intercept the potentially damaging impact sufficiently soon and *preharmonize* internal and external environments protecting valuable acquired harmonies.

The area of external sensitivity allowing for sensing unwanted impacts quick enoughand far enough for proper counter measures will be called the *comfort zone* (CZ). Although far extended sensitivity might be taxing, it supports a good vision in the situation and is capable of advanced warnings. CUI characteristics of environment as well as harmonization abilities and harmonic structure of MSOS influence the shape, size and other properties of CZ. The balance between the possibility to support HH and, yet still receive advanced warning is necessary.

VS Consideration in AES Choice

The biggest problem in AES mapping onto VS (harmonization with VS) is the incomplete information about and the limited sensitivity of external DPCS. In order to design an adequate internal CS-map there should be a way in assessing the S-map of the environment or reconstruct it from major external DPCS with their dynamic trends. For example, organizations might be sensitive to regular assessment commissions but not to its customers. It means that some important external patterns might not be accessible and their information could be delivered later, through a destructive DPI rather then in the form of a signal. In the case of customer-insensitive organizations, it could be a loss of business that is a direct physical impact, which could have been avoided if customer sensitivity were included in the area of external sensitivity of such MSOS.

Since MSOS includes a number of VS and LVS they, as DPCS, have their own AOS, together forming an AOS of the whole MSOS. The activation of some of LVS in the process of HHz leads to a different AOS formation (focusing) for the same MSOS at different times. All intermediate products of VS/SI harmonization like the LVS of various levels are then harmonized with each other. But any changes in DPCS structure of MSOS affect the set of its AOS. It means that in the process of internal harmonization AOS dynamically changes, reflecting the dynamics of VS harmonization. At the same time AOS influences the internal structure of V-level through specific signals (SI) MSOS must become harmonized with. It means MSOS, by activating or developing a certain state of OM as a harmonized set of active VS and SI, can affect the shape of its AES which, in turn, affects the dynamics of its HHz. An example is human preconception when the previously created mindset affects vision which selectively works along the established sensitivity lines, attempting to support that mindset. The change of the mindset (like in those role-playing games) can create different sensitivity to the various aspects of the current situation.

Initial Rx Balancing of V-level

Once the general adequacy and possibility of beneficial AES incorporation is determined and proper VS are ready to participate in new SI harmonization, the initial Rx balancing of the V-level has to be done. This step is important because the proper levels of health indicators from the start will not disturb the future HHz and will contribute to its efficiency.

The most important areas of Rx balancing include:

1. Rud balancing of LVS in chosen VS as the degree of decentralization and self-determination of particular views of AES by LVS. The too poor selection/design of LVS leads to inadequate sensitivity and excessive filtering of information, while too rich selection (active pattern complexity is much higher then the situation) leads to the problem of an excessive use of harmonization resources (time, support) for integration and alignment of all different views on the selected AES.

2. Rcs balancing of relations among LVS and VS/LVS where disproportionally domineering LVS or VS can distort the proper perception of AES. Special Rcs balancing of individual vDPCS might be required if a more advanced vision (like group human VS) exposes beliefs in the higher stability of certain LVS (as concepts, beliefs, patterns) or the lower importance of some of the evolved patterns as fluctuations. Such a situation is typical for data mining with necessary human corrections and the analysis of computer-discovered patterns.

3. Other possible indicators of health have to be tuned up.

Connecting the V-level

After V-level is prepared to accept the flow of harmonization from the newly designed sensitivity to AES, it is time for starting the process, but initially only on V-level without immediate impact on P-level. The existing organizational practice partly parallels this process as initial research, after the areas of engagement have been determined as viable projects.

Allowing for V-level to get tuned to the AES using individual and necessary group and automated procedures is an important step toward harmonizing vision with the V-level structure and functionality. Remember that the idea of HE is in self-organization of various DPCS using advanced sensitivity and other features of VO.

The difference introduced by VM architecture is that not only people are involved, but also the whole V-level including means of automation, group vision reconciliation, and individual vision development. The result of VS development is in the V-level readiness to influence the highly automated fashion in which the P-level processes (V-management).

Use VM for AHS Harmonization

Once V-level matures enough to get sufficiently harmonized with AES, it is time to pass this harmonic understanding onto the P-level. As an example, a design team has to understand the situation, the requirements, and get the right vision of the main processes before starting the actual organizational changes. VM mechanisms have to provide the leading role of advanced harmonization on V-level for P-processes. One of the important features of such an influence is the "reinvention" of MSOS on P-level to match the new V-level structure. V-identity (or VID) has to influence the change of P-identity (PID) or VID→ PID.

A change of PID modifies coevolution with environment, influencing VID in its turn. After a while such a process has to converge to the new VID/PID. The organization is reinvented. The new VID might include the understanding of a company as a service versus manufacturing organization. Then this vision has to influence the physical level (P-level) structures and processes to match that VID.

Toward HE in Existing AHS

When the initial connection of an AHS (like an organizational MSOS with self-harmonization abilities) to the chosen/designed AES is completed and the force of harmonization starts working, the next stage of vision management begins. This stage supports **continuous** efficacy of the HHz in the new environment. Organizations built as AHS are capable of affecting the whole process of their HHz including internal Hz and operations on their environment. They can use all the necessary forms and patterns of AHS behavior. Such activity is naturally directed by the laws of harmonomics to higher levels of HH in all areas of sensitivity (that continuously evolve in a smooth or abrupt way, as in AES design). Another energy-saving aspect, in addition to the effectiveness of harmonization, is its efficiency.

HHz can be improved as a result of:

1. More efficient harmonization processes on existing S-maps
2. Reuse of the existing DPCS on all levels, like reuse of the results of the past harmonization in similar situations

The second method has a very serious impact on MSOS harmonization. The inability to reuse previously preharmonized structures leads to a serious inefficiency in repeated harmonization of the same information. This is why the requirement of efficiency implies the viability of all adequate and reusable DPCS within MSOS on all its levels, which can be supported in balanced AHS. Here the OO/C concept of reuse is transformed into the concept of DPCS viability which includes the possibility of modifications, while reuse is a strict repetition of the structure/process. Adaptive reuse is the middle ground which shows the shift from OO/C to a more PO/H approach in this matter.

Rx balancing is the main guiding tool in this approach, allowing for the best fulfillment of HE goals, and is supported by the proper mix of the following activities:

- The engineering and care of proper DPCS forms (orientational models)
- The engineering and care of harmonization processes (orientational skills)

Both engineering activities attempt to use free self-harmonization "energy" and guidance as much as possible.

The Methodology of Continuous Support

The direction of holistic engineering as it "felt" by AHS and as it goes along the lines of Natural Harmonization: The maximization of the efficiency of HHz at maximum possible level and volume of Hi (but not at the ultimate expense of viability). More precisely—it is the attempt to keep the LCh of OM/OS efficacy at its optimal attractor's position and shape. It is a dynamic balance of tactical adequacy of orientation with strategic orientational skills that, if left to themselves, tend to decrease with growing stabilization.

Approach: the design of balanced AHS with Rx balancing as a diagnostic and treatment method. Such an approach includes:

- **Rx treatment/support** in dynamic ASA of DPCS on all levels and locations (including necessary stability or disintegration/ separation) **including OM/OS** as a main global balancing concern, detailed on the lower levels into Rcs, Rud, and other Rx.

- **Support of the continuous ability of Rx balancing** (use of necessary shortcuts in H and Hz support) because even a short-term disharmonization on a large scale can destroy (death of AHS with its identity as acquired Hi) the regeneration ability which is based on existing pattern-context combination

Comment: notice the focus on Rx balancing at this stage versus intensive creation of the proper DPCS within OM engineering, which is the dominating focus on the Initial Stage of HE when the organization is not converted to AHS yet.

Role of OM/H/DPCS engineering: using free Hz for form/channel management

- **V-level engineering**

  - **PCCE**—engineering as the determination of the proper **common** context focusing and abstractions from other contexts, Carrier and Environment. Compare to ontologies and organizational design charts and diagrams
  - **Engineering** (as shortcuts or initial grafting) of necessary **Hz-forms** with the proper level of self-stabilization and other patterns-features
  - **The support of adequate continuous DPCS dynamics** (formation/change/stabilization) **based on AOS** (where possible) **for harmonies and disharmonies** (as internal and external VCs)

- **Maintaining leading role** in higher (advanced) levels of vision (VM principle) via **VCP** for all levels, for the best use of free Hz
- **Internal/external channel-DPCS engineering** (what

should be sensitive to what and subsequently harmonized) as **OM/OS (for V-level)** or **H/Hz** (in general) **tradeoffs**, where more Hz work slows OS and its efficiency

- **Shortcut risk/benefit management** (considering risks of DPCS—shortcut mistakes)

Role of OS/Hz/CSI engineering: using free Hz for process management

- **CSI engineering** supporting DPCS forms, their changes and Rx on all levels and locations
- **CSI shortcut engineering in OS/Hz**
- **Shortcut risk/benefit management** (considering risks of CSI and shortcuts)

Using: HE tools for development and enhancement

- **CSI matrix enhancements** including human integration
- **H-development** (as H-theories, Harmonizers, Interpretation) for **HT**
- **VMS/VMT** as distributed support for all decomposition integration/communication/Hz leading to VMS with its **specific methods/tools/ technology of HE implementation and support**
- **Support of adequacy for all decompositions** (PCCE, VCP, SCT, VS-AOS)

Chapter 3

OM/DPCS ENGINEERING

Introduction

The orientational model (OM) of the V-level carries all the discovered harmonies as a number of various vDPCS evolved or embedded during the initial design. They constitute the experience, knowledge and current personality traits of MSOS. UVO use in organizations means, first of all, the ability of OM to find and reflect the maximum holistic harmony in the given situation. Such findings are then propagated through MSOS, supporting the holistic harmony of the whole system led by its vision level.

V-level development can be done using one of two methods, depending upon the availability of resources and tolerable risk:

1. The gradual enhancement of existing DPCS to the level of AHS (based on SOS methodology), following with the integration of the V-levels of every local AHS

2. The development of the whole organizational UVO—
    based V-level, following with the "attachment" of
    various pDPCS in its guiding role using VM-technology

In both cases, after the V-level is formed the process of its
support works in the same fashion, including:

1. **V-level engineering**

    ♦ **PCCE/SCT/MLS**—engineering as a
       determination of the proper **common** context
       focusing and abstractions from other contexts,
       the Carrier and the Environment. Compare to
       ontologies and organizational design charts and
       diagrams. AES coordination → Vmod design
    ♦ **Support of adequate continuous vDPCS
       dynamics** (formation/change/stabilization)
       based on AOS (where possible) **for harmonies
       and disharmonies** (as internal and external VCs).
    ♦ **Engineering** (as shortcuts or initial grafting) of
       necessary **Hz-forms** with the proper level of self-
       stabilization and other patterns-features.
       Compensate for lack/abundance of Rcs

2. **Maintaining the leading role** in higher (advanced)
    levels of vision (VM principle) via **VCP** for all levels
    for the best use of free Hz
3. **Internal/external channel-DPCS engineering** (what
    should be sensitive to what and, subsequently, be
    harmonized) as **OM/OS (for V-level)** or **H/Hz** (in
    general) **tradeoffs**, where more Hz work slows OS and
    its efficiency
4. **Shortcut risk/benefit management** (considering risks
    of DPCS design as potential developmental shortcuts
    capable of carrying various mistakes versus natural
    DPCS evolving)

AHS/SOS Engineering

This task is involved in the design or grafting of SOS as
self-supported harmonizers into the main MSOS (like whole
organization). This explains why the idea of *ownership* was
not as rotten (Lenin's view) as it might seem. It just means
that objects, entities and more fuzzy forms of physical DPCS
are being connected to the proper SOS-owners that instantly
add a much higher level of sensitivity and harmonization
abilities to their physical level existence, responding mainly
to the violent hits of the environment as direct physical
impacts (DPI). This is why ownership was a cornerstone of
further sensitivity development and harmonization in the
capitalist economies. The owners actively treated their
property as P-level which could be harmonized according
to their vision. In a socialist economy there should be some
controlling impact forcing people to start harmonization and
instructing how exactly it should be done. Such an approach
removes the connection with LVS and makes the
harmonization of pDPCS much less effective. Of course, as
we have already mentioned in Part 1, there are other views
on SOS design (OO/C in particular) that introduce special
ways of using ownership methods that might be difficult to
sustain in the age of the explosive growth of sensitive systems
in a man-made world, similar to the life explosion in the
Cambrian Period.

The first big change in the design of SOS was in the
development of various forms of professional
management responsibilities, rewards and fears. It was
caused by the increased CUI-nature of the environment
with its turbulence, and the need for professional SOS-
led harmonization of assigned DPCS as areas of
responsibilities.

With further blurring of the boundaries of organizations
and increasing organizational networking the need for fast
local solutions grew and it became practically impossible to

clearly define the domain of management and its necessary reactions under all local circumstances. The time of distributed local team management and project leaders has come with largely unspecified domains of harmonization and a growing reliance on PO/H vision, formulated as "doing the right thing." Not all organizations could be successfully converted to MSOS. The needs for complex synchronization among small teams and group decision-making problems created a new breed of communication technology and artificial intelligence (harmonization) tools.

The latest change in the SOS controlling organizational DPCS happened in e-economy times when inverted e-organizations switch to the idea of submission to environmental control (external SOS-consumers and other influences). This completes the loop of market harmonization when all parties are sensitive to each other in the process of seeking certain harmonies and producing means and services for covering these needs. They are tied together into SOS-complexes managing all necessary DPCS based on VM—methodology.

Such changes stimulate an SOS merger with DPCS for harmonization purposes and do not mean fully switching from one form to another, but rather the domination of the new forms with a reasonable coexistence of the old forms wherever the dynamics of the environment and its stability allows it. A small group of people (SOS or MSOS) can effectively manage some resource transformation into products (DPCS modifications) and their delivery to the market. The described method does not pre-assign SOS to DPCS but rather supports dynamic and flexible SOS corresponding to DPCS evolution. It uses the modification of connectivity and sensitivity between SOS and DPCS leading to the possibility of self-adjustment and, finally, to the vision of the whole e-organization as one effective and efficient SOS. Being properly designed such organizations can enjoy the free resources of natural harmonization.

Decomposition/Focusing

Seeing the world as a bunch of DPCS and using the various forms and patterns of DPCS harmonization requires the ability to focus/connect to particular DPCS chosen out of the web of CS-interactions in the holistic reality. The value of DPCS discovery is in the ability to see the encapsulated harmony (with surrounding it AOS). Such a search for DPCS replaces an OO/C search for objects.

Growing problems in defining the whole-part and unity-subsumption categories of OO/C vision with the growth of complexity, uncertainty and instability in the entities of interest show the need in UVO with T-mode platform. Using UVO as a communication tool requires solving such problems as vision organization using special methods for all major VO features:

- Vision **connectivity/focusing** can be based on **PCCE** decomposition allowing for DPCS recognition and focusing on holistic all-sensitive environments with high CUI.
- **Sensitivity** as a form of receiving information from the AES can be based on different types of **Vmods** (S, C, T) delivering such information onto an internal carrier for harmonization with existing VS.
- Decomposition into supporting V-mode types determines the **interpretation** processes when SI is harmonized with VS (like logical consistency for S-modes or sensitivity harmonization for Tmods). The need for the current adequacy of the vDPCS map to its external source has to be supplemented by the mechanisms of additional sensitivity (Rx balancing) in order to preserve such adequacy/harmony in the future. **Multilevel Rx balancing** of vDPCS plays the role of a grantor of long-term adequacy/harmony sufficient for use in the communication processes.

PCCE Decomposition

HE analysis and synthesis of VS/SI harmonization dynamics has certain problems that have to be solved:

- Partial knowledge of holistic harmony limited by the AOS and harmonization abilities
- Limited sensitivity (that limits vision) of engineers and MSOS to all DPCS involved in MSOS harmonization
- Limited availability of resources

The first two problems lead to possible errors in the process of design and implementation of particular harmonization schemas because of the inability to design fully adequate S-maps of an arbitrary scale. The third problem leads to the necessity of splitting the job into parts in time and among the participants in the project. In spite of the necessity of decomposition, all methods of HE are supposed to decrease the errors of handling of holistic tasks and entities.

DPCS can be detected in AOS and seen in a number of ways. SOS can focus on particular features that form particular contexts with their own patterns. For example, relations between people in a group could be seen in a personal relation context, in work communication context, or as statistics of physical bodies moving in space. DPCS discussion has to be carefully clarified to compare views on the **same** DPCS, to synchronize switching of individual sensitivity from one DPCS to another to form a group opinion and orientation.

In this section we will describe the methods of decomposition of holistic reality with the possibility of the following synthesis of harmonic solutions. We will focus on concepts of the *carrier* and the *environment* as well as discuss the interaction of all four concepts of holistic abstraction: *pattern, context, carrier, and environment* (as components of PCCE-model). Since DPCS features have been described earlier, we will concentrate on the carriers and the environments.

Carrier

The idea of a carrier in one form or another has been known for a long time and sometimes causes numerous debates. In signal communications, a carrier is openly used as a separate and important component allowing for message delivery. For example, a modem uses modulation and demodulation of regular oscillations of a *working frequency* carrying the useful signal. After delivery, the carrying frequency is filtered out and the message-signal is decoded. On the other hand, in neuroscience attempts to reduce all forms of intelligence to underlying neural cell networks and their functionality still remain viable. Are economic relations a carrier for behavior of individual stocks? Is culture a carrier for economic relations? Is organic nature a carrier for life phenomena that can exist in any other carrier (a computer, for example)?

The complexity of these questions lies in the differences among analyzed DPCS. Well-structured objects like a train or a telephone signal, where functionality and implementation of carriers are separated by design, are more likely to be considered as carriers for passengers and signals. Carrier separation (filtering) in the analysis of the whole situation of signal transfer is rather simple and has a low level of uncertainty. Object-oriented analysis and the control type of engineering are the most appropriate here. Separating the train and the people and studying both separately, using different methods and processes, could decrease the complexity of understanding of the whole DPCS, like the train with people. Most likely the meaning of acts of human communications will be independent from the type of the train they are on.

On the other hand, DPCS with a higher sensitivity among their components, as well as a higher instability of patterns in contexts, are more likely to be considered as one system. In such systems carrier separation is much more difficult. Applicability of object-oriented methods of distinction, as well as cause-effect analysis, is becoming less useful then pattern-oriented methods in sensitive systems.

Carrier as Abstraction

The main mechanism allowing for carrier separation from other parts of a given pDPCS or vDPCS is in the structure and mutual relations of groups of disharmonies or tensions to be minimized. They form DPCS of their own. For example, sinking the *Titanic* represents a nice harmonization according to the law of Archimedes, but we can focus on people's lives and reassess the situation. Certain human relations and dramas can become more important than the exact execution of physical laws. We are able to separate the sinking ship as a carrier from the new meaning of communications and relations among people in various groups, despite the fact all of them are one physical system. From another point of view, people, as well as furniture and water, represent a carrier for physical processes in the dynamics of sinking. In this case the carrier is in a specific context, which could be isolated from other parts of DPCS using sensitivity/tolerance of a given set of disharmonies.

In addition, various contexts could be separated as carriers on each level, creating multilevel hierarchical systems of carriers and contexts. The difference between the two is in their use. Sensitive contexts will most likely be used in the further harmonization of a given DPCS while the carrier will, most likely, not be considered at all on a given level of context abstraction.

The carrier can separate a large part of AOS from its harmonization attempts if they do not add much to the evolving meaning determined by a set of disharmonies. Carrier boundaries are permeable and further investigation can determine certain sub-areas of sensitivity that could be considered a carrier and visa versa.

The observation of similarities in DPCS dynamics in

various carriers leads to the conclusion that reductionism can, actually, be redundant, duplicating studies of the same type of DPCS harmonization on multiple carriers. A special unified methodology is necessary for the study of general dynamical pattern-context behavior, like systems theory was created to observe similarity of more stable components or Chaos Theory for the description of deterministic dynamical models. In addition, interpretational processes can effectively use DPCS similarity in order to find out the future results of harmonization. The last area belongs more to art, semiotics, language studies, cognitive science and other fields creating, discovering and analyzing a variety of interpretational techniques as simulations of DPCS harmonization.

Carrier as V/P-space Independence

The idea of the whole as something bigger than the sum of its parts was perfectly known at Aristotle's time and is heavily used in various oriental philosophies and religions. Dynamical Systems Theory showed the existence of certain dynamical patterns becoming as real as "firm objects," yet not existing without sensitivity among all systems components and determined by it. It showed the similarity of these stabilities or *attractors* in dynamic behavior regardless of the underlying system structure but depending only upon its dynamics.

Actually, the existence of characteristics of systems that are homologous to all systems simply because they are all systems, and despite the differences in their phenomenal implementation, can be traced directly to Ludwig Von Bertalanffy. As he put it: "An open system that imports free energy or negative entropy from the outside can legitimately proceed toward states of increasing heterogeneity and order (Bertalanffy, 1968). The concepts of organization, holistic features that cannot be reduced to the sum of the parts, and self-organization were seen valid in all contexts including social, engineering, and biological. This led Von Bertalanffy to postulate a new discipline called "General System Theory." Ervin Laslo (Laszlo, 1973) explained the same idea this way:

> *Thus, if one can show that the schemes are isomorphic in regard to the basic underlying invariances then these invariances (or uniformities) can be held to "signify a unity of the observed universe and hence of science. Their presence does not mean that all areas of reality are reduced to a single level, e.g., that of biological or sociological organized complexity, but that the various levels of reality, ranging from the atomic to ecological nature are "vertically" interrelated by means of properties lending themselves to isomorphic models, i.e., those which exhibit fundamental invariances of basic constructs, conserved throughout a range of transformations. It is not the analogy of phenomena, nor yet the identity of properties, which signifies the possibility of General System Theory, but the isomorphy of invariant constructs, such as laws of development, structure and self-maintenance, occurring in differentiated form in the manifold realms of nature.*

Harmonomics states that this mysterious something, which is in the whole and not in the sum of the parts and which could exist independently of the particular physical properties of the parts, is their mutual sensitivity. The whole DPCS, then, could be perfectly described by its CS-map, which, if existing on various carriers, will demonstrate isomorphic dynamical characteristics and patterns extending General Systems Theory to CS-map dynamics.

The carrier in this case could be seen as a cluster of sensitivity or a special type of context. Its specificity is based on its ability to perceive an S-map from another carrier and embed it in its own tissue of sensitivity. After foreign DPCS is mapped onto a particular carrier, the natural dynamics of harmonization takes place producing the same results for the same S-maps. Such a possibility as mapping DPCS from one carrier onto another and "playing it there" makes DPCS a special form of being. Of course, as we mentioned earlier, some context sensitivity might be preserved for various reasons and becomes a residual sensitivity making such "model" life. This residual sensitivity links mapped DPCS to the original sources of its sensitivity that were not captured during the mapping process.

This possibility of DPCS existing independently from its carriers and being multiplied in various mappings-recordings makes the world of Plato's ideas as real as the physical properties of carriers. Considering the fact that DPCS could be harmonized on one carrier and be mapped in the initial stage of harmonization on another carrier where the final result of harmonization could be obtained, makes such 'substitution a valuable forecasting and modeling mechanism. From this point of view, DPCS could be considered carrier independent models . . . still requiring some carrier to "play them" (perform the harmonization process).

Each carrier, as well as DPCS, could represent a multilevel hierarchy of carriers and DPCS, allowing for further simplifications of AOS perception and distribution for parallel harmonization and analysis. The distinction of carriers in such multilevel models is not a simple predefined procedure and could be done using the following methods:

1. Utilizing full predictability of underlying specifics of carrier dynamics (if it takes place) in order to filter out its influence on DPCS behavior. For example, knowledge of the carrying frequency in telecommunications allows for the filtering and amplifying of the transferred signal itself.
2. If the carrier is a more fuzzy and unstable entity, then methods of holistic analysis could be used including recognition, pattern resonance, learning, and others.

Good Carriers

Considering the important role of carriers, what are the requirements for an ideal carrier? What features should it have to play its role more effectively in MSOS harmonization? How should design and management of carrier quality be handled?

Organizations usually have several types of carriers whose combination could be seen as a general carrier of organizational DPCS. Among these carriers are people with their body/mind sensitivity, information systems, technology and various forms of assets, legal and accounting contexts, etc.

The most important role belongs to information and communication technologies (including people) carrying information images of real processes. This type of carrier is special because it was partly consciously, partly evolutionally designed as a special artificial carrier, capable of integrating DPCS from all other carriers and providing for their efficient harmonization in various ways. In a sense, it alone can support the V-level of MSOS existence.

A good carrier is supposed to have the following features allowing for S-map recording, harmonization and the simple interpretation of results:

1. Allow for the quality mapping of various types of vDPCS and SI. It includes such areas as data mining, statistical analysis, knowledge discovery in databases, multimedia and virtual reality systems management, various methods of visualization and online analytical processing as in OLAPs and data warehouses. Other types of vDPCS can be based on human interpretational abilities in cross-system communications.

2. Provide for various types of harmonization among Vmods of all types (Smods, Cmods, Tmods), and between the levels and contexts of system architecture with the possibility of supporting evolving patterns,

detecting them and maintaining their newly obtained communicational properties. These features also mean the constant possibility of distinguishing between carrier and DPCS.

3. Allow for the dynamic mutual sensitivity of object-oriented and pattern-oriented parts of the system by discovering all stable patterns and reflecting them in OO/C description and systems logic (business rules, logic of carrier functionality, etc.). In this case all emerging patterns could be represented as changes in systems' description and be analyzed using traditional scientific methods. Such experience-knowledge combination and mutual enrichment can help using the full potential of all forms of harmonization of all types of Vmods.

Carrier Design

PCCE—model allows to use physical carriers and environments and build a number of contexts where patterns will be determined with all their dynamics. It is similar to the idea of Java Virtual Machine working on any computer and allowing to run there same language patterns. Here the virtual machine is a context or rather DPCS played on some carrier, which can be any physical machine. Same DPCS can be played on any carrier with the following requirements:

- Predictable dynamics
- Sufficient richness (for the class of possible changes on some interval)
- Proper Rcs balance
- The carrier has to be protected from environment
- The carrier can have many layers increasing independence from the environment and other layers similar to **OSI communication model**
- The carriers in multi-carrier systems could be

optimized for particular types of Vmods and VS but, after all, have to be able to use some interpretation for inter-carrier mapping.

Environment

The environment is a combination of all AES. DPCS might not be sensitive to many external areas at all times because of poor connectivity and tolerance boundaries. Then it waits for impacts as periodic changes in connectivity (usually when something gets closer). DPCS, the carrier and the environment have permeable boundaries.

The environment can be seen as an MDPCS existing within AES boundaries. LH2 determines the dynamics of the coevolution of MSOS and its environment. One of the errors in the design of the environment is making it too small for simplified HHz allowing for the maintenance of existing Hi. The Comfort Zone concept directs engineering activity to sufficiently full AES.

Basic separation from the environment is not an object-like distinction with firm well-definable boundaries. It is just based on better clusterization of sensitivity within DPCS and preservation of some external sensitivity (Se), which plays a very important role in the process of HHz. The duality of relations with the environment requires necessary procedural support:

a) The management of Carrier/Environment and DPCS/Environment interfaces as tolerance boundaries

b) The process of constant MSOS redefinition of itself (re-recognition) from carrier and environment. Such recognition is based on sensitivity, which might require changes in Hi.

c) The proper PCCE decomposition of the environment in order to detect DPCS that can be used for enhanced HH.

PCCE dynamics

The concepts of DPCS, the carrier, and the environment allow for the modeling of context similarity in various situations, hiding their differences in the carrier/environment systems. DPCS will be considered the primary objects of our interests. The patterns, contexts, carriers and environments can have a complex structure themselves, representing systems consisting of various components. The same environments can have numerous carriers and each of them can have several pattern/context systems. More then that, such systems can communicate with each other.

The model <Pattern, Context, Carrier, Environment, Time> describes pattern relations with its context forming particular DPCS on a certain carrier and with a particular environment at a particular time interval. As an example of the usefulness of introduced modeling abstractions, we can describe a famous test allowing for the discovery of a solution based (in our interpretation) on DPCS and the carrier/environment model.

First, the fortress story is offered as a problem-solving test (used at Harvard). According to the story, one bad guy (in some kingdom) with his associates and supporting forces were hiding in the fortress from the local citizens' angry backlash. To secure their position they set landmines on all the roads to the fortress so small groups from the fortress were able to go around, very carefully, in search of food and supplies. The citizens' army could not directly attack the fortress because the mined roads prevented a massive invasion of troops. What to do? The majority is able to find the solution fast, such as splitting the army into small groups, using different roads, and gathering near the fortress for the attack.

The second test story was sad. It described a patient with a cancerous tumor which could be treated only with a certain, strong dose of radiation. The directed beam of such adose would destroy all tissue on the way to the tumor. What to do? The problem seems more difficult. A hint to use the solution pattern of the previous story leads the students to suggest the use of several beams of radiation from different sides, concentrating on the tumor area. This way none of the beams is strong enough to destroy the body tissues.

In each story, the splitting of the attacking army, as well as splitting the dose of radiation into several beams. are the patterns of the solution. The description of the situation with the impossibility of using one direction in both stories is the context. Military and clinical specificity play the role of the carriers of these patterns with their codes of roads, armies, fortress and radioactive beams, tumors and sensitive tissue. The historical, social and political situation in the country, as well as all other factors of the situation in the first story and the health and hospital situation factors in the clinical story are their environments.

By setting carrier harmonization effectiveness and efficiency apart from the problem of SI/VS harmonization as maps of DPCS that are important for MSOS environmental adaptability, it becomes possible to discuss vision harmonization as a problem of its own, separating it into a distinctive architectural layer. This approach will be further explored in the present chapter.

SCT Hz and HT

Another area of vDPCS classification, which can be discussed on this introductory level, is the distinction of vDPCS types according to their design and harmonization methods and procedures, corresponding to their position in the VO-pyramid. As it was shown in the "Vision" part, we can distinguish three types of vDPCS: symbolic, connectionist and sensitivist.

Symbolic types

Symbolic vDPCS (Smods) can represent more stable external DPCS to an extent allowing us to consider them as object-type entities, capable of carrying a label/name matching a stable collection of features recognizable by other processing elements. Because of their stability, such DPCS could be designed and harmonized using traditional OO/C methods.

Smods can be used within the UVO approach as shortcuts of harmonization, that can be more efficient in terms of required resources (including harmonization time). The more the situation is PO/H-like, the less effective and efficient OO/C methods are. The use of Smods can also be justified by existing investments in OO/C methods, but only to the degree of their adequacy for the situation and usefulness of the viewing system.

Connectionist types

Cmods can be used at the low and middle levels of the VO-pyramid. They also can play the role of Tmod approximations of Smods or Smod approximations of Tmods. The biggest area using connectionist models is artificial neural network design. It uses the notion of nodes and connections, where nodes exhibit a certain level of sensitivity (described in their weights) to connections (inputs) and can generate an output signal (fires) if their excitation is above a predetermined threshold. Excitation itself could be represented by a number of functions, varying from step-like functions to more smooth curves. The combination of connection weights leading to the nodes form a distributed pattern representing system's Hi. Operations include only weight adjustment in various learning paradigms. Artificial life, genetic algorithms and other forms of "soft math" can also play a role of Cmods.

Such models are very different from symbolic models and their processing in their pattern-like representations. There is a long history of discussions about their independent role from symbolic models in the representation of human thinking (e.g. Smolensky, 1988).

Sensitivist types

Tmods are the most consistent foundation for the methods and dynamical processes of harmonomics. Their ability to automatically acquire the features of the proper level of the VO-pyramid according to the specificity of the situation plays the central role in the possibility of building UVO implementation.

Poor harmonization tools, low sensitivity, and the difficulties of supporting true CS-dynamics might hinder their use on V-level. The methods of vision integration of all types of Vmods are required for multi-type system architectures.

Multilevel Rx Balancing

If PCCE permits coordinating the vision of DPCS, multilevel system (MLS) decomposition allows for the handling of macro DPCS engineering when we build super DPCS (MDPCS) out of other DPCS. What methods and logic can we use to understand the proper engineering design of this DPCS Lego game?

VM represents the enhancement of the SOS method possible in the MSOS context. In reality, the harmonization abilities of MSOS necessary for successful intelligent MSOS organization could be limited for various reasons. In such cases it might be appropriate to develop multilevel holistic harmonization (**MHHz**) processes allowing for the maintenance of optimal Rx indicators for the whole system where different levels might compensate for each other's deficiencies in CSI-abilities (connectivity, sensitivity, interpretation).

If the physical P-level of MSOS does not provide sufficient horizontal ratios of Rch and Rud, then the coordinating response becomes imperative and forceful methods of P-level harmonization should be used. They can come from a higher level of MSOS architecture. This level is responsible for the adequacy of the coordinated response on a P-level, which cannot evolve to the proper state on its own.

The higher level is supposed to have the following properties based on its more advanced abilities to maintain proper Rx:

1. Be **sufficiently sensitive** to important signals
2. Be able to develop (evolve to) a **good OM**
3. Maintain **continuous** functionality, which means that it has to possess **good orientation skills**.

The idea of this scheme concerns Rch/Rud compensation on the lower level by improving these ratios on higher levels so that the combined multilevel system will have optimal Rx. For example, if Rch on the P-level is too high, then Rch on the V-level will be sufficiently low to support the proper Rch on the two levels combined.

This method could be further applied within V-level itself, making it a multilayer structure. With the growth of CUI, as it was shown in the previous chapter, vision itself could become too stable with past knowledge negatively influencing changing conditions. The higher level of OM could be created supporting strategic vision stability but relaxing tactical vision forms, allowing for easier evolving and matching of the patterns of reality. Ultimately, the system will develop something like the Ten Commandments on the very top level guiding its MHHz process on the lower levels.

Such use of MLS could be seen in the integration of LVS on a higher level (VS), which is capable of inter-LVS harmonization developing a more **global vision**. Different patterns could be stored on different levels where local tactical fluidity will be later harmonized with perceived global patterns of strategic importance.

VM architecture, then, can be seen as a special case of a MLS when necessary levels of Rx support exist on different carriers (the physical level world of sensitivity and a V-level carrier like the Internet). MLS decomposition could be further applied to such architecture, making more levels on both the P—and V-carriers as well as adding possible new ones.

Continuous growth of management pyramids, utilizing the method of MHHz, was caused by the growth of CUI and, hence, the need in higher pyramids with more flexible vision on higher levels. But the more levels are there, the higher the problems of inter level and intra-level harmonization leading to the overall inefficiency of further MHz growth. At a certain level of CUI this method alone becomes inefficient. A new direction was taken by using flatter, but more intelligent, structures (more Rx balanced) with better harmonization properties on each level.

VCP Design as a Special Case of MLS

VCP Decomposition

The existence of the V-level in MSOS does not guarantee its smooth management of the P-level because of the complexity of harmonization of multiple vDPCS, pDPCS and their mutual relationships. A multiplicity of SOS participants with individual V—and P-levels adds to the problem requiring synchronization of all levels between all participants. The traditional solution to the use of harmonization (vision) on the human and the device carrier was the development of information systems/information technology (IS/IT). This technology is rapidly deviating from the original goal of just informing people about past events to the role of a communication/coordination level.

This intermediate level, which could be called control/coordinating or C-level, will consist of the two sub-layers: the upper *vision layer* and the lower *system layer*. The vision layer deals with vDPCS coordination, synchronization and interpretation to the system level for further control of the P-level. The vision layer generally supports C-level sensitivity to V-level changes. The system layer is a controller/coordinator for P-layer and mainly consists of various software objects, whose changes in the state or interaction logic cause changes in DPCS of the P-level. For example, the removal of a particular supplier object from the system leads to a disconnection from this supplier in real life. Adding a product object to your shopping cart leads to its delivery and payment transactions.

In such three-level architecture the upper V-level is responsible for clear vision and orientation with the P-level to follow. The C-level is placed in between, assisting the V-level in coordination of its vision processing and management functions. Since C/P level architecture is already in place, traditionally supporting human management operations, what remains is to connect the V-level to its leading role, determining birth, destruction and modification of C-objects as well as their communications and coordination. It is important to note that the direct V/P mapping can also exist and often can work without C-level coordination. Animal behavior is an example of such vision-management without the use of S-modes and inferential OO/C "thinking."

The VCP-architecture of communicating parties explicitly acknowledges the necessity of considering the harmonization of the received information with all the complexities of internal organization. The scientific method supported systems design (as well as some ideas of general language role) as mainly C-level communications. Smods, after receiving inputs, modify their control actions by changing system states. Oversimplification of such an approach was discussed in the "Vision" part. The growing intelligence and sensitivity of system components require the development of an interpretive communication theory which considers the existence of at least VCP-levels as active parts in the communication process, which becomes the harmonization process.

The switch from the idea of communication to the concept of harmonization has a very profound impact on the concept of meaning. Interpretation is not an attempt to reconstruct the meaning that the sender tried to put into the communication's message but is, rather, a harmonization act of an internal adjustment to the received information. Different adjustments bear different "meanings." In the following sections we will analyze the consequences of such harmonization using a VCP model of communication parties.

Harmonization Between VCP Levels

VCP decomposition is based on the type of existing Hi in SOS and their VCP specifics to provide for the best HHz later. It considers which VCP type is presented (like V/[C,P] or C/[V,P], etc.) where for C/[.] types (C-dominant types, harmonized with any combination of other participants) C-level will play a bigger Hz role and should carry more functions then for V/[.] types (V-dominant). VCP decomposition can be used iteratively when any part of what was previously considered as P-level can be seen, in its turn, as the whole VCP microstructure, with its virtual or physical vision implementation and more rigid P-level parts harmonized with its own V-level. The same can be done for the V-level itself, where more stable vDPCS with insufficient Rx balancing or sensitivity could be supplemented with higher and more flexible constructs playing the role of the V-level. It means that any VCP decomposition and analysis should proceed with joint focusing on the ultimate DPCS, which is being decomposed. The switch of the focus to lower or higher levels of DPCS changes the arrangement of VCP. In this sense VCP decomposition is just one of the ways of using MLS decomposition, discussed before in the case of multilevel Rx balancing. Its special role is based on serious differences in carrier implementation and methods of operating in the case of whole organizations (MSOS) or their macro parts. Future organizations with increased fluidity and sensitivity of P-level components will have less dramatic differences between VCP levels, allowing for smoother and more efficient Rx balancing and coordination. Some of the so-called virtual organizations and "dot coms" are moving in this direction already.

Interaction of VCP Architecture Participants

There are several levels of MSOS participants with certain differences in harmonization:

- SOS/LMSOS as the harmonization of several SOS within some local MSOS (like people in a group)
- LMSOS/LMSOS as the harmonization of lower level structures supporting some higher level organizational structure (groups/department)
- LMSOS/MSOS—same as previous but supporting the whole organization
- SOS/MSOS—contexts where all SOS (mainly people) in an organization have to agree on some vision concerning everybody

Matching the description of VM, we can say that each kind of participant in a higher-level DPCS has three main architectural components: V-level, C-level, and P-level. The taxonomy of the possible architectural compositions of these levels include ten combinations:

1. All levels are well connected and naturally harmonized within one cluster of mutual sensitivity <V, C, P>. As with individual human beings, we would like to see holistic harmony of the body and mind (C/P, V/P) as well as reason and harmonization power of the emotional perceptions (V/C).
2. The other nine combinations are based on three harmonization classes where two levels are harmonized

with each other much more tightly than with the third level. For example: [V, C]/P, or [V, P]/C, or [C, P]/ V.

3. Each of these three classes can have three possible harmonization schemes with the external third component:

- Two schemes with a better connection to either one of two clustered levels (like in [V, P]/C class C-level could have more influence on P through which V—level will be affected in its turn, and the whole [V, P] cluster will be harmonized with C-level).

- One scheme of harmonization where the third component directly affects the fabric of a new context created by the holistic harmonization of the other two components (levels), like in the [C, P]/V tight holistic harmony of [C,P] which could be found in automated processes, can be influenced by the V-level affecting both the controller and the physical equipment operations by implementing, say, fuzzy logic mechanisms.

One of the interesting examples of such harmonization schemes includes the separation of control in the old Russian army between the ideological (communist vision—supporting) officer—commissar and the military officer synchronizing military behavior of the whole unit. The first one was responsible for the harmonization of the individual and group vision with the official party vision, the second had to take care of the viability and efficiency of the group of individuals as a military unit. In some units commanders were very popular, creating one harmonized system with the soldiers. Commissars had to find ways of influencing individual vision, either through exercising their management power directly over soldiers, or attempting to influence the commanding officer. Readers can trace the similarity of some modern military organizations with politics as well as some corporate dilemmas between managers, employees and stakeholders.

The creation of the general V-level, as well as using the same approach in local MSOS, allows for the creation of support for new context development within the system of local visions, with evolving global VS and their integration into the OM of MSOS. VM supports the dominance of the V-level over C-and P-level roles. Such a step will mark the beginning of the transition to the effective VM. Further steps will include improvements in the effectiveness and efficiency of the interlevel harmonization within the general process of HHz of each participant, and all of them together within the MSOS context.

Inter-Participant Harmonization Specifics

The multiplicity of methods of communication and harmonization of such MSOS participants is based on the possibility of one multilevel participant affecting another through harmonization or impact on any single level (V, C, or P) or affecting any cluster of these levels created through their internal holistic harmonization. For example [V1,C1]/P1-P2/[C2,V2] scheme reflects a direct physical impact of one SOS on another, through which other V—and C-components will be influenced in the process of the subsequent internal harmonization. [V1,P1]/C1-C2/[V2,P2] scheme describes harmonization on control levels with various degrees of mutual sensitivity up to the scheme [V1,P1]/C1 $\rightarrow$ C2/[V2,P2] with one-way sensitivity only. C-harmonization is carried out by mainly using Smods as control and information signals impacting upon the logic of DPCS performance.

Recognizing three architectural levels within SOS and

LMSOS participants, we should not forget that on the more complex and dynamic V-level the same ideas of the interaction of levels with different and compensatory Rx in MLS fashion exist, too. How does inter-participant harmonization happen with multilevel participant architectures?

The complexity of a multilevel HHz stems from the existence of the internal harmonization of all Vmods and DPI received on all levels, whether we are talking about VCP-levels or additional sublevels within these main architectural parts. It means external signals do not directly change the states of all these levels, but only after the stabilized procedure of internal harmonization. These Hi and Hi/e parts of HHz that include intensive use of internal models of external communication partners and communication channels have to be accounted for by holistic engineering. It means the recognition of the phenomena of multilevel communication processes among MSOS participants.

Multilevel harmonization (MHz) through organized communications of SOS or MSOS—type entities require methods of the development and handling of the special communication tools designed or used in such situations. Although in PO/H vision we can use the term *signal* like in OO/C-vision, it's understanding is different. It is seen as an active period of mutual harmonization of the sender and the receiver with the development and recognition of certain DPCS of meaning—SIs that later have to be harmonized with existing vision systems. Of course, there are cases when, especially on C-level, such Vmods have a form of Smods that are well-shaped and designed to contain all their meaning with them, causing a universal similarity of signal interpretation. But this only describes how they are designed . . . which does not mean that the situation they are good for always happens.

The MHz of SOS presents a big problem for such

Cartesian treatment of signals as self-contained communication objects. Not only Shannon's information theory but also the subsequent use of the information richness theory created a foundation for single-level communication devices, where such signals are uniquely interpreted and provide a predictable effect on the whole communication process, making it work as some kind of strictly logical device. The idea behind such an approach was in the increased power of control when signals are treated as direct physical impact (DPI) controllers capable of modifying the states of receivers in a predictable manner. In order to give information signals the power of DPI resulting in direct state-space modification, they have to be designed and used as stable, well-recognizable and measured information objects. The latest wave of object-oriented technologies attempts to save this approach in the face of a growing complexity and the challenges of multilevel communications.

In addition to the growing role of people in organization communications and the rising knowledge management wave, there are a growing number of intelligent devices and communication processes that are not single-level with direct mechanical interpretation. Quantity here becomes a new quality. The implementation of intelligence in a growing number of simple interactive objects or mobile agents could be seen initially as a way AI can develop. But, at the same time, the growth of even simple intelligence modifies the communication structure into a multilevel one when following a creative interpretation of the signal is assumed. And, after it obtains the distinct features of multilevel harmonization with the growing use of internal models, sensing and filtering incoming information and, later, responsibility for internal harmonization of gathered signals, the intelligence has to jump to another level. On this level we deal with signals that are not self-contained and are only a part of the holistic harmonization process, including internal Hi of the participants as well as their mutual harmonization as whole DPCS. Information is not fully contained in the signal anymore. It does not even exist as information per se, but rather is an HHz process.

VCP Structures Based on V-level Integration

In VM design the task of the V-level formation could be achieved by using several methods of connection of the V-levels of various SOS or local MSOS:

1. Advanced V-level connectivity and sensitivity as one integrated level supporting its further harmonization.
2. The use of autonomous vDPCS mapped from their SOS onto some common carrier capable of supporting their mutual harmonization processes. In this case ideas and vision systems have a life of their own, being separated from the C—and P-levels of individual SOS. After common harmonization is achieved, results could be interpreted by each SOS. This is the most promising type of V-level organization, using special designs of multiple common carriers to better serve independent VS/SI harmonization.
3. Communication with some SOS could be done through other levels (C, P) with the V-level playing its role only inside particular SOS. For example, in wrestling, communication is on the P-level, which can involve internal interpretation of the contender's movements later. In the army it is usually on the C-level, saving time on interpretational procedures. C-level there during the training is well-mapped onto the P-level so that a command causes immediate physical response.

As was shown in the previous section, communication between VCP structures can be supported on all levels. It means, as in the case of the shown differences in V-level connections and overall integration/decentralization, the same three types of design could be applied to C—and P—levels. Thus separate V-levels of different SOS can have a joint C-level (like an integrated computer network). A more elaborate example of the joint P-level and isolated C—and V-level structures can happen when several VS are so disharmonic with each other that when one is active, others are dormant or their control over the P-level is functionally split. Multiple personality disorder is one example, as well as the differences of opinions in management about some important matter, which results either in their functional separation, or a strange mix of inconsistent operations or in periodic changes in management with resulting changes in behavior (the two-party system in the US).

Group Coordination of DPCS Harmonization

Before any DPCS harmonization is organized in a distributed manner, the parties should be focused on a particular DPCS, like in the case of a OO/C group analysis, the focus is on a particular object. Tuning vision connectivity to external DPCS is done by focusing on the same AES, similar to throwing a net in the waters of the sensitivity of a particular area and pulling out various DPCS. Such synchronization of concentration on AES uses two mechanisms: PCCE and MLS decomposition, where all participants are informed about what is considered as a carrier, context and potential DPCS that each of them should get using their own fishing nets of sensitivity. The structure of MLS also has to be generally understood.

MLS and PCCE mutually complement each other as methods of focusing on DPCS in holistically complex environments. PCCE decomposition is about pattern and context development as a DPCS, with internal harmony supporting its boundaries and its relationships with the outbound sensitivity of such DPCS to its environment and relationships with the carrier. MLS decomposition is about the whole and its parts seen as two levels, where the whole evolves on the higher level, supporting maps of local harmonies on the lower level as well as the harmony of local DPCS with each other. This additional harmony is what makes such wholes bigger then the sum of their parts.

PCCE could be applied to an MLS structure containing all inter—and intra-level harmonizations within the same context, or each of the levels, as well as the interface between them, could be seen as two DPCS with the third one as a channel. The opposite operation as an MLS application to a PCCE architecture can expose several local DPCS connected with the one which is their higher level as global two level structures or the context could be seen as a higher level for the DPCS it contains. PCCE serves the goal of DPCS identification and its HHz with the environment. MLS decomposition supports visions allowing for a more detailed view of inter DPCS relationships.

V-level Design

Once the system of DPCS recognition/formation is in place, it becomes possible to start designing DPCS on the V-level (vDPCS). The V-level design of DPCS includes the following tasks:

1. The creation and improvement of vision systems as the orientational model (OM)
2. The development and implementation of effective orientational skills (OS) as a system of harmonization mechanisms on V-level.
3. The planning for proper coordination and balance between OM and OS.

These procedures interact with each other, forming a spiral type of evolution where initial steps in V-level creation or improvement will be supported by the implementation of harmonization methods and tools. That, in turn, will support the enhancement of vision and its involvement in MSOS functionality. The fine-tuning and balancing of OM and OS is then the main concern of V-level care.

V-level aspects requiring HE attention include:

- The type of V-level (virtual or physical)
- MDPCS architecture including various types of vDPCS (SI, LVS, VS, OM) and processes of their mutual multilevel harmonization (MHz)
- Ways of V-level incorporation into VCP-architecture of the whole MSOS (for example a company)

V-level Features

Virtual V-level

The virtual V-level phenomena was, probably, first seriously analyzed in "Mind in Society" (Vygotsky, 1978), where he described his experiments with children when a group was able to demonstrate a higher level of intelligence then any individual participant tested separately. Such intelligence could be measured as success in special tests that prove the existence of a certain level of development. As a result, the level of the group development in the intelligence tests was higher then individual before and after the test. It shows that this intelligence was not gained individually but could only exist in a group in the process of its creative communications. The difference between the zone of *actual development* of participants and the results of the group development he called the *zone of proximal development*. Such a zone is the achieved level of the group VS development and harmonization ability with respect to incoming SIs.

The virtual nature of V-level implementation is in its CS-dynamics, supported by communications only, without harmonization processes running on the physical carrier with the ability to carry resulting C-maps over time. The virtual nature of the network of periodic communications, like in Vygotsky's case, places the burden of harmonization (as connectivity, sensitivity and interpretation) on communicating DPCS, not offering the support of physical harmonization processes on the physical carrier. Sensitivity in all our DPCS forms doesn't have to be physically implemented as a series of contiguous channel states, but can be based on periodic messaging and reactions to it, regardless of how such information gets to local participants.

Vygotsky also emphasized the necessity and role of *play* in development, which in our interpretation is the process of harmonization when children, in addition to internalized SIs, learn the rules of group harmonization that become the grounds (carrier) of the VS/SI solutions of the higher level. Kurt Lewin's studies (Lewin, 1951) showed that high sensitivity to external DPCS (quasi-stationary equilibrium of the force field), and the need to harmonize them with the game, support the phenomenon of *management-by-environment,* similar to e-business management by external sensitivity. In his conclusion, things dictate to the child what he must do.

Physical V-level

In case of physical V-level implementation, there is a specialized carrier allowing for the externalizing of vDPCS in all their CS-map existence as well as supporting their external harmonization and evolving. The nurturing of a plant by several people, when each attempts to support a necessary level of plant harmony with its environment and the aesthetical ideas of beauty of each person could serve as such as example. In this case, the carrier is the plant's physical structure and the processes sensitive to external impacts (DPI type in this case) implementing VM procedures. The beauty and viability of a plant is the next level of individual ideas (LVS) of the participating SOS (people). For example, lianas could be forced to grow in a certain direction and fashion to supplement the structure and harmony of a building exterior. Here the V-level has an autonomous carrier capable of HHz and sensitive to the ideas of the participating SOS.

Communication among SOS-planters (if they do not speak to each other) can be achieved by the impression they get from the integration of the efforts of each while just looking at the plant. The physical V-level could be *dynamic* (with its own harmonization processes) and *static* (just with memory). An example of a static V-level is a game where every participant draws something, thereby continuing the work of others. The created picture, at any moment, communicates the state of integral imagery to the participants of the game, harmonizing their perception and ideas with others.

A management group taking care of the organizational workability is a similar example. Here an organization with its self-adaptability and internal Hz processes based on the workers' understanding of their job and means of automation becomes a carrier, supporting the vision of the management group. Individual mind/body systems capable of seeing the integral result as an internalized dynamic CS-map could be considered another carrier. If communicating sides can see only partial local aspects, then they need a more advanced communication system working like a virtual V-level, capable of representing the full OM. The proper language and the means of human vision synchronization facilitates the use of UVO in discussions, procedures, and changes in organizational behavior. With vision automation its power will only grow.

DC Design

Concentration or focusing on active problems is an important feature of MSOS, allowing for a fast and efficient response with even insufficient sensory and harmonization resources. More than that, it is an ability to take everything the system is generally sensitive to and scoop out the meaningful parts that are important for particular tasks. It is an ability to focus on the most important harmonization problems. Problems in UVO are disharmonies appearing in the system, while problem solution is their harmonization to a satisfactory level. A *disharmony cluster* (DC) is a cluster of mutually connected problems (disharmonies) that create tensions in the system. These tensions of harmonization processes that attempt to find the minimum energy solution are very valuable indicators of problems. Similar processes are known in neural networks, when disharmony frustrates the processes of harmonization, keeping energy levels sufficiently high, kicking out possible "solutions" from their local "energy wells" and searching to discover the global "energy wells." This property was noticed and is actively researched in "smart matter" projects. An example of such disharmony signalization triggering additional harmonization resources could be seen in a situation when the crack in the wing of an airplane creates micro-tensions in the properly chosen material that are perceived as signals by the specialized local harmonization system capable of patching cracks "on the fly" without the use of centralized monitoring.

Similar to other clusters of sensitivity, DC is a DPCS having harmonization problems with other DPCS of the system or within itself. The internal harmony of the DCs supports their relative stability. There are several ways of dealing with DC:

1. Harmonization with other clusters
2. Channel modifications that, according to LH3, decrease connectivity between disharmonic DPCS or absorb part of such disharmony, mediating their coexistence

In work groups the vision harmonization importance of the

DC is shared among the members as well as the similarity of its understanding. Consequently, DCs can be derived as variables of some analysis or object components that have to be explored further, or they are perceived as commonly understandable problems or areas of necessary attention, or they are the results of the new vision, having evolved in the process of communications. The utility of DCs is based on the fact that for different people it is much easier to agree on problems of importance as some relatively stable parts of the whole environment they are sensitive to then on the forecast, assessment and analysis of this environment. After such sensitive components are determined as problems to study, it is time for the restoration of the whole DPCS they belong to.

The process of DC utilization includes the following steps:

1. Based on the areas of sensitivity of each participant of the group harmonization process, the common DCs are discovered and agreed upon.
2. Each DC is a basis for special research leading to the discovery of the area of sensitivity (AOS) of a given DC. For example, if it is a lack of funds, then AOS will include all aspects of reality that can affect the funding problem. At this step, no conclusions should be drawn, but focus should be on the discovery of all relevant aspects. Something that J. Christopher Jones called *divergence* in the process of design, which has a certain similarity to our AOS. At the stage of divergence participants try to find all relevant matters without rejecting any. AOS design, in comparison, is seeking not only possible solutions but everything relevant to the matter (affecting AOS) in order to be able to build the model of natural DPCS harmonization.
3. The third step includes the harmonization of AOS which could result in additional DPCS evolving during this process. Such harmonization, which could be partly automated and partly a result of a specific rhetoric

procedure in the distributed parallel communication process, could result in evolving DPCS with sufficient stability, thus becoming new DCs and causing an additional search for their new AOS.

4. Finally, harmonized AOS is becoming a flow of SI including initial DC as a part of its DPCS structure. Such SI have to be harmonized with the local vision system and, later, with the higher levels of VS.

SI Design

Roles of SI in MSOS

Various roles of SI in MSOS require a number of specific features:

1. SI of External Sensitivity

    a. SOS within MSOS have to have mechanisms of focusing on SI, singling them out of the holistic AES (as *perception* SI), and developing the necessary sensitivity to them, allowing for SI to play their role in SOS vision formation.

    b. Synchronization and coordination of such SI focusing and sensing among all interacting SOS-participants in certain MSOS Hz-schemas in order to provide for synchronous SOS harmonization and response required by VM procedure which has to result in coherent physical action (P-harmonization).

2. SI of Horizontal Sensitivity (communication of SOS on the same level)

    a. SI creation (*communication* SI) by one SOS (or VS) in order to improve communications with other SOS (or VS).

b. SI collaborative development and redesign (harmonization) among several SOS

3. **SI of Vertical Sensitivity** that include the collaborative development of SI on lower local levels for the higher level of VS, ultimately supporting the vision of the whole MSOS as a SOS.

SI of External Sensitivity

In MSOS context, comparing the relatively simple reception of SIs by SOS from its AES, SI processing becomes more complicated. Since there are multiple interacting SOS within MSOS, they all have to be able to obtain proper SI of the external sensitivity adequate to the level and importance of external changes. Also, there should be a way of synchronization of their harmonization reactions since the results of such harmonization will control the P-level. For example, all of the volleyball team members have to understand the movement of the players of the other team and synchronously read them as preparation for an attack along a certain attack line, in order to enforce this line with proper blocking movements of several players and proper defensive positions of the players in the back line in the case of the ball passing the block. In our example the signals come from all the movements and changes in physical configuration of all opponent players, as well as new relations appearing among them, creating possible attacking structures of players passing the ball and players performing the attack as continuous changes. The players of the opponent's team have to be able to read/see such signals as SIs requiring intensive VS reharmonization leading to different P-level activities. Such interpretation has to be similar and coordinated.

On the other hand we do not want to maintain a too-high Rud by forcing and teaching everybody the same interpretation. Some variety is necessary because it allows for a broader sensitivity and even evolving SI variability, in case somebody notices the attacking team is just simulating the attacking signal, which is a deceptive move covering up the preparation fo a different attack.

Internal SI of Horizontal Sensitivity

Created as a means of inter-SOS communication and sensitivity management, such SI have to be understood as externalized vDPCS, which in comparison with the SI of external sensitivity created inside the SOS V-level using AOS-PCCE processing methods, should be able to achieve externalized existence and access by different SOS or VS. Such SI (vDPCS) should support appropriate mapping onto various carriers, preserving its patterns as well as the ability to interact with other SI in the process of harmonization with the vision of different SOS/VS. For example, a message as information concerning product quality should be delivered to various people for joint work on that product development. But if it is a product in the process of its creation by several participants, they should be able to understand quality according to their own VS, see corresponding disharmonies and modify the product and accompanying message of the quality to be harmonic with their vision of quality. For a painting process, it could be a quality of coloring to harmonize with their concentration on color perfection, for an automobile body shop it is the quality of the car body with its designer shape and functionality, for the buyer participating in the car design process it could be the feel of a "cool" car that could be easily perceived by the others. Each of the participants will modify the specs and the description of the ideal car, which will result in a product harmonized according to all their visions (with eventual compromises as certain disharmonies appear, different for each of the participants).

This means that communication SI should ideally be designed in a way supporting such harmonization activities. The important features of SI designed this way include:

1. Proper PCCE design supporting carrier and environment independence of the harmonizable context. It includes special interfaces among V/P levels supporting SI dynamics on its V-level, but allows for physical delivery via means of physical connectivity.
2. Mechanisms of SI sensitivity for possible interactions with other SI, providing for mutual harmonization, as DPCS in its communication context.
3. Mechanisms supporting its HHz of such SI including the means of internal harmonization even without external impacts. An example of a simple function of this kind is the AutoCorrect function in MS Word, when a typed message will automatically be harmonized with the rules of spelling based on the best guess of the embedded harmonizer.
4. The forms of interpretation management by the receiving SOS or another VS when we would like to ensure the necessary level of Rch in such harmonization. We can provide for 100% definite interpretation by maintaining clear definitions accompanying an SI and harmonization instructions known to the receiving side. But it might also be beneficial to allow for a more liberal interpretation which can increase efficiency of the whole harmonization process, making it easier to harmonize the new SI with existing VS by slightly modifying it, filtering it or using other interpretational techniques. Or we might be willing to deliver the purest possible CS-map of the situation, allowing the receiving side to perform AOS establishment and PCCE reconstruction of the sensitivity, creating SI as it was in the case of the SIs of external sensitivity (like sending a picture of the car without our conclusions).

SI of Vertical Sensitivity

Multilevel Rx balancing can be used in the communications of sensitive systems. The same way as the V-level could be virtual or physical, any higher level within the same V-level could be virtual or physical. Such upper levels allow for communications of various physical sensitive systems and communications of various local VS forming one global VS. The latter can be seen when we are trying to "get into another person's shoes" during a discussion in order to harmonize our vision of the situation with another person's vision into one more general and mutually acceptable picture (VS).

The complexity of such a multilevel system (MLS) design depends upon the type of Vmods that are used and the accompanying harmonization methods. In case of Smods, like in the communication of software objects, the local logic can be rather easily integrated on the level of coordinating software objects, sending and receiving messages from lower-level objects. All such messages can be properly interpreted and integrated by internal higher-level objects' logic into a certain pattern of behavior realized by those objects. Such upper-lower level communications can be designed not only in a top-down control fashion, but also as a mutual collaboration. The global picture (calculations) formed by an upper-level object will be sent to lower-level objects allowing for their better coordination. As an example of such an MLS communication pattern, we can see a system where local software objects send information about local demand and upper-level objects calculate the best prices for all localities based on the global demand information as a calculated global pattern of growing or decreasing demand. Such an approach works well for the Holiday Inn communication system, where local information forms a global picture in their headquarters' computer system, which then calculates the proper local behavior consistent with such a picture. Centralization, in this case, serves not the purpose of higher and tighter control, but better vision coordination, which explains its success in the times of dominating decentralization of computing.

A number of fields include the study of MLS dynamics based on non-symbolic, non-logical processing. They include psychology, psychiatry (especially psychoanalytic research), various forms of economic and social phenomena, art, culture, religion, and so on. Kroeber, analyzing the phenomena of the variety of styles and their mutual evolution based on communications within the same civilization, notes (Kroeber, 1952) that "styles are the very incarnation of the dynamic forms taken by the history of civilization." Started as an individual attempt to harmonize internal vision with the new carrier (canvas/oil, dance, music, etc.) but resulting in an informal exchange of vision between people of art, style development and evolution represents a non-symbolic way of expressing VS as externalized SI, implemented as various types of DPCS on various carriers. The existence of such carriers adds physical means to this new V-level of the evolution of civilization. The observation of the evolving style and its influence on artists represent the top-down feedback of the higher vision level. Resentment of the acknowledgement of the importance of such a V-level on civilization (as a sensitive system) development is a result of OO/C domination, which will change with the growing efficiency of non-OO/C communications. Some researchers still share Bagby's (Bagby, 1958) opinion that we should analyze civilizations in terms of ideas and values. We can say that such overblown domination of "hard evidence" was the style of the modernist era. Nowadays, even the analysis of computer networks is supplemented by such vision systems (from higher levels of the VO pyramid) as economic and social (Alstyne, 1997), offering terminology and references to some dynamic human experiences that reflect the fact that modern computer networks are much more sensitive to human and organizational patterns then it was thought before.

An interesting way of designing vDPCS and SI for the higher level of cultural experience can be seen in so-called "non-objective" art. This is a type of expression where there are no recognizable objects, but impressions from the system of lines, colors, forms, and textures which creates T-mode SIs can change the internal VS of observers to the intended state. Already Impressionists stated that the full vision of reality includes not only hard objects and their connections, but also more vague patterns of light, color, air, and other forms of environmental sensitivity. Followed by Purism, Constructivism, Synchronism and other forms of non-objective expression, the design of culturally significant non-symbolic SI took off. Kandinsky managed to develop this idea to the level of commonly recognizable Tmods that have practically no assigned symbolic meaning, but are capable of mapping the perception of such non-object types of observations as "Contrasting Sounds" or "Small Pleasures" and others. Rene Magritte was famous for his ability to combine symbolic and sensitivist (in our terminology) means of a T-mode SI creation, like in his "Liberator," where certain objects and their combination with the background figure and landscape play the role of symbols that simultaneously activate T-mode style perceptional feelings and interact with them in a S-mode style tide of thoughts clustering around the picture.

The use of sketches, diagrams, and charts that can be modified by any of the discussion participants is a way to create an external carrier which, due to the use of interactive technology, becomes sensitive to local visions and affects them as an integral result of MLS dynamics. The development of various types of SIs for human and system "consumption" is a matter of serious and important research. Some interfaces for airport dispatchers don't show planes in specific situations, but rather special patterns with constantly changing shape and color under the influence of real-time data, representing patterns of danger or safety that dispatchers are trained to recognize and act upon. An Artificial Neural Network can send a Cmod or Tmod of their perception of the evolution of a membership function pattern, which might be used by a fuzzy logic expert system. In this case the V-mode is a pattern expression of the sense of harmony developed by ANN from the harmonization of its external and internal sensitivity.

LVS

Local VS (LVS) will be seen here in two incarnations:

1. As VS belonging to local SOS participants of MSOS
2. As local vDPCS communicating with vDPCS of the higher levels

In the first case, the LVS belong to the existing well-established SOS, like people or whole teams with a high degree of internal harmony and its own V-level support. The design of LVS for the benefit of HHz of the whole MSOS includes two main methods:

1. Grafting the right SOS into MSOS (like hiring the right people)
2. Subjecting existing LVS to a special stream of SIs designed to deliver some information about the current situation and converting the existing LVS to the one most appropriate in Hz sense

In the second case (teaching/learning), there could be a feeling that the system's vision is not adequately rich and sensitive. Then, the decision could be made to create a series of LVS in order to handle either specific types of SI (allowing for faster and more effective harmonization) or support specific locations (like by placing LVS near the source of incoming Sis). A pattern specialization purpose for LVS development could be supported in the process of learning/training while the localization will be a matter of proper allocation.

Specialized LVS will support a more diverse sensitivity (low Rud) of the system, allowing for improvement in the external harmonization and overall HH. It might be useful in handling and understanding rich external signaling. VS will have to integrate specialized perceptions of LVS into the whole picture, like signals coming from various video and sound patterns.

Properly localized LVS can lead to lower connectivity costs as well as better local harmonization based on the higher fit and sensitivity of the newly placed LVS to their local environmental specifics. The designers should be aware of the situation when the newly developing harmony could be strong enough to force SOS to focus more on its local harmonization then the final purpose of achieving HH of the MSOS.

VS Design

The VS in comparison with the LVS is the top level of the current vDPCS harmonizing all LVS and SI into one integrated system's vision. VS determines the meaning of any new event for the whole MSOS.

Note that there could be several VS active at different times and invoked in connection with different roles of MSOS or different situations better understood (harmonized) with a particular VS. Only one VS should normally be chosen for the global harmonization in the MSOS of various LVS and IS. Of course, it is possible to apply several VS in a very short interval in order to see which one delivers better harmonization results (meaning of the situation) in connection with the particular goals pursued by the system.

VS creation is based on the proper use of the decomposition methods discussed before. They include the determination of the global Hz schema of DCs to be harmonized at a particular time. After that, the familiar steps of AOS design and following PCCE/SCT/MLS decompositions are done considering the specifics of the involved VCP-structures if several SOS/MSOS host the VS.

At the core of MSOS specifics as a special type of SOS is the potential multiplicity of vision systems due to direct human involvement and the dynamics of small groups and substructures with various roles and sensitivity/control functions in a whole MSOS. For example, different classes of situations and different roles can invoke different VS even in the same person or department. The orientational Model (OM) of MSOS is a system of all VS with their interactions in the process of harmonization of new Vmods with existing OM. The criteria for effectiveness of the whole system is its ability to create global meaning for the whole MSOS based on local sensible inputs (local meanings) and the usefulness of such global OM for local orientation.

The relationships between various VS and the general OM include the following features:

1. Various VS can work together interchangeably or in parallel, choosing the best VS for interpretation. This calls for a certain level of mutual sensitivity among various VS despite their largely independent existence. Ultimately, several VS can create a multilevel distributed system of VS. This whole system with its communicative dynamics represents OM of MSOS.

2. The existence of a variety of VS reflects an existing variety of global clusters of sensitivity and the possibility of inter-cluster harmonization. Such decomposition is one of the methods of harmonic analysis based on context preservation. Several global clusters of sensitivity can exist only if some of their parts are hibernating or dormant in one VS and are activated in some other.

3. OM also covers different frequencies of changes or signal harmonization. For example, faster changes can be

harmonized or make sense on a tactical level without considering strategic problems with slower changes and visa versa. Usually, such frequency differences create layers of analysis on different time horizons. The problem of their integration can be solved as a problem of a multilayer harmonization of various VS with different weights or the influence of a situation on one frequency layer on the decisions of the other.

VS design and management is based on the previously discussed types of implementation (virtual and physical). In addition to the goals of balancing the effectiveness and efficiency of harmonization with incoming SIs by using limited VS contexts requiring less harmonization work, VS is the most important architectural MSOS component determining modification of the areas of external sensitivity and whole connectivity structures with Hz schemas. Finally VS is responsible for the whole coordinated P-level performance of MSOS in VM context. VS flexibility and efficient self-harmonization ability is the basis of MSOS success (like in e-business case).

Similar to LVS there are three methods of VS influence:

1. The right choice of existing VS such as grafting the whole VS (either in merger or acquisition moves or something similar)
2. Subjecting existing VS to a series of predesigned SI, also considering their impact on existing LVS that have to try to harmonize with the new organizational vision. Sometimes management can allow for negative external DPI "hitting" the organization and causing people to realize the need for the change. Sometimes it can happen by itself and, only at this point, when LVS become reshaped and sensitive to the ideas of reharmonization can the change really take place.
3. In addition, since VS could be partially externalized,

the third method is in the designing of VS by a properly chosen design team (a group of SOS capable of produce the right vision) and then to present it to SOS for harmonization with it and future self-support, based on LVS/VS harmonization processes.

Hierarchy of vDPCS Types

Generally, vDPCS (all types of SI and VS) are DPCS with their own Hi perceived as *sense* that they make by themselves. For example, it could be a message verifiable as true/false or according to the degree of harmony among its components. Such a message could be a picture of some situation, musical phrase, text or some other type of information, which potentially could be harmonized with VS. Such a message is treated as a cluster of sensitivity (internal and external) like a Web page with links, or a collection of signals from various sources to be integrated into a whole picture.

VS/SI harmonization is the process of developing *meaning* out of components that make sense. The challenge here is obtaining the meaning and not just the information, which could be cut out of reality in any way we wish. Meaning cannot be separated from the context in such a forceful way. It requires the natural context of the problem as a cluster , of sensitivity where meaning will be seen as a result of the natural harmonization in such a context.

VS is a system of harmonized LVS that consists of harmonized SI. OM is a set or a system of VS that could be used for meaning extraction out of SI to support or change existing CS-maps. LVS/SI harmonization creates local meaning which, later, could be harmonized with VS and full OM. Rud adequacy often calls for a number of local LVS communicating with each other and with local SI and VS of a higher level via hierarchies of SI derived from their AOS.

The Specifics of OM/OS Development

Despite the tight relationships between OM and OS we saw that their differences and dynamics of mutual influence is one of the main factors determining the theoretical ability for growth, the sustained effectiveness of Hz and the viability of MSOS itself. It is important to understand that evolving vDPCS of all types affect the **efficiency** of harmonization with new SIs because the volume of harmonization work is proportionate to the number and levels of involved vDPCS. In MSOS the existence of multiple vDPCS beyond the adequate Rud can cause extra harmonization work which, in the situations of limited time, might be counterproductive or even dangerous.

The importance of the proper OM design (using VS harmonization of the design team with respect to the given MSOS) is also based on considerations of the **effectiveness** of Hz. Different areas of sensitivity to environment as well as different Hz-schemas of harmonization among different vDPCS determine totally different *personalities* of SOS based on their VS. Inadequate VS design could lead to inadequate results of harmonization when the proper information will be filtered and excessive attention paid to secondary features of some situations creating distorted Hz results and, hence, behavior induced by VM.

But in the same way, even initially adequate OM could get distorted by the inefficiency and ineffectiveness of OS. Weakness of the V-level Hz can result in excessive use of the C-level coordination mechanisms or OO/C methods which can rapidly reverse the system to the narrowest V-level capable of coherent and coordinated MSOS management (like the lower levels of management trying to guess the vision of the upper-level management and enforce it down the pyramid). The latter can affect the scale and adequacy of OM as well as provide for the source of too high Rud stimulating too high Rcs.

Any VS by its role and design has to be able to handle the class of situations that stem from the state of MSOS sensitivity as a state of its DC system playing the role of the focusing tool. Harmony achieved within particular VS determines its reaction to current AOS and the way sensitivity is shaped into SI and harmonized with VS. Similar to this, being in the management role described by the general organizational culture as a control position, often forces managers to respond to various situations in a particular way they are expected to, while being in the role of the low-level employee restricts responsibility and creative thinking (within the old pyramid system). At the same time, the role of the fellow human being among other humans deserving love and support leads to a different VS and different ways of SI and vDPCS Hz processes.

The existence of several VS leads to the necessity of the mechanism choosing the best one to deal with the current situation. For example, participation in sports brings a very competitive and fighting vision, while the time spent reading a bedtime story to your child calls for a different VS stimulating different sensitivity. Incompatible VS can, according to LH3, create strong tolerance boundaries with each other, being totally unaware of each other's existence and avoiding painful and useless mutual harmonization attempts. Multiple personality syndrome serves as an example of such disassociation.

Gradual Improvement and Adaptation Versus New Design

The described approach could be used in the design of a new organization. But what if we want to empower an existing organization with elements of HE?

VM architecture and procedures **could be implemented gradually,** providing for further levels of organizational evolution in search of more advanced forms. In general, evolutionary methods (versus revolutionary reengineering and transformations) are typical for HE seeking the utilization of harmonization resources existing in MSOS.

The particular tasks of V-level implementation depend upon the structure, scale, plans and procedures of the C-level implementation, which usually happens first because means of control and OO/C-vision of the management are better developed. General schemes of implementation of the V-level could vary, for example:

1. Special control schemas using specific connectivity and sensitivity in communication procedures could coordinate some sub-clusters of internal MSOS sensitivity. Each cluster could be reinforced with the advanced local vision system connecting members of the cluster with further development of proper communications among clusters evolving into a global V-level of the whole MSOS.

2. The hierarchy of control schemas manages the whole P-level and could not be broken into sub-clusters. In such a case, the V-level could be implemented top-down. First it could be the development of a good vision system for top management with further proliferation of this method down and connecting the local V-levels.

3. There is no serious control but also no good coordination among SOS participants (human or automated). A combination of the V—level with supporting coordinating mechanisms of C-level could be designed together.

Three major steps lead to VM implementation:

1. V-level design as OM and OS implementations
2. The live connection of designed components to the existing P-level, providing for V-level evolution and

fine-tuning as well as *V-level grafting* from SOS with properly evolved VS

3. Gradual tuning of all balance tasks on all MSOS levels to provide for effective and efficient Rx balancing.

Chapter 4

OS/HZ PROCESS ENGINEERING

Introduction

All decomposition and types of vDPCS discussed in the previous chapter are not isolated objects and, within the HHz process, have to be harmonized with each other. The implementation of such processes can differ based on the type of entities we are dealing with.

Basically, in every situation, there are always several DPCS in the process of harmonization with each other. Compared to OO/C methods, the above-mentioned harmonization is not (or very rarely) based on predefined models expecting controllable and tractable results. The main approach of HE is in setting the proper means of mutual vision (the UVO for each DPCS) including connectivity, sensitivity, and interpretational (CSI) mechanisms. After that, the process of natural self-harmonization takes place, substituting the enforced logic of the system models. S-mode and C-mode approaches to modeling could be used, but only as shortcuts balancing the trade-off requirement between efficient harmonization and the need to support AHS viability at all times (which might add serious response time constraints).

It means that HE attempts to convert DPCS/DPCS harmonization to AHS holistic harmonization based on the SOS technology that effectively responds to signals before the real dramatic environmental impact happens. In some cases there are no other tools for enhancing sensitivity and harmonization abilities, but a human presence as SOS attached to controlled DPCS in the MLS manner, balancing Rx for the man-machine combination. This also offers a partial solution to the problem of reliability and risk in such a control-free procedure when model control is omitted and self-harmonization is supposed to deliver comparable or better results. What if the sensitivity was insufficient and all other UVO parts (connectivity and interpretation) do not work properly because of that? Well, then we use people in places with poor means of sensitivity and harmonization. Human participation in HE is only increasing, but the role of such participation with all resulting interfaces is different from OO/C systems. The use of sensitivity as a self-regulating mechanism has a certain similarity with the use of various models where the guarantee of their use is only as good as the convictions of the model designers that the model captures the situation adequately, and the computations will be precise and fast enough to provide the proper harmonization effect. We are not discussing here the correctness of mathematics in such models but the applicability of the captured patterns as a harmonization result of the real-life situation. The same with sensitivity: The adequacy of sensitivity to the task of proper HHz is based on human convictions, perceptions and, eventually, results. Being used in situations with little statistical help in uncovering the essence of harmonization patterns, HE uses people not as OO/C stability finders (in the form of models) but as PO/H sources of advanced sensitivity and harmonization/interpretation abilities, as evaluators of vDPCS adequacy.

We have to remember that harmonization does not mean enhanced communication at all times. According to LH3 the channel might behave quite the opposite by disconnecting certain disharmonic DPCS (like in security cases). Sometimes, a proper boundary has to be maintained limiting mutual harmonization dependency and allowing each side its own independent internal harmonization. This might be done for security, efficiency and other purposes. Again, all these decisions are direct results of laws and patterns of harmonomics and, ideally, do not require any extra system decisions or models, although human abilities can be seen as supplementing MLS technology and are used as a part of such harmonization.

A decrease in sensitivity to certain types of influences from some DPCS might be used when we do not want negative or overly chaotic behavior of one DPCS affecting others and visa versa, allowing that DPCS to stabilize, find its harmony and then join the others. There are many examples around such disassociation, but in the case of system design, it usually takes a form of multilevel structures with a certain degree of independence of the levels to some changes in other levels. OSI and TCP/IP protocol layers are examples of such an approach.

When is it better to acquire independence from some DPCS and when is there a need for increased sensitivity? AHS with properly balanced Rx and adequate OM can self-organize the level of necessary sensitivity in accordance with LH3. But how to make such decisions when we are only building AHS and human interference is important? The answer could be given by a well-developed and adequate SOS, where such decomposition already has evolved by itself. Then, using its vision, such SOS can guide the development of the initial MSOS. In dot com businesses, a well-prepared designer group does such work after multiple discussions and evolving of the adequate vision.

After the initial decomposition of OM components (see previous chapter) are made, it is time for their mutual harmonization, which can result in new DPCS and produce harmonization dynamics as MSOS behavior and re-development. The main areas of harmonization analysis include relationships between VCP-levels, PCCE parts, all types of vDPCS on the V-level, the interaction between different (S, C, T) Vmods, and communications among various SOS/AHS as complex multilevel participants. All these processes constitute a continuous evolution of MSOS in their environments seen in a more detailed and constructive way according to the performed decomposition but preserving their holistic integrity.

V/C/P Harmonization

VCP structures, like all HE components, are not stable concepts with well-defined boundaries, but rather are DPCS in their environments. As such they are sensitive to each other and **require a certain level of harmonization** in order to represent a coherent SOS on all levels, which can function as AHS. At the same time VCP decomposition means that each level has its own role and should be given a certain level of independence in finding its internal harmony. The careful balance of level separation with their mutual sensitivity results in interfacing and communication technology determining their mutual CSI features as DPCS vision, where each level could be treated as DPCS of its own. Sensitivity also does not have to be symmetric and some levels can have a more controlling state at times, when it is necessary.

Harmonization of the V—and P-levels doesn't have to work through the C-level all the time. Direct V/P harmonization in a VM context is a direct mapping/ harmonization of vDPCS from the V-level onto the P-level carrier bypassing C-level. Such mapping is possible only when there are sufficiently advanced means of the P-level carrier sensitivity to the V-level patterns capable of their effective and efficient Hz.

The latest works in neuroscience showed the existence of such a dual mechanism in the human brain. In one scenario external sensory signals (from eyes, ears, etc.) are mapped onto the thalamus as a primary V-level component of the brain, then they are transmitted into the neocortex (the equivalent of our C-level with OO/C type of thinking), and then are mapped onto the limbic brain, which manages signaling to the P-level of the rest of the body. This is a nice VCP sequence with the C-level controlling the logic of the evolving models and, after analysis, sending the solution signals to the P-level. People feel in control here and praise such a way of functioning.

Another recently discovered scenario (LeDoux, 1994) showed the possibility of sensory signals bypassing the C-level (neocortex) and being directly mapped onto the amygdala (part of the brain, which deals with patterns of sensitivity as emotional maps). In such a scenario, the amygdala can start a response much faster then following the operation of full registering in neocortex. The neocortex does not have the full idea of such mapping, which can play a big role in "unconscious intelligence." Experiments show that people can develop preferences like special harmonization operations working only on T-mode kind of maps without cortical involvement (Kunst-Wilson and Zajonc, 1980; Bargh, 1994).

The described method of acting on perception was used by the best cowboy shooters and martial-arts fighters: train your direct reaction, bypassing thinking (which takes too long). Having a duel situation, you are not supposed to think about the best reaction to the signal, but rather bypass your mind (neocortex), letting the P-level respond immediately (V/P). Direct perception and mapping your opponent's movements in fighting is a serious part of Kung Fu training. Often, before the actual fight happens, the fighters walk around each other, showing their reading of the opponent and checking the speed of the responding matching movements (still not fighting). Sometimes, when one contender sees the speed of direct mapping of his movements onto the P-level reaction of another side as superior, he gives up the idea of fighting.

In addition to the speed, there is another consideration of adequacy, which might be lost in OO/C translation of T-mode patterns to the P-level. The serious part in Zen training (Sekida, 1985) is dedicated to the creation of a pure vision, not affected by logical cortical thinking or even by harmonization with the existing VS. In some cases the development of a totally new VS from incoming SIs building VS from scratch is desirable. The search for a pure vision not affected by OO/C vision, but using direct T-mode patterns of sensitivity, was characteristic of many artists. The famous Jackson Pollock tried to paint faster then the cortical OO/C brain could register and comprehend, thus designing externalized patterns matching internal PO/H-like patterns of sensitivity. Exhibiting such art makes it a form of T-mode also designed for direct mapping back onto the viewer's emotional pattern memory.

The harmonization of the V—and C-levels requires the interpretation of the evolved harmony on the V-level as a model for action management and coordination for the C-level, enforcing it for the P-level of DPCS. C-level functionality does not mean that it is all developed as an OO/C system carrying out a strict control function based on the model evolved on the V-level. It is possible to use all types of Vmods and harmonization on the C-level, but the goal is not the HHz of the C-level of DPCS, but rather the channel-type harmonization between the V-and P-levels with much higher P-level sensitivity to V-level than visa versa. Such asymmetry in mutual sensitivity only means the superiority of the V-level in harmonization (remember MLS) and its control domination over the P-level as it is formulated in VM-approach. Such sensitivity asymmetry can be better carried out by a specialized channel (C-level). An additional influence for the C-level comes from the Comfort Zone patterns determining the timing of the response and the need for forced harmonization of the P-level if constructive dialog takes too long. The necessity of harmonizing vDPCS with pDPCS, including CZ considerations and the usual lack of time, determines predominantly Smod harmonization (synchronization and coordination) for the C-level and C/P harmonization.

C-level can get so complex that its own functionality incorporates a number of SOS-type internal harmonizers and methods of holistic integration. Modern distributed systems previously grown out of the simple Turing model are getting increasingly complicated, exposing many features of sensitive systems. Next Generation of Networks (NGN) includes multiple mechanisms of intelligence and self-organization. Such systems could themselves be decomposed into VCP parts.

An interesting role of the C-level supporting its coordination activities in the P-level is in the recognition of the V-level patterns **in their entirety** in order to provide for coherent mapping and following processing. Such recognition is not trivial even in simple cases. Imagine a several step pattern (transaction) involving several people working with the same bank account while depositing and withdrawing money at different locations. Depending upon the view of the sequence of such operations, the result could be different. If there were $200 in the account and John is seen as the first to withdraw $300, then illegal operation detection could be a possible response. On the other hand, if Jane is seen as the first person to start working with the account and depositing $100, then John's withdrawal, being the second operation, will be seen by the system as perfectly correct. Now, if Jane is in New York, John is in Moscow, and the system is in Sydney, the vision of the sequence will depend upon the speed of signals traveling in the network (whichever comes first). To make it a little bit more complicated, imagine that John is paying from obtained resources for two dozen nesting dolls that have to be ordered from a New Jersey warehouse. Since this is one whole harmonization pattern, an error in any operation should result in the error of the whole pattern (transaction), which should be rolled back or not committed. It will be nice if such wholeness (a transaction consisting of several smaller operations) is defined prior to the procedure execution. But, in real life, complexity might grow far beyond all expected object compositions and various patterns (especially on the V-level) can multiply like rabbits. The ability of the system to recognize DPCS and respond to their **whole** meaning is as important in a discussion when we do not respond immediately to the pronounced words, realizing it is not the whole meaning of the speech yet and we have to wait a bit longer and, only then, respond to it.

The related function of the C-level is the coordination of such a perception of the whole meaning of the connected vDPCS among participating distributed processors/harmonizers. The differences in such perception can create chaos in multiple responses to different parts of the whole vDPCS. Such synchronization works for all levels, including the V-level itself, when multiple LVS have to synchronously harmonize incoming SI and then support the adequate evolving of VS. Imagine that different parts of the human body respond to different signals, like the brain responds to the tiger attack with panic and a desire to run, while the legs respond to the nice feel of sitting on the grass and relaxing, staying calm. The mechanisms of the synchronization of harmonization responding to the VS managing the whole P-level reaction to various SI is necessary.

This is why the pattern recognition component of the

C-level has to be sensitive enough and use C-mode or T-mode technology allowing for the proper cluster evolving and distinction. From a multilevel Rx balancing point of view, the role of the V-level in C-level formation is a compensation of its insufficiency of its own sensitivity on the lower levels.

VCP-VCP Harmonization

As it was discussed in the previous chapter, one of the harmonization tasks after the VCP structures of participating SOS are determined is to ensure smooth mutual harmonization among these SOS, using channel/hub DPCS on all levels and determining the best connectivity and sensitivity schema for these levels: V-V connection or P-P or V-P connection and so on. The understanding of the best way of SOS harmonization with each other is determined based on the role of each level and the types of Vmods it sends and receives. For example, an automated device might be better contacted through the Smods of its C-level by the Smods of the C-level of another device, creating a mutual harmonization schema. Or an airport dispatcher would better receive a visual pattern of the airport load balancing situation then columns of numbers since his V-level harmonization in T-mode was trained to be more effective in complex situations.

In order to achieve the global connectivity and communication effectiveness there is a need, in addition to local choices of levels supporting VCP-VCP harmonization, to develop a general communication procedure. As it was proposed in the "Vision" section, such a procedure should be vision-based. We called it UVO. The UVO use schema recommends the use of the Tmods on the V-level as a universal communications method. In this case, the VCP-VCP harmonization of the different SOS uses the V-level's internal sensitivity, leading to changes in the VS and subsequent mapping onto the C—and P-levels.

PCCE Decomposition and Harmonization

PCCE decomposition and harmonization are the major functions contributing to UVO design, allowing it to deal with the world as a system of DPCS. PCCE decomposition (described in the previous chapter) and harmonization should be seen not as acts of engineering control and triumph of the model supporting particular decisions, but rather as processes resembling natural clusterization and harmony of the pDPCS as much as possible. It would be incorrect to see vDPCS/pDPCS relationships as traditional signifier/signified. We should just see vDPCS as maps of pDPCS onto the V-level carrier that are subjected to the process of harmonization with each other (following and trying not to miss the natural harmony which might support properly captured patterns later). It is not a representation mechanism but a process of mutual coevolution of the two levels.

Vision patterns are not less real then pDPCS. This is the key to the problem of intentionality, since all DPCS develop toward HH as the necessary process and direction. The necessity of such progression transforms vDPCS at a higher speed (as vision is expected to do), then such harmonization spreads to pDPCS and the newly found Hi requires harmonization with the existing environment in any form (changing, searching or accepting it). This chain forces mental and then physical actions while the target harmony is being developed on the V-level before its implementation on the P-level can be called intentionality (as the behavior according to the laws of harmonization).

The idea of combining differentiation with harmonization in PCCE implementation might sound strange. In Western culture differentiation is usually based on opposing various features to each other: black/white, soft/hard, big/small, and so on. This approach has a long history and can be traced to pre-Socratic philosophers and their vision, which is often seen as "dialectical." It means that truth and the whole dynamics of external and internal processes are based on the tensions and interplay of the *opposites*. This idea was somewhat formalized in Aristotle's logic. Later Hegel, Marx, Heidegger and some other thinkers were heavily influenced by the dialectic approach. Such an "oppositional" vision led to perceptions such as "Those who are not with us are against us" or "The enemy of my enemy is my friend." Final "purification" of dialectic thinking led to the vision of direct conflict, the power struggle of opposites (Marx, Lenin), the value of power and the control necessary to overcome opposites as "obstacles." But there was another aspect hidden in dialectic thinking where the holistic unity of the opposites was seen (already by Heraclitus) as a very important part of their struggle. This aspect was gradually fading away in Cartesian vision. The Newton's vision of the result of several forces acting upon one object as a simple sum of their respective vectors was taken as a much more general approach then it should have been. No feedback in the resulting situation, no force interactions in a mutually influencing way were a concern.

Derrida, in his post-modern deconstructionist position, brought the oppositionist vision to its logical opposition as the inability of having a vision at all since the meaning as the result of the struggle of differences can never be achieved because "the play of differences involves synthesis and referrals that prevent them from being at any moment or in any way a simple element that is present in and of itself and refers only to itself. Whether in written or in spoken discourse, no element can function as a sign without relating to another element which itself is not simply present." (Derrida, 1981). Constant interplay of the differences leads, in his opinion, to the phenomena of *deférrance* as constantly deferred meaning. Frontal conflict of the opposites leaves no room for anything else to just be present or absent or to have some creative evolution stabilizing somewhere. This absence of creative stabilization in endless deconstructionist interpretations allowed postmodernism to fight Cartesian and, later, the positivist OO/C vision of logic and certainty, but prevented them from understanding the phenomena of creative emerging and the stability of such self-organization.

Meanwhile, in some forms of oriental thought, the conflict was seen as a creative and self-stabilizing form of opposition (Yin/Yang concepts) being a much more advanced vision of the integration of differences and mutual harmony. Such an approach received support from the Theory of Chaos, where constantly interacting and mutually sensitive tensions lead to never repeating in details, but quite stable in pattern, form dynamics of such interactions. Such stable patterns are called *strange attractors* that, compared to point and periodic attractors that either converge to some stable situation or produce periodic oscillations, behave in a chaotic manner. As an often-cited example, there is a strange attractor called the "chaotic pendulum," (Mosekilde, et al, 1988). This attractor is a trajectory in a two-dimensional phase space where a unique variety of swings can be seen by the human eye as a distinctive pattern caused by the similarity of repetitions of the cycles. Such a resulting pattern, despite its Derridean interplay, shows a creative pattern-like form which can be seen as a converged "meaning" of the whole commotion.

PCCE decomposition/harmonization is closer to the third type of unity-opposition vision and are very similar to the pattern-context or connectivity/sensitivity dynamics. The necessity of designing systems that will expose such features leads to careful engineering, balancing the desire to freeze the differences and continuing the control-type of system development in OO/C manner.

Since PCCE engineering does not create stable systems with clear boundaries, but is, rather, a DPCS-type design for all components (DPCS, carriers and environments), it has to be constantly harmonized (preferably in the AHS self-harmonized manner). Harmonization among the three parts (PC/C/E) is based on the following processes:

1. Harmonization and decomposition of the **natural** DPCS/C relationship where there is not much control over the carrier (C) largely interwoven with DPCS. The main task is in the proper vision design, determining the focusing procedure, showing what should be seen as a context, and the DPCS itself and what should be seen as a carrier. This requires:

   a. **Context/carrier boundary recognition** of the DPCS/C harmonization maintaining the purity, independence and clustered character of the DPCS context.

   b. **DPCS recognition** which, a in changing context, can lead to changing harmonization and the evolution of new DPCS within the same context which redefines the context as well as its influence in DPCS evolution.

   c. **Carrier recognition** as issues and features that have to be separated from the recognized DPCS and be clearly understood in their harmonization mechanics in order to maintain DPCS evolution separately from carrier problems.

2. **The design of a special carrier** for good DPCS mapping, requiring the same procedures as above, but providing for a much higher level of understanding of the boundaries between DPCS and carrier (by its design).

The environment is seen as an AES of the current DPCS. Exact DPCS determination can be based on the natural T-mode tolerance boundary detection or on the use of S-mode

(OO/C-like) methods of cluster analysis only as necessary shortcuts (still with attempts to reconstruct the whole AES of DPCS).

PCCE-PCCE Harmonization

The possibility of communications between carriers leads to the possibility of mapping of the same DPCS onto different carriers, which is the explanation of multiple pattern similarities in totally different systems. MSOS generally include multiple types of natural and predesigned carriers that have to provide adequate mapping for designed connectivity and Hz schema. An example of such a task is in the discussed above need for harmonization among the V, P, and C-levels of SOS, where each of them has a specific type of carrier and harmonization methods, yet requiring DPCS on all levels to cooperate in a coherent manner leading to the HHz of the whole SOS.

PCCE/VCP Balancing and Harmonization

VCP and PCCE engineering is supposed to lead to self-harmonized substructures (DPCS) and their mutual co-dependence is supposed to support effectiveness and efficiency of the MSOS HHz. There is always a possibility of a carrier on the V-level as an environment of the P-level or the environment of the V-level as the carrier specified on the P-level and so on.

VCP and PCCE decompositions based on the harmonization of the vDPCS of the design team, as all design HE operations, should be amended through their mutual evolving co-design in order to have minimal perceived disharmonies of the whole MSOS. Holistic engineers should carefully consider options leading to the vision of a certain dynamics as the context of DPCS and, seeing it from another angle, as a carrier or DPCS for a different VCP level. This ability of components to be seen from different points of view (VCP or PCCE) makes the architecture and harmonization dynamics much richer then just working with registered DPCS on predesigned VCP levels.

V-level Hz

DC-Based Harmonization in Communication and Perception

After the discussion of the main concepts of V-level architecture, we can build the *general model of the vision harmonization process*. It is possible to describe such a model, despite the high CUI conditions of some MSOS situations, because the concepts used do not depend on particular Vmod harmonization characteristics and MSOS specifics on a physical level.

Depending upon the source of SI we can create different models of SI/VS harmonization procedures:

1. Observational
2. Communication

The observational model is based on the transformation of the AES of a given MSOS into a series of SIs that are supposed to be harmonized with its VS. Here, unstructured general sensitivity is split into smaller DPCS or SIs as their mapping onto the V-level, describing various *episodes* of the current situation. Such SIs first have to *make sense* as possessing a necessary level of Hi, and then be harmonized within a much smaller group of other SIs from connected episodes (meaning and coordination of the perception), and later *obtain a meaning* as harmonization with whole existing VS.

The communication model of vDPCS harmonization is based on the existence of a number of SOS within an MSOS, that can and should cooperate in the sense and meaning-making process. Such cooperation is based on a certain level of *trust* of one SOS to the SI/VS harmonization abilities of another, substituting the necessity of SI recreation from the AES for the direct use of *preharmonized* vDPCS of another SOS in its orientation as meaning-making (SI/LVS/VS). Such a description of cooperation is sufficiently general to include any communication output of the work done in one SOS as a preharmonized set of SI, since SOS behavior on the V-level is interpreted in harmonomics as meaning recreation after situational changes.

These two models on a more detailed level can harmonize two groups of SI: external SI responsible for He and internal SI responsible for internal Hz. LH2 states that external AES disharmony could be adjusted by some balance of changes in internal harmony (Hi) and external harmony (He) supported by Hi/e process. The inability to harmonize certain SI with the VS internally or externally creates disharmony clusters (DC) as elements that might change location, being shifted from an area of external harmonization to becoming a problem of internal harmonization. Preferences for external harmonization usually mean actions, while internal harmonization is encapsulated from the environment. In other words, this is an old dilemma: to change or to accept.

The Observational Model

The simplified observational model could be described as a causal chain of harmonization processes:

$$DC \rightarrow SI/SI \rightarrow SI/LVS \rightarrow LVS/VS \rightarrow DC$$

,where active DC first has to be harmonized with its AES (which also has to be determined), producing a series of SI describing the current AES situation as a series of *observations* (in time and space) that, later, should be harmonized with each other in order to preserve a sense of the whole observed episode, while coordinating focusing on it without shifting to disconnected aspects of reality. After that, the SI that make sense should be harmonized with the active LVS specialized in that kind of situation and, therefore, are more sensitive to them and more activated by them. After that the LVS changes have to be harmonized within the whole VS. If such attempts are unsuccessful on any step, another DC or a series of DC is activated (as tensions emerged in the process of harmonization causing higher levels of energy and directed toward its minimization) and the procedure starts again.

· · A closer analysis of the observational model leads to the conclusion that not only should such a procedure be recursive, as a continuous loop shifting focus of observations from one episode to another, but also should allow for parallel work of multiple procedures of the same kind following any harmonization problem on any stage of the described process. It means that instead of a linear loop it is better to think of a dynamic network of similar harmonization threads generating each other at various harmonization points and attempting to harmonize various results of their work. For example, if some observation becomes a cognitive puzzle, then it could be split into several smaller DCs, activated in parallel where the generated SI also have to be harmonized with each other and the appropriate LVS/VS.

All harmonization operations on all stages are conducted with a preliminary PCCE design allowing to arrange for a better understanding, focusing, and decomposition of complexity. Every PCCE design is a dynamic context structure, which changes according to the necessity of new views, vision harmonization decomposition among various SOS, the sensitivity of new vDPCS, and the solution methods of various harmonization problems. It means that PCCE design is not an established model but is a co-evolving process alongside the main holistic harmonization action.

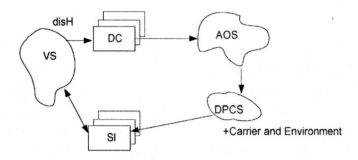

Fig 6. DC/SI Dynamics

The Communication Model

The model of communication harmonization is similar to the previous schema of the observational model, except that the DC seeks harmonization not with AES but with some existing SI or LVS of other SOS partners in MSOS.

Various vDPCS play the role of a AES for emerging SI and DC, but instead of shaping episodes into a series of SI, the task is in the detection/design of the most suitable SI (message) for DC harmonization. After the best candidate is established the harmonization procedure looks like the following:

$$DC \rightarrow SI \rightarrow SI/SI \rightarrow SI/LVS \rightarrow LVS/VS \rightarrow DC$$

Such schemas could be nested and interlinked, like in the previous model, and might work for any level of disharmony shaped into a DC, whether it is a local or a more general problem. It is important to remember that this is only a snapshot of the real harmonization process, where the mutual sensitivity context can evolve into a new vDPCS or lead to the dissipation of the old ones. This is why vDPCS do not have to correspond, element by element, to the external DPCS of the environment and could contain a number of "visions" or concepts without adequate real life mapping.

PCCE engineering is especially important in this case because vDPCS might not belong to the same SOS and carrier (like in the SOS "thinking" case) but require recreation of the V-level commonality for communications between different SOS. Instead of the problem of finding a set of SIs matching our interests in the AES, in the case of the communication model there is a problem of adequate understanding and interpretation of the "foreign" vDPCS, which is well known in hermeneutics. In the HE such interpretation is a matter of searching/having sensitivity for pattern similarity (using all SCT types of Vmods) by varying carrier designs. It means that the solution to some business-particular problem, for example, could be found in Nature as a different carrier for the same type of pattern dynamics.

Even properly chosen communication levels and the VCP-structures of interacting DPCS cannot guarantee their successful harmonization. The Vmods from one DPCS might not be easily harmonized with the VS of another because of the difference between the vision systems of the sender and receiver of the Vmods.

These differences could lead to problems in the understanding/interpretation of the Vmods sent from the V-level of another communication partner. In order to overcome this potential problem, communication partners can try various *interpretational systems*, attempting to find the most common ones shared and agreed upon by both sides. In this case, if the difference between the sender's VS and the receiver's VS is small, then the SI, which was harmonized with one of them, has a high chance of being harmonized with another.

Various kinds of tropes could be used for this purpose by encoding Vmods into various symbols suitable for the interpretational abilities of the receiver. Thus, saying that each cloud has a silver lining, people appeal to the most common level of mutual experience, which immediately accepts the truth of the cloud symbol harmonizing it with low-level vision systems. Knowing that it is a Vmod designed for interpretation, the receiver can harmonize this meaning with a lower and more specific level of Vmod abstraction received from the environment. For example, by bringing the harmony and comfort (silver lining) of such vision into the, possibly, unfavorable situation the receiver might be in.

Vmods can be used for initial harmonization at any level of abstraction/generality. Thus a mathematical model could be explained to the receiver as a general Smod, from which the particular character of the immediate low-level assessment (Cmod or Tmod) could be deduced. In this case Smod is used not only for possible calculations, but for the purpose of harmonization with the theory the receiver believes in and the mathematical model will be consistent with. Then, a more general and abstract understanding could be used for lower level explanations or interpretations that could be expressed in other types of Vmods. In (Polya, 1990) there are numerous examples of Cmod, Tmod and Smod harmonizations and interpretations (our terminology), helping to arrive at the best understanding of certain mathematical results. All religious books heavily use symbolic texts in order to fit the higher-level principles of harmony into everyday life situations, appealing to conscious or/and unconscious (Pmod-type) multilevel interpretations.

In all these examples, the received T-mode SI are not just self-contained truths but are designed for the subsequent internal harmonization when the sense or meaning arrives as a result of the whole communication/harmonization process. The future improvements of such a scheme could be seen in the improvement of multilevel interpretation.

DC-Schema Design

Using the described generic methods of DC harmonization,

holistic engineers have to develop specific DC harmonization schemas, especially for persistent DCs. For example the following schema:

$$DC1—SI/VS1$$

means that all disharmonies of the DC1—type are supposed to be seen or interpreted as some SI that are already in harmony with a particular VS1 or could be easily harmonized with it. In another example:

$$DC1—AES1 \rightarrow SI/SI \rightarrow SI /VS1$$

The area of external sensitivity in AES1 is determined for the DC1-type and the task is in finding and creating relevant SI from AES1 with scanning led by DC1, that are capable of harmonization with predetermined VS1, which resolves the current tension of the DC1-type.

Further details could be supplied about the choice and implementation of the observational and/or communication model of DC-harmonization, including:

- SCT details about DC (whether it is closer to Cmod, Smod or Tmod)
- A relevant harmonization method to be used with its resources and specifics
- A method of AES1 establishment (as natural DC-sensitivity, or specially designed sensitivity channels, etc.)
- The scale of SI/SI harmonization before the episode will be considered as evidence for further meaning development in harmonization with the VS1

The system of persistent DC-types demonstrating the ongoing harmonization process between some DPCS largely determines the specifics of MSOS harmonization efforts and can describe the structured part of the MSOS environment. The unstructured part of environment consists of ad hoc harmonization problems of an unstable nature.

Harmonization on V—level

The main harmonization process determining V-level dynamics is based on inter and intra-level sensitivity of the VS, in the form of incoming local SI (LSI) from all local sensors. Such LSI play several roles:

1. Support LVS harmonization
2. Support harmonization among several LVS, exchanging LSI of a perceptional and communication origin
3. Support harmonization with the VS of a higher level when the LVS work on LSI harmonization to be mutually acceptable, which becomes an SI of a higher level

In the first case, the LSI sensitivity of the LVS is largely controlled by the existing Hi within that LVS, which either filters LSI that did not pass the threshold of LVS tolerance or partially accepts influence of such LSIs. The second and third cases use several LVS or VS. LSI then could be seen as the work of sensitivity channels, where the necessary mutually acceptable harmonies evolve, capable of harmonizing connected parties. The mechanisms of LSI harmonization influenced by various LVS and VS should provide for LSI sensitivity to communicating parties and the ability to evolve in the direction determined by LH3.

Such a mechanism differs from the traditional design of the LSI as self-contained signals that could be used for communications only, due to the interpretational skills of the sender and receiver. In our case, the message as an LSI has to have abilities to adapt to the end-party VS, either by itself or through a special iterative collaboration assisting the evolution of a common language and message structures. Seeing LSI as states of harmonization channels creates a new incentive for the design of *context-sensitive* messages-communications.

Another problem, which has to be solved, is in treating the upper-level VS as a real communication partner with certain vision harmonization specificity, like an appeal to the collective mind of the group. The VS could be implemented virtually as an effect of communications of the lower levels (called by Vygotsky "the proximity zone") or using its own carrier in a physical implementation version. In both cases LSI/LSI harmonization is the process of LSI harmonization in the context of mutual LVS acceptance and a **certain harmony with the VS** of the higher level. Such multilevel parallel harmonization determines the properties of the whole to be more then the sum of the parts (LVS).

The effective and efficient LSI harmonization in all three cases described above should allow for the faster evolution of harmony on the V-level of MSOS. Then such harmonization takes place in the environment, offering the possibility of staying in its comfort zone by choosing the necessary Hz schema and ways of HHz. Slow V-level reaction leads to the higher probability of being DPI-controlled by the environment, which could irreversibly change pDPCS and vDPCS without regards to their achieved harmonies. This can potentially destroy an important and adequate state of Hi and, ultimately, the VID and PID as they were before—the death of MSOS.

VS/VS/SI

OM level harmonization of various VS has its own special features because of the possibility of having a dormant disjointed VS and VS complexes. If each VS determines harmonization of all the SI in a given situation, in the long run, different VS could be invoked by choosing the best one to suit the goal of HHz in a given situation.

For example, certain political situations could be viewed through democratic or republican platform VS. It will determine a different sensitivity to various SI and result in different types of evolution for each vision. But the necessity of coordination of national behavior requires special processes of harmonization between these two vision systems, where each provides for its own LVS harmonization of the participating members and blocks. Various situations are seen here as SI-level sensitivity, which might not respond to smaller events or those that are not reflected in a VS sensitivity context (ignoring issues). In some cases, only the vision of one party is used for the VM of the national behavior (national-level management decisions) suppressing the other side or using its dormant state (non-responding to certain issues, management of which is a traditional domain of another side).

Inter-VS harmonization is based on the SI circulating among active or specially activated for this purpose VS. The necessary variety of the VS is based on Rud management for the whole MSOS. On the other hand, such variety should not be too disharmonic because of the importance of P-level coordination in order to stay in the comfort zone.

The inability to maintain close (not necessarily full) harmony among the VS and their variations can lead to an effect similar to multiple personalities, when the change of the VS leads to dramatic differences in the P-level Hz behavior. As it was discussed in harmonomics, sufficiently big disharmonies among the VS could lead to their further differentiation and the development of tolerance boundaries between them, blocking possible harmonization under normal circumstances.

The possible self-feeding growth of the VS disharmony creates problems in the normal HHz process and either will naturally lead to a V-level ID (VID) split into two different SOS on the V-level which, most likely, will be followed by the same kind of split of PID or will require special engineering actions, splitting the MSOS into several disjointed sub-MSOS. Two HE approaches could be used here:

1. To allow for the natural flow of events to support efficient ID separation
2. To prevent such a direction for the natural Hz by providing for extra harmonization of the disharmonic VS

The latter approach should be used only when there is full confidence (supported by the VS from the HHz of the trusted SOS) in the necessity of splitting or artificially increasing Rud. In general, any shortcut toward natural harmonization is a risk of the same kind as using a model in Smod control schema which might turn out to be inadequate.

The highest level of risk and possible dramatic effects on the P-level could happen when several VS belong to different SOS that are required mutual harmonization within the MSOS. Here both the logic of Smod harmonization and the accelerated evolving of Cmods or Tmods as shortcuts of natural harmonization bear a big risk of inadequacy. Broadening the number of participating VS and the simultaneous use of different types of SCT-harmonization seem to provide for the necessary level and proportion of Rch/Rud in a difficult harmonization situation with a high cost for the wrong Hz engineering decision.

OM/VS/VS Harmonization

Not only the Rud of all the VS should be carefully maintained with concise decisions about the level of possible differences among the VS, but the whole set of the VS as a system (OM) should lead to the best HH and HHz of a given MSOS. It means that all the VS together should be capable of providing an effective P-level HHz. The efficiency of such harmonization leads to the appearance of smooth dynamics, using the best discovered and applicable methods of P-harmonization, creating sufficiently stable patterns of responses or traits and, finally, the PID as mapping of the Hi onto the P-level.

Very turbulent MSOS environments with a high CUI lead to lower chances of using the VS intact and, hence, to sharper drifts in the OM and the P-level ID features and the perception of its own identity to be preserved. Such destabilization can have a snowball effect when the SOS of the environment sensitive to a given MSOS will have to change their He and internal vision, leading to sharper changes in their behavior as growing environmental changes and so on. This is the way disharmony introduced locally to the context of communicating SOS can spread quickly throughout the whole system.

(LVS/LVS)/VS GL

Although, somewhat similar to the problem of VS harmonization within one OM of a given MSOS, VS/LVS harmonization is more intensive because most of the LVS are not dormant and cannot be shut out of harmonization. The same as with VS/VS harmonization, the two HE actions are possible in the case of the growing disharmony among several LVS:

1. Allow for the natural harmonization and subsequent VS harmonization or the split into several irreconcilable VS/LVS systems in accordance with LH3
2. To prevent such a direction of the natural Hz by providing for extra harmonization support of the disharmonic VS

The necessity of the VS functionality with all LVS being active makes the second type of HE intervention a dominating choice, leading to the three possible implementations of such action:

1. The leading role in such LVS harmonization/direction is on the upper VS level
2. Delegating the necessity of this harmonization to the LVS level, which through inter-LVS communications can develop a virtual upper-level harmonization (global vision) which then will be imposed (with various degrees of certainty) on all the LVS
3. Allow for the evolving dialog of LVS/VS where VS and LVS are capable of mapping each other's states with the VS being just a broadcaster/transmitter of the evolving picture provided by the LVS and which, then, is mapped onto the LVS as a vision of the whole (example: The way a group jointly modifies some diagram of the system, which then, being understood by each participant as a whole, can lead to its further improvements)

The design leading to the natural flow of the second and third types of global/local harmonization could be extremely beneficial. It allows LVS to "see" the bigger picture, which could be invisible on the local level, and draw conclusions about the best way of achieving local harmonization knowing the global harmonization patterns.

There is an old Buddhist story about several blind men touching different parts of an elephant, trying to figure out what it was. One thought it was a tree since he touched the trunk; another thought it was a wall and so on. Given a choice of the proper harmonization of their LVS into a VS (whole picture), they would have been able to arrive faster at the conclusion that it was an elephant and better coordinate their research of particular details.

VS/LVS harmonization is an example of the previously discussed MLS architecture, allowing for the best multilevel

Rx balancing. The delegation of the upper level job (of the VS) to some lower level vDPCS (the LVS) can also be done and should be based on their harmonization and mapping abilities.

DC-AOS

As at the initial design phase, the role of the disharmony clusters (DC) remains crucial in harmonization stimulation. There are two basic mechanisms of the DC emerging and harmonization attempts: internal harmonization as trying to find harmony inside the SOS and external harmonization attempting to increase or reshape the area of external sensitivity, hoping for the correction of the misunderstanding or its better understanding consistent with the broader situational context.

In the first case, a new DC activation/detection should be designed as a self-exposing situation, due to the increase of some equivalent of heat, tensions or other indicators; that is usually the case in natural harmonization. The VS changes its state resulting in the SI reaching other vDPCS. It has to stimulate the process of the mutual harmonization with other LVS or the VS that were the source of the DC activation. New SI, reaching another LVS or VS and having its origin in DC, carries certain disharmony which stimulates those VS to emit SIs to other VS or LVS that fall into the area of DC sensitivity. Finally the process will stabilize, resulting in either some mutual harmony among all participating vDPCS or into the localization and a certain insulation of the problem with minimal impact on the others, but still sending signals requiring harmonization ("couldn't find internal peace").

The second mechanism of DC activation has to initiate a part of the area of external sensitivity (AES) relevant to the particular DC (as disharmony in a certain context). Activation of a specific part of the general AES in many cases naturally leads to the specific problem context development and its natural harmonization. This mechanism of disharmony stimulating relevant sensitivity, which leads to its harmonization, corresponds to LH2 and is the basis of external focusing seen as following the shift and the development in SI tensions, with LVS or VS possibly shifting during harmonization attempts.

AOS-DPCS-Vmod

On V-level, the stimulation of a certain AOS has to lead to a SI creation that can penetrate the tolerance boundaries of the existing VS or LVS. Such SI, if it were not created for communication purposes directly by a VS as it was pointed out above, has to be designed/born as an observational SI. PCCE decomposition should be applied to the activated AOS in order to determine the necessary context of harmonization and find the DPCS of importance. These DPCS after SCT decomposition and under the influence of the active VS are shaped into SI to start LSI/LVS or SI/VS harmonization. Any new problem of such a harmonization represents its own DC, which starts the process again until it converges to a tolerable level of disharmony.

Harmonic Transform and Vmods

The three types of Vmods (Smods, Cmods, and Tmods) represent three different vision organizations in all major vision components, including the way they are harmonized with the existing VS that could also be of the same three types. The use of a mix of Vmod types could be justified by the need for increased efficiency and risk management. Slow and inadequate harmonization can be counterproductive. For example, when the situation is more stable and structured, the use of OO/C, favoring harmonization of C-maps as stabilities, can be justified as a shortcut. Similarly, neural networks or other soft models (Cmods) could serve as a more adequate approximation of non-linear functions that periodically change and require retraining (re-mapping). In addition to symbolic and connectionist types, there is a growing area of sensitivist applications especially based on various holistic experiences (like in sports, driving, human relationships, etc.).

The mutual harmonization of several vDPCS of various V-mode types is based on the final harmonization and adequacy of the CSI patterns in them. It doesn't mean that C-maps should be the same, like the patterns of the forest shapes mapped on the features of human bodies (although some live forms use such direct approach), but those structures could find their match in sensitivity or interpretation patterns of a life form supporting adequate **behaviors** as a response to the **structural** changes in the environment.

Advanced Vmod processing and VS/SI or LVS/VS harmonization could use this result for the following purposes:

1. Decrease time and increase efficiency of harmonization
2. Increase effectiveness or adequacy of internal harmonization to external situations
3. Reuse harmonization results obtained in one type of LVS/VS or SI/LVS for harmonization in other types

The time of Tmod or Cmod harmonization could be decreased when it is possible to create an Smod which, with sufficient precision and efficiency, will allow for the symbolic harmonization on a symbolic VS. Usually such symbolic VS are logically preharmonized formal theories. It is important to note that sometimes soft computing can be faster then hard model computations subjected to so-called "dimensionality curse" when the need in computing resources necessary for the model solution grows exponentially with its complexity (which, as they suspect, always exist in real life SS-problems), making it NP-hard. Then the reversed transformation can be applied. Similarly, sometimes Tmods can work better.

Such use of different Vmods will be called an *harmonic transform* (HT) consisting of the forward harmonic transform (FHT) as a switch to a different type of Vmod and the reverse harmonic transform (RHT) back to the original harmonization problem. Interestingly, the HT of a particular type could be applied to only a part of the whole harmonization problem, while the other parts could use the HT into different types of Vmods or even VS. For example, the OS interface could be seen as a desktop object space, while the controls use the dashboard metaphor for easier orientation.

In general, it can be done as a shift within the same type of V-mode (not only shifting between different types of Vmods) but different contexts and other PCCE components, altogether providing for an isomorphism of the HT. As an example of the HT use, we can point at metaphoric transformations when some situations are converted into others which are more familiar and easy to harmonize. Saying that some business situation is similar to war or a particular sports situation allows for finding a solution in a familiar field and applying it to the original situation. Tropes, as good tools for the HT, are widely used in literature in the form of metaphors, similes, allegories and all those ways of shifting readers to a VS different from the current one supported by the main text. That new VS is supposed to be either well-known with many known results of possible harmonization or at least be the one people/systems are very comfortable with and can provide for very effective and efficient harmonization based on that VS. If on one of those trusted network channels they say Saddam Hussein is a new Hitler then most of the possible actions toward Iraq and its government could be foreseen as the ones that are used to fight ultimate evil. And Saddam's death will be the best harmony achieved. The Hitler term brings us into a different

ALEXANDER VENGEROV

VS already known and emotionally experienced with trained reactions. If they say on the trusted channel that Saddam or comrade Stalin is like our father, than crowds of people will stand up to fight and die for him in a different, but also trained and largely preharmonized, vision system.

Davidson (Davidson, 1978) thought that the metaphor doesn't carry any content on its own but makes us notice certain things. Such noticing is based on switching to another VS, which might be richer, more familiar, easier to play on the body/mind carrier in order to find the Hz solution. Such use of the human body as a carrier/player for various patterns provided/awakened by metaphors was stressed by Lakoff and Johnson (Lakoff and Johnson, 1980).

The same use of the HT can increase the adequacy of harmonization by comparing the harmonization of the same situation in different types of Vmods. Another benefit of HT use is in the possibility of using previously developed VS of a particular type for the harmonization of different situations. The teaching process is based on this feature when the explanation of new material is in its harmonization with the existing VS, and finding the proper VS for a particular group of students with their specific backgrounds and experiences can significantly reduce comprehension/ harmonization efforts. The use of more abstract terminology or hints in interpretation of what was said allows for the choice of the most effective VS, usually from everyday life practice. This method is widely used in poetry, rhetoric, and religion.

Harmonization of SOS in MLS

SOS/SOS/DPCS—LSOS/LSOS

Harmonization between participating SOS and DPCS creates a context of its own. The design of the original connectivity and sensitivity among them constitutes the choice of Hz schema. After it is chosen such harmonization has to be maintained, using either natural harmonization if supporting its sensitivity is sufficient or using SOS-managed (or sometimes DPCS-managed) sensitivity with assigned responsibilities.

Such harmonization can be designed using the choice or combination of various VCP level communications in this participants as well as the choice of SCT-types of harmonization. The main challenge here is in the use of LSOS-level harmonization in order to maintain the viability of the higher SOS level. In OO/C vision it is known as an integration problem where a balance of local and global harmonies is sought. Sometimes it requires sub-optimal local performance to maintain optimal global harmony. The goals and control models on all levels should ideally be harmonized, not to create tensions based on their differences, like in the case of different goals of employees and the organization as a whole.

(SOS, SOS)—(PCCE/VCP)

Inter SOS harmonization has to correspond to the state and constant redesign of the PCCE/VCP decompositions that work like a digestion machine. Disharmonic SOS or DPCS that are incapable of maintaining He are subjected to a series of DPI destructive to their Hi. According to LH2, decreased Hi leads to the increased sensitivity of such a context that can either result in its restructuring or decomposition by other VS or LVS pulling that DPCS apart. According to LH3, pattern similarity results in better connectivity which is the basis of the ability of external DPCS to select chunks (sub-clusters) of the original DPCS and pull them closer to external clusters with CS-maps similar to such sub-clusters (digestion).

VCP redefinition means that a new DPCS was created during communication of several SOS, which could be directly (DPI style) affected from its new environment versus its higher new V-level. Then, some pDPCS of one SOS could become more sensitive to the V-level of another SOS which gained control over them (through expanded C-level) as a form of digestion of the P-level of another SOS. This is how some regions of some countries disassociate themselves from the ex-host countries and attempt to join (or be forcefully joined to) the other country. This changes the control structure as well as creates modifications on the national V-level.

The Use of Rx Indicators

The complexity and volume of harmonization maintenance seems very large for the goal of the development of a viable MSOS. Fortunately, being properly designed, most of the tasks are self-supportive, based on the understanding of the patterns and the direction of DPCS harmonization. In order to be able to "catch" the DCs that might arrive in case of improper or poorly working self-harmonization, such general indicators as Rch, Rud, Rie and some others might be very helpful.

The mechanisms of Rx indicator development for all SOS and DPCS could be built on a hierarchical basis when deviations on the higher level show indicators that have to be analyzed next. The detection of indicator deviation should be supplemented with a set of processes (preferably triggered automatically as disharmony of the desirable indicator state and current—DC) that correct the balance or uses special HE methods, including PCCE/VCP decomposition if the design team allows for such an intervention. It then will make it possible for the natural dynamics of DPCS harmonization to evolve in the right direction.

Chapter 5

UFO: GENERALIZATION OF HE METHODOLOGY

Generality and Universality of UVO

How to Use H and HE

T-mode based harmonomics and holistic engineering (H&HE) are trying to find the general forms, patterns, methods of engineering, and principles guiding the world of sensitive systems. Such generality is not limited to only the top levels of system description, but can be used on any level, no matter how high or low it is in the abstraction hierarchy of vision. And here is the thing . . . The OO/C vision mainly connects (in its focusing) to stable elements, which is somewhat natural in human evolution, because stable objects leave longer lasting imprints on the retina of the eye and have higher chances to further proliferate as representations in various sections of the brain. The analysis done in OO/C favors hierarchies of abstraction of object-like entities. For example, when we look at a car we can see a particular car, or we can see it as a particular car model, or, among other levels of abstraction and generality, we can see it as a generic car with very general car features (a "car"). But one feature remains in common among all such views: it is the superiority of an object (physical or conceptual) that is stable enough to be named or labeled.

In the UVO it is always a DPCS with the focus on the state and dynamics of sensitivity harmonization. In our analysis we should not decompose DPCS into a bunch of objects and processes. Mutually sensitive DPCS with their contexts seem more appropriate. Same refers to the higher levels of generalization like seeing an MSOS as just a DPCS. Such analytical or synthetic consistency with T-mode nature results in a situation where we always deal with various types of DPCS and harmonization processes and can use acquired knowledge and experience, and can even use harmonization shortcuts obtained from the previous experience, and showing what it is going to be after the harmonization is completed.

The richness of the possible ways of PO/H abstraction provides for a sufficient complexity, allowing for the reflection on the specificity of particular situations, and yet, offers a sufficient generality of forms and patterns of harmonization. The possibility of DPCS describing both OO/C and PO/H like phenomena greatly simplifies the use of the same experiences, observations, methods, principles and laws in the *world of DPCS*.

H&HE supports the ability to notice DPCS among objects and processes and the possibility of deeply embedding UVO vision into systems functionality by incorporating all its major features. The latter is necessary because vision compared to language uses internal experiences that are being "played" on certain internal carriers (brain, body, computer system, etc.). Such playing, being connected to vision mechanisms and actuators, guides all the main functions from self-adjustment of the vision itself to other behavioral aspects. It allows for the full use of DPCS harmonization, which affects the life of the system, not only via symbolic communications and reasoning but through the use of S-modes and the direct use of T-modes. The latter changes state-processes using sensitivity changes, like an experience which might not be expressible in S-modes. Such an approach is already used, say, when very simple fuzzy rules can invoke very complicated operations on sensitivity patterns (also known as *membership functions*) like in "smart" camcorders and point-and-shoot cameras.

The use of UVO doesn't mean that OO/C cannot be utilized too. Remember the discussion in the "Vision" part. UVO Use Schema allows for other types of VO to communicate, with UVO **interpreting** the results between S-modes, C-modes, and T-modes. The interpretation of a T-mode into an S-mode or C-mode is a "lossy" operation which looses some information. For example, the S-mode will capture only stabilities. But this is what OO/C does in the processes of vision anyway and the vision of reality mediated by the richer T-mode systems can be seen through OO/C-type vision operations.

People can use both sides of the brain that seem to deal with OO/C and PO/H types of the VO. Leonardo Da Vinci was capable of seeing harmony and rationalizing it through the system of calculations of the harmonic components in his paintings. Systems can also use T-modes in UVO use schema as middleware, additionally applying a variety of VOs in appropriate cases and locations. Group use of UVO as a tool of integrated harmonization efforts, in addition to the knowledge of H&HE as well as the ability of each participant to use the UVO, requires a certain coordination of focusing and vision processing.

Generality and Vision

OO/C generality is based on the use of object-oriented abstractions and the reductionist possibility of drilling down into the carrier for details. PO/H generality is based on language **description simplification, which relies on hidden specificity** (information richness) **in the CS-maps** of the vision experience. This is similar to the simplicity of fuzzy-logic expert systems with only a few rules supported by specific CS-maps of the membership function shapes. The whole communication system uses the following main parts that constitute not only descriptive components but also the main **embodied** mechanisms:

1. Vision **connectivity**/focusing. Being an act of connectivity switching, it can be guided by simple descriptions pointing at particular stable patterns as orientational indexes. Also it requires describing the PCCE/MLS structure of sensitivity tuning, in order to work properly and in sync when there are multiple participants. Here OO/C language could be used. Focusing also refers to the internal VS (Hi) which is used in conjunction with sensitivity

2. **Sensitivity** as mapping of the context around the chosen by connectivity patterns and trying to detect their boundaries (through a net of sensitivity, fishing for patterns in their context "to keep them fresh")

3. **Interpretation** of these discovered/evolved SI by proper VS (VS/SI)

4. **Harmonization** on the V-level and the P-level that guides further individual and group focusing as DC-based (but not the success of control)

The use of pre-existing VS with embedded experience-knowledge in the process of the Hz, which includes all CSI steps directed by the drive toward the HHz, is the way the PO/H can simplify descriptive parts, making them very general and universal. But it works **only for those with embodied UVO to support the hidden non-describable—** especially in S-mode—DPCS dynamics (like fuzzy rules are good only for those with embedded CS-maps, such as the membership functions, and the mechanism of their use).

Then essence of H&HE is in their general and applied engineering logic and experience written in the language which uses logic (of the stabilized connectivity) together with references/invitations to particular experiences. Interpretational work is the second difficult point here. This is why many religious texts are written in language requiring serious interpretational efforts (which also is taught by various religions through periodic public readings from the Books). Poetic language is the most compact and general form of the use of Tmods in communication, allowing for a simplified and compact language, but intensive interpretation. There could be a number of vision-based teachings differing in **their ease of interpretation** for various fields, as well as in **richness** and **universality** as a communication and group meaning-making device. Completeness is a nice feature for such teachings to have, but the possibility of adding new generalized observation/experience is more important (in any open study like harmonomics) as well as a study of the best engineering methods (HE). Top-level generalizations in these approaches can form a complete system, able to support all necessary survival modes of vision, but at the expense of the ultimate generality and the need of interpretation or mapping of these forms (like rules, commandments, sayings, etc.) onto the context of any particular situation.

A hermeneutical or interpretational solution is based on the widespread use of UVO supporting the similarity of experiences and visions between communicators. Like in the understanding of complex poetry, people have to have similar interpretative experiences grounded in similar harmonization experiences and practices; the use of UVO requires its adoption by all participants.

In the following sections we will offer some tools as examples of the generality of the UVO and the DPCS (AHS) analysis and management methods that could be utilized, regardless of the level of their abstraction and locality in the system (meta DPCS). These methods and tools could be applied to the whole organization, departments, groups, various clusters, projects, and other entities seen and treated as DPCS.

The first group of methods and tools is based on the idea of Rx balancing as a dynamical system, when its trajectory forms a limit cycle (LC) whose stability is the equivalent of the continuous Rx balancing. Such a pulsating character of CS-dynamics as well as of other Rx indicators was discussed in harmonomics. The analysis of an LC for various Rx, and finding ways of supporting its adequacy, allows for tactical harmonization assistance within the VM approach. We will call this method—**limit cycle analysis** (LCA).

The possibility of compensating for inadequacies in a LC is based on the flexibility and some other properties of connectivity, sensitivity, and interpretation (CSI) as the main tools the HE attempts to work with. The analysis of the compensatory possibilities of these means and ways of its enhancement form the area of strategic analysis and management (harmonization support). This approach will result in a **cost-control analysis** (CCA) methodology of the required efforts in CSI modification.

It can be shown that the holistic engineering goal of the maximization of the HH of a given MSOS is similar to the goals of LCA/CCA optimization as the minimization of the total level of tensions in the long run. LCA and CCA could be applied to all indicators, patterns, and forms of harmonization on all levels and locations becoming universal and ubiquitous.

LCA as a Tactical VM Tool

Model-Based Adaptability

Technology today plays the double role of destabilizing the environment and, at the same time, offering protection from such destabilization, thus starting a positive feedback loop leading to the need for the special treatment of technology as a major factor in business development. In its destabilization role, the broad use of the TCP/IP standard has led to increased connectivity among various parts of business context and environment. Such connectivity led to the growth of sensitivity among the various organizational entities.

Dynamical Systems Theory and Chaos, in particular, showed the importance of system sensitivity contributing to its growing *complexity, uncertainty and instability* (CUI) that, with higher level of sensitivity, lead to chaos and then random behavior. CUI is a situation which could be characterized by *model instability* or *concept drift*, which means rapid adequacy deterioration of the control models, causing an increasing risk of their continuing use. The time from the development and implementation of a new model through its growing inconsistency and failure constitutes the model life cycle. Models are understood here in a broad sense as relatively stable solutions, rules, practices, and structures that are supposed to remain stable due to their presumed adequacy in existing situations. Management support of model stability is based on this presumed adequacy and usually considers deviations as "noise," which should be just filtered or resisted in order to stay the course of the chosen models of behavior. Such support is grounded into the OO/C vision and constitutes *model-based adaptability* (MBA), which leans toward BPR methods of rational organizational remodeling at times, when old models fail and the damage caused by their inadequacy outweighs risks of model change. Attempts to find the application of forces to a system for the purpose of maximizing some measure of performance or minimizing a cost function in optimal control (Stengel, 1986) serve as an example of OO/C vision and its inherent problems of dealing with real world complexity that make "the treatment of control problems very difficult in almost all standard model formulation cases" (Hangos, 1993).

An Alternative to MBA

Another option of organizational response could be in considering noise as signals of growing environmental changes that have to be adjusted to. The methods like social embeddedness (Granovetter, 1985), institutional forces (Powell and Di Maggio, 1990), hereditary traits (Hodgson, 1993) and cognitive effects (Argyris, 1990) are proposed as more realistic approaches to strategic behavior. Ideas of emergent strategies under environmental conditions were expressed by Mintzberg (1994) and Whittington (1993).

CUI growth does not mean the environment becomes worse, just different. It offers troubles for an old model-based school, but allows for the new communication-based approach to thrive. The avoidance of the problems and thriving on the potential benefits of the new environment is the challenge of the new economic "order-disorder." Under CUI conditions *strategic business adaptability* as a system's feature becomes more important than the development of an *adaptive strategy* based on the constant adjustment of models, solutions, or best practices. Adaptive strategy should work as a natural result of strategic adaptability.

This alternative: to ignore/withstand or to change is becoming the major tactical choice under growing CUI conditions. Then, the ability to make good choices between these two alternatives for all kinds of models consistently constitutes the basis of strategic adaptability.

Not all seemingly adequate behaviors are based on stable models. The choice of adaptability based on high sensitivity to changing situations offers two possible options. One is based on *reactive coordination* widely used in the development of situated agents. It uses fields of forces (Zeghal, 1993 and De Medio, 1991) or marked environments (Deneubourg, 1989) methods to support reactive adequacy without model control. Actually, most human automatic reactions and activities use these methods, like walking without conscious control of every exact step and instantly/reactively responding to minor obstacles on the road. "Managing by the wire" is an example of such a reaction, when there is no time for theorizing or the situation is specific enough to prevent attempts of finding general strategic remedies to it.

Another option is in the use of the phenomena of self-organization. The Singularity Theory and the Theory of Complexity offer some insights into this process. The main idea is in the increased mutual connectivity and sensitivity between a system's components as well as the environment, which can lead to the point of being at the "Edge of Chaos" (Goodwin, 1994 and Langton, 1991). Such a particular level of sensitivity provides for an automatic self-dissolution of the wrong models and the self-evolving of the new adequate ones as stable attractors or critical points.

Such an alternative to MBA is based on the PO/H VO and could be described as *communication-based adaptability* (CBA), which actively uses the benefits of connectivity and distributed sensitivity. The first described option, then, works with a lower level of sensitivity, the growth of which (to the "edge of chaos") allows for the creation of the second option.

Comparing MBA and CBA we should distinguish MBA from the centralization of control and CBA from decentralization. MBA is rather an excessively supported controlling power of model stability, which could create even more harm being distributed as a set of local models and rules. Often being too rigid and conflicting with each other, such model implementation can be of a higher degree of MBA then aligned centrally controlled structures with fewer models to be used and changed when necessary. On the other hand, too high sensitivity and desire to easily change strategic position under tactical fluctuations could be counterproductive. Such a situation means that there is a measure in optimal MBA/CBA balancing which, according to Ashby 1956, should depend upon the dynamics of the environmental stability.

Both MBA and CBA can be expressed in fuzzy cognitive maps of their respective categories where the membership function of belonging to either style of adaptability is based on the level of model sensitivity to its environment. The lower levels support rigid control methods while a higher level of sensitivity could lead to the possibility of self-organization with some dissipation or evolving effects. The separation of MBA and CBA is justified by the existence of different management cultures and techniques making them appear as rather distinct approaches.

CUI growth and PO/H proliferation, coupled with the traditional abuse of the MBA approach in OO/C seeking more control as a defense against instability, leads to the necessity of counterbalancing it with much more attention to CBA.

Technology and CBA

The main problem on the way to the broader use of CBA was an insufficient level of communication technology allowing for the necessary level of mutual sensitivity. Advanced networking/integration technology and explosive proliferation of Internet communication/s provided a few further steps toward CBA than were possible before. New methods of automated learning and reasoning, allow for the future use of "soft" information versus well-defined self-evident information units.

The Cartesian idea of *self-evident* as ultimate truth in modern rhetoric as a theory of argumentation was reinforced by theories of probabilistic reasoning accepting non self-evident facts as possible evidence. Such an approach was seriously used in the judicial system even earlier (Bentham, 1839) where no evidence was supposed to be excluded from consideration at trial. The idea of using all kinds of information and the success of the use of various multimedia formats suggests the shift away from strictly logical control to broader types of communication/s among system components. Representational approaches to linguistic sign exchange as a unit of information in itself, like in Information Richness Theory (Daft and Lengel, 1986), has been sharply criticized lately (Ngwenyama and Lee, 1997) in favor of communicative methods where information is used not to convey the controlling message, but to evolve its meaning in the process of communication. Such meaning evolving is an essential step on the way to distributed communicative model/solution development.

In addition to technological advancements, scientific methods of fuzzy, evolving and distributed adaptability could be found in new AI approaches offered by fuzzy logic, neural networks, genetic algorithms, artificial life, theory of chaos, etc. Thus, combining fuzzy logic reasoning and neural network recognition might result in more adequate systems under a broad range of environmental uncertainty. Successful neuro-fuzzy systems are rapidly becoming an important part of general systems adaptability (e.g. Tsoukalas, 1997; Sun, 1996; Chin-Teng Lin, 1996).

E-commerce is a leader in the CBA approach expanding outwards to customers and suppliers as well as inwards by changing relationships and communication within the same organization. Such a shift to CBA rapidly becomes a distinguishing feature of the EC. The main achievement on this path was in much better communication with customers, to the extent they are becoming a part of the organizational context.

Electronic Business and CBA

CBA does not only include the organizational structure in its traditional sense and even the extended network organization, but also customer organization with its increased connectivity and sensitivity rapidly becoming a part of the organizational dynamics. EB is the leading force in this area since there is no possibility of really controlling the customer's needs and satisfaction. This is why we can define the first generation of EB as a CBA type of business, which includes customers as a part of the organizational dimension.

Enhancing customer connectivity with suppliers and virtual communities creates a real basis for their participation in the learning about and the formation of a growing sensitivity to emerging demand patterns. These patterns are becoming more diverse and are arriving increasingly fast because of the various mechanisms of social learning. Intensive email, chat, web pages, and forum communications with specific clusters of people of various psychological types, views, and situation patterns increase the role of social cognition and speed up the evolving of the demand/satisfaction pattern. Social cognition has its roots in social psychology which attempts "to understand and explain how the thoughts, feelings, and behavior of individuals are influenced by the actual, imagined, or implied presence of others" (Allport, 1985). Bandura (1977) states that: "most human behavior is learned observationally through modeling: from observing others one forms an idea of how new behaviors are performed, and on later occasions this coded information serves as a guide for action."

New forms of EB explicitly design systems to be used on the customer side of organizations, like customer decision support using fuzzy logic, expert systems, neural networks, data mining, and other forms of intelligent assistance which, in fact, help customers to generate models or patterns of needs in a form suitable for automated communication with other organizational systems. Some companies offer intelligent search, information and analysis of existing trends among other customers as well as the best ways of customer satisfaction including quality/price/risk analysis. More and more Web sites use instant statistical polling on customer preferences with a generalized display of the results. All these and some other methods lead to intensive customer learning and the resolution of the tensions between their needs and market capabilities. Companies that include customers in their organizational contexts will be able to implement CBA in its most advanced and effective form, using mapping of the evolving patterns of customer satisfaction onto production, marketing, and other processes.

The necessity of moving to CBA with a sufficient control of the organizational ability of maintaining an adequate level of models reflecting situational stabilities is growing. This task of balancing MBA and CBA methods by balancing the controlling power of models with the dynamics of communicative sensitivity is becoming the major strategic goal. Such management of strategic and tactical adaptability requires new tools and methods of measurement and visualization of communicative sensitivity and model control.

It is easy to see that the MBA/CBA problem, as well as many other problems of supporting proper DPCS harmonization by balancing various features, could be generalized as Rx balancing problems. For example, **Rcs could be interpreted as an MBA/CBA** proportion in the context of methods chosen to support organizational adaptability. Another aspect of MBA/CBA is in the balancing of control and harmony intentionality where there is a need in additional means of group analysis, visualization and the adjustment of organizational dynamics.

LCA-Chart as a Tactical Vision Tool

LCA-Chart

Initially, we will clarify the nature of the proposed MBA/CBA visual balancing tool/method. The tool is a visual model representation based on ideas of dynamical systems theory and the analysis of the viability of AHS limit cycles discussed in harmonomics. The presentation of particular features of balancing dynamics should not be based on any "frozen" symbolic model description, but rather include perceptions and observations of the involved personnel. An important aspect of the model design is in its evolving character, based on human sensitivity and communication of a perceived MBA/CBA balance in business processes of various degrees of generality. It could be a particular marketing program, a product design process, or whole organizational behavior as the adaptability to CUI conditions. The need for a broad discussion and Rx limit cycle analysis (LCA) stems from the fact that it is based on the perception of tensions, the adequacy of communicational harmonization of problems and the effectiveness of their solutions. The possibility of the group development of the LCA for various Rx (like for MBA/CBA) is based on the human ability to draw from knowledge, experience and the emotional state in the evaluation of the pressures and effectiveness of Rx balancing. The need in such a vision exchange and its integration into a global vision requires the possibility of its expression in a very simple form (a graphical representation seems a good choice), accessible directly for logical and perceptional assessments.

The importance and effectiveness of such types of visual tools were emphasized in Japanese quality control methodologies (Mizuno, 1988) that, in the communication area are focused on:

- The ability to assist in the exchange of information
- The ability to disseminate information to concerned parties
- The ability to use unfiltered expressions

LCA in Dynamical Systems Interpretation

Situations where several conflicting forces influence each other while creating non-linear patterns of instability are usually described within the framework of the dynamical systems analysis. For a simplified analysis of stability/sensitivity dynamics we will employ Lotka-Volterra model explored by Goodwin (1967) in socio-economic modeling. We will show a general picture of the MBA/CBA balancing problem as CS-interaction dynamics, which will be analyzed in a more detailed way in subsequent sections.

Our main variables here will be the perceived sensitivity of communications (*s*) and the controlling presence of connectivity (*c*) in all forms. First, we assume that sensitivity $s(t)$ among entities of an observed part of the organization is growing at a rate *b* (i.e. s' = bs) mainly due to the proliferation of communication and networking technology. Parts/processes of the system that became more sensitive due to enhanced connectivity tend to pass their increased sensitivity onto other connected parts/processes. On the other hand, implemented control models (automated or bureaucratic) tend to decrease sensitivity on its connections by blocking natural communications and imposing a pre-designed model of functionality for all the encounters of the communications channels of the sensitivity at a rate— *nsc*.

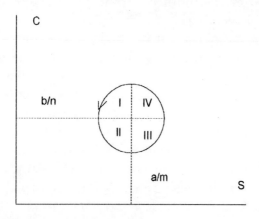

Fig. 7 MBA/CBA or Connectivity(C)/Sensitivity (S) dynamics

At the same time, the controlling presence of the models $c(t)$ forcefully changes the controlled entities in order to make them function according to the established control requirements. This makes the model presence grow due to encounters with sensitivity/communication channels that could be used for control purposes at a rate *msc*. But environmental changes make the models obsolete, decreasing their use at a rate—*a*. Then

$$ds/dt = bs - nsc$$
$$dc/dt = -ac + msc$$

, where *a, b, n, m* are positive constants.

Since the model now looks exactly like the Lotka-Volterra model, it was shown that such a system has two critical points on the s/c coordinate plane. One is a saddle point at (0,0) and another is a critical point at (a/m, b/n) with neutral stability (see Fig. 7). The speed of rotation is proportionate to *ab*, or to the speed of changes that make models obsolete and the communication sensitivity growth allowing for the new models to evolve, both contribute to the speed of rotation (model redesign).

The chaotic properties of the management in multi-stationary environments, as the model demonstrates it, explain the poor success and the principal system flaws of the model-based management with control domination. It shows there is an MBA/CBA balancing and management problem growing with the rapid proliferation of technology. The use of LCA allows for vision integration of all the participants in their perception of MBA/CBA disproportions. A more detailed analysis of the chart includes LCA—*shape analysis, area analysis, frequency analysis* and *critical point position* (CPP) analysis.

In reality, given a large variety of particular organizational situations, possible non-linearity of all the presented model coefficients as well as their dynamical instability, there is a need for the substitution of a model-based LCA chart with the one constantly updated based on the current situation and the perceived future system reactions. Common awareness of the real characteristics of MBA/CBA dynamics can allow for necessary strategic and tactical adjustments.

LCA Shape Discussion

The described model demonstrates the expectations of circular type fluctuations between the growth of the model control and the sensitivity expansions. Each sector has its own meaning and specifics depending upon its shape and relative size (see Table 6).

Table 6. LCA Sector Analysis

Sector	Role	Meaning of size variations
I	A new model introduction and control of its initial implementation with dropping the most radical components of the model that cause too many tensions	Bigger or smaller sector size indicates smaller or bigger tensions of the new model enforcement with existing harmony in component/process relations
II	All players and parts tend to overcome increased tensions brought by the model change adapting to the new situation	Bigger or smaller sector size reflects bigger or smaller collective power in fighting disharmonic models and to management decisions.
III	Communication sensitivity has found ways to its own harmonization and with additional recovered effectiveness is capable of seeking real tension and problem resolution	Bigger or smaller sector size reflects bigger or smaller sensitivity growth from improved communications accompanied by improvements of local tensions/problems as evolving models.
IV	Found compromises are stable enough to be considered as new models. This continues control growth, but emerging models are slowing further sensitivity growth	Bigger or smaller sector size corresponds to faster or slower freezing of the new order which suppresses communication sensitivity

Use of methods such as online fuzzy logic interfaces, individual shape amendments statistically processed into an integrated resulting shape of a current and future CS-chart, various expert methods, and others can support the task of local CS-vision aggregation of MBA/CBA balancing into a global vision. Direct evaluation of the emerging global CS-patterns could be another approach, which might include factors not presented locally.

The sensitivity/connectivity periodic orbit of the CS-chart is a result of all processes in organizational dynamics. A very important contribution to the shape of the CS-loop comes from organizational learning, which tends to demonstrate a similar circle of the working model stability, learning, and innovation (Brown, 1991). Learning itself, in a more general sense, includes the necessary phase of unlearning. Unlearning is a process that shows people they should no longer rely on their current beliefs and methods [Kuhn, 1962 and Petroski, 1992).

The discussed LCA shape also coincides with the views of the applications of complexity theory to organizational dynamics ' (Nonaka,1988). Gould (1989) sees change as consisting of long periods of stable structure (equilibrium), followed by change and reconfiguration. Attempts to implement e-procurement and other e-business processes have the same cycle. They start as a result of CBA, form a cluster of sensitivity, such cluster gets formal or informal vision management leaders that try to secure their own position first. They start opposing free environment-based evolution in favor of the Hi of their own Holistic Harmony, switching to MBA regime. After it fails, the crush/weakening of the old model brings different ways of clusterization and its coordination.

CBA/MBA balance is seen as an organizational effort using technology, special business organizational measures and human cultural dynamics to maintain the proper state of readiness for general and particular realignment with CUI changes of the environmental patterns.

Speed of Rotation

The strategic, high level of abstraction of the CS-loop purposefully omits the traditional question of gradual or revolutionary change by having no direct reference to time. Each sector or its part can have a different speed of completion depending upon internal and external specifics. Although lately organizational development is becoming more accepted due to its incremental approach to organizational modifications, organization transformation theorists might respond with the notion of possible environmental shifts, that have to be addressed fast with a lack of time for incremental changes. The application of dynamical systems' vision in the chaos theory, the theory of complexity, and the complex adaptive systems allow the reconciling of these two visions in one complex dynamical type of behavior. Here timing of the various sectors depends upon the level of CUI, affecting the model stability and the organizational efforts in MBA or CBA in the various CS-sectors.

The general goal here is to increase the speed of rotation (the model update according to the rate of real changes) in order to decrease the risk of functioning under inadequate model control. As was shown in the discussion of the CS-model, the speed of rotation mainly depends on the speed of environmental changes and the organizational sensitivity to them. This last factor could be managed in all possible specific implementations. In the task of speeding model adaptability as an increase in the frequency of rotation, the size of the area covered by the CS-cycle becomes very important.

Area of the CS-Cycle

The big radius of the CS-cycle shows inefficiencies in organizational adaptability. Thus, a big projection on the M-axis shows the inertia of the model adaptability, allowing for serious model inadequacies accumulation (unless it is a really dramatic change in environmental situation). In addition, the big model changes involve extra time, resources, and the risk of reengineering failure. The big size of the projection on the C-axis indicates excessive communication sensitivity, leading to unproductive human discussions and long system design time. Some other concerns of the CS-cycle size include social stability and harmony, inertia in creativity and new model acceptance, and organizational viability in general.

Technological and business organizational advancements can decrease both types of MBA and CBA inefficiencies. The growing role of IS/IT in this process was widely noticed, but the roles played by technology could be different. Rockart and Short (1989) suggest that the most important role of IT under competitive forces would be in providing for the "effective management of interdependence" as a CBA approach. On the other hand, IT/IS can excessively support model control rigidity and resistance to change. "Firms operating in new world markets will increasingly be at a serious disadvantage if they are unable to firmly control their worldwide operations and manage them in a globally coordinated manner. Investments in information technology can give firms a basis for increased coordination and control or can provide direct competitive advantage in world markets." (Ives & Jarvenpaa, 1991, p. 33).

In our opinion, technology is becoming the leading factor of organizational strategic adaptability with a business readjustment to follow. But benefits of technology do not come automatically with its use. They can heal or they can hurt. Understanding of CS-cycle and adjusting the proper use of IS/IT is becoming of ultimate importance given the size of investments in technological development.

Critical Point Position Analysis and the Move to DEA

The possible positions of the critical point of the CS-chart are shown on Fig.8. Attempts of a dramatic reduction in the area of the CS-chart, as well as the increasing speed of the model adjustment in increasing the speed of loop completion, could be based on the shift of the critical point to the zone of higher sensitivity (the right side of C-axis on Fig. 8). The position of the critical point also influences the shape of the CS-loop pattern. The far left position (P1 on Fig.8) determines a tall loop with a much smaller use of CBA, dominated by a BPR-style model or periodic paradigm shifts following current fads. The far right position determines a "wide" shape based on multiple discussions and communications of opinions and requirement changes. Kaizen or QFD methods (Akao, 1990) with advanced communication technologies and user involvement are some of the alternatives supporting this shape. It causes small but often model changes based on the serious participation of all involved parties.

The previously given example of e-procurement with periodic tendencies toward bureaucratization and MBA-stabilization opposing free ways of its CBA evolution, behaves differently when the support for sensitivity and harmonization technology grows. From management attempts to acquire and hold decision-making power, it switches to smaller and softer loops of personal preferences of some methods, models, and particular suppliers, showing indestructible preferences for "strategic partnerships" as an example of the "economy of thinking." Finally e-auction technology undercuts the possibilities of MBA attacks by successfully holding positions longer then necessary. Still certain patterns of dynamics can evolve and stabilize, but be only adequately stable compared to the real world stability of the represented DPCS of the situation.

Poor decision making, as well as the poor organization of the CBA, can lead to excessive time and resource waste in both cases. If local sensitivity does not lead to new model evolving drowning in chaotic reflections, it means that the main point of CBA evolving is not addressed properly.

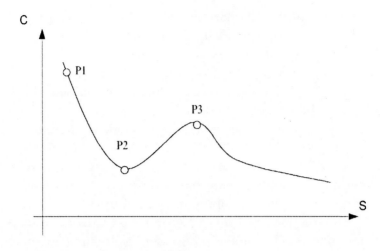

Fig. 8 Critical point positions

The ultimate goal is in moving toward position P3 (Fig.8) of the critical point location, where a small area of the loop compensates its frequent rotations and results in a fast model adaptability with little transformational energy needed. The largely model-based methods of automated adaptive control understand signals too narrowly and should be definitely supplemented with CBA methods heavily involving people, sensors and the use of all types of available information, human sensitivity, and experience. The necessity of being in a non-equilibrium state, and demonstrating a self-organization effect in adaptive behavior was emphasized in (e.g., Nonaka, 1988; Leifer, 1989; Stacey 1995).

According to the CS-model (Fig. 7), the movement of the center to the right could be done by increasing a/m ratio as the position of the center on the communication ,sensitivity axis. Here a could be increased due to the higher awareness to model inadequacy and rejection of the use of such models, allowing for self-adjustment effects. Similarly, the decrease of m is in lower rigidity and higher flexibility in conflict situations, in not attempting to revert to the power of controlling models such as rules and regulations. Together these requirements could be considered as an increase of the yielding approach to the natural forces of self-harmonization based on sensitivity versus model implementation and stern control.

On the other hand, we have to keep the center of the loop on a certain level of model effectiveness, thereby not allowing for too sensitive and irrational random-type reactions, but supporting creative attempts to find new balances and stabilities fitting the situation. Another ratio, b/n, is responsible for a model control decrease, but only to a certain point, while moving the critical point down. The relative decrease of b and increase of n with stabilization at the point of "criticality" means there should be some slowing in sensitivity expansion when encountering tension zones that should be resolved by finding mutual satisfaction as a new low tension model of dynamical coexistence (which, eventually, will change again).

It could be seen as the implementation of the organizational learning methods using internal and external connectivity intensively. These methods are aimed at conflict resolution, not by using old models but creating new ones learned in a CBA-like approach. The business tactics in choosing the best current position of the critical point, as well as its desirable future location, should be based on the analysis and the forecasts of technology advancements supporting CBA or MBA effectiveness. It, also, should take into consideration the organizational specifics in its ability to adjust to new types of behavior and architectural changes.

Toward Dynamical Evolving Architecture

Position P3 of the CS critical point (Fig.8) could be characterized by the effective and efficient evolving of adaptive models, reflecting environmental changes as well as communicative sensitivity, allowing for the reactive adaptability of poorly structured conflicts with the

363

environment. Both the evolved models and the reactive adaptability are important for organizations. Dynamical evolving architecture (DEA) as constantly updated "rules of the game" should be coupled with CBA, which, in addition to its DEA evolution support, provides its own input in the area of unstructured adaptability. The two roles of CBA correspond to the two types of organizational learning (Senge, 1990) where proper balancing of generative learning result in new models and adaptive learning which result in reactive coordination without special model formulation being necessary.

The style of learning can also be subjected to MBA/CBA balancing (Vengerov, 1999a). For example, the balancing of coercive learning (Schein, 1961) as a result of MBA pressure with the methods supporting the creation of learning environments (e.g., Slavin, 1990; Kuhn, 1972; VanLehn, 1994).

Here we see that as with the use of technology, organizational learning implementation could also be of the MBA or CBA style, supporting either model control, or communication adaptability, or some mix of both. Depending upon the level of effectiveness of MBA and CBA tools, the critical point position could be shifted closer to position 1 or position 2 (see Fig. 8), until the organization is ready for a transformation to point 3 (DEA implementation). CS-visualization could be a valuable tool enabling the discovery of the right use of technology, learning, or other modern trends by balancing MBA/CBA with the final goal of moving toward automatic self-balancing at P3 as the implementation of the DEA/CBA approach. Insufficient CBA capabilities can force companies to move back in the direction of position P1, getting burned on attempts to move further to the right. Such a movement can also occur in the case of the application of very effective modeling tools and methods, while a shift to the right can reflect the existence of advanced CBA implementations.

The move to P3 for businesses is not a simple and gradual advancement, but rather could be described as a revolutionary move from traditional business features to the new ones determining a totally different organizational culture. The new features together describe the essence of the future shift to CBA up to the point of a fast (catastrophe style) switch to a new quality—DEA. The traditional approach to enterprise architectures as a choice of stabilities (models) securing enterprise long-time stability is gradually shifting from strategic to more tactical choices deviating from the initial idea of architecture as a very stable set of decisions.

The main cultural shift could be seen in full reliance on self-organization. The management role, then, will take the shape of the care of the workability of the main CBA/DEA processes, similar to taking care of plants while trusting their ability for uncontrollable growth and blossoming. The main CBA processes to be taken care of include the proper connectivity, sensitivity, and interpretational freedom necessary to stay at the "edge of chaos.".

Planning for a transformation of such a revolutionary nature includes the ability for a fast switch to the new vision, culture, and value system and is the main challenge in growing global competition. The evolving role of the EC and its increasing influence on business-as-we-know-it is bound to be readjusted to the new position at point 3 (Fig.8), based on advanced CBA and DEA features. Such a new quality of the EC could be called EC2. It will deeply affect the role of customers, market dynamics, competition and the way companies are doing their business. It definitely will coexist and cooperate with MBA-oriented types of businesses that are less affected by CUI and such cooperation will be another challenging task. The CS-vision is capable of improving the organizational competitive advantage while moving between P1 and P2, (Fig.8) as well as at point P3, in order to remain there under various situational changes.

CCA as a Strategic VM Tool

Connectivity, Sensitivity, and Interpretation Management

The preferred use of CSI methods is based on the benefits of making natural harmonization work in the proper direction without attempts to manage and harmonize all problems, without constant designing of "solution" forms. They should evolve on their own if proper connectivity, sensitivity and interpretation is applied.

But what is "proper"? How can adequacy be obtained. The answer to these questions lies in the design of the AHS where CSI methods support autoharmonization dynamics. One of such AHS is the Design Team itself, as well as other human and automated forms that will substitute for this team when fully functioning AHS is born. The perception of insufficient or excessive sensitivity in certain areas and channels leads to the perception of incorrect Rx and the need for their balancing. As we saw in the discussions of harmonomics, the emergence of particular DPCS forms is based on the specific features of connectivity, sensitivity, and interpretation at different times and in different contexts.

According to harmonomics, the orientation of MSOS as the meaning of the situation is not only in representational complexity, but also in the dynamic features of the processes of communication or harmonization. With the increasing CUI of the environment, the latter part is becoming dominating. The adequacy of the harmonization characteristics to the environmental CS-map features is becoming crucial. Actually, it means that just by organizing, the adequate CS-map harmonization process automatically delivers adequate representations and situational meaning. As Dwight D. Eisenhower put it: "Plans are nothing; planning is everything."

The success of the CSI methods of the HE is based on the detection of CSI deviations, the understanding of the necessary changes and the existence of the proper tools capable of the delivery of necessary patterns of CSI. Since all DPCS activities could be reduced to CSI dynamics (as a Hz activity), the effectiveness and efficiency of the CSI changes are the main values. The requirement of advanced CSI tools includes the need for and the ability of constant evaluation and improvement of the means supporting connectivity, sensitivity and interpretation. The following methods show the possible ways of analyzing the quality of the CSI-patterns and developing the strategies for their improvement as the only strategies that hold true under all circumstances for the sensitive systems in the CUI environments most of businesses are.

Patterns of Connectivity

In the old economy, the production of objects and their optimal distribution was the main concern of the market and other economic mechanisms. The types of used services were very similar to the objects in their finality, the possibility of clearly describing the terms, the boundaries, duration and location. This is why they fit the same economic model of supply-demand balancing.

Already, network economy and later e-economy see the value in connectivity and attempt to optimally distribute it (where its value is the highest). The main difference is that connectivity, unlike consumable products, increases its value with produced quantity. For example, the more areas that are connected to the Internet, the higher the value of my personal connection to the Internet because I can use a bigger volume of connectivity by accessing all other connected places and files through my little ISP connection.

An overwhelming deficit of proper connectivity everywhere in our current world environment brings us to the situation where all major value creation in the new economy is either the creation of new patterns of connectivity or their enhancement. We see public and private funding directed to customer-to-product connectivity via online storefront catalogs, B2B connectivity, connectivity of workers to their benefits and many other more general or more specific patterns or types of connections. The telephone as P2P connectivity and television as people-to-news or people-to-movies connectivity are the early examples of the power of the new value.

If understanding where connectivity adds the most value is more of an art then a science, the evaluation of the quality and viability of any particular pattern of connectivity is an area of systematic analysis. It is based on the situation in modern economic environments when the snowball of changes causes a need for faster and bigger system counteractions, which in turn creates more and faster changes in the environment and so on . . . It is usually called *acceleration of evolution.*

The two major dimensions of pattern analysis under environmental pressures include (see Fig. 9):

- The need for lower costs of changes in various connectivity parameters (including the ability of new connectivity establishment and the disbanding of some existing connectivity)
- The need for less control over changes in connectivity in response to environmental pressures. This allows for less rigid (more flexible) adaptive actions).

The Cost Dimension of Connectivity Patterns

The connectivity in e-business systems arranged by decreasing cost of changes can include connectivity to **members, products, services/processes, and other entities and phenomena.** We distinguish the following classes of connectivity that have fuzzy boundaries and have additional gradations within each class:

- **Fixed**: when the cost of changes is very high (like when adding a new long-term supplier to Ford Co.)
- **Scalable**: with management efforts as possible redesigning, incurring some tolerable costs (like adding a new client to the client-server network)
- **Dynamic:** no design efforts, low (or no) cost of connectivity changes (like we do not have to do anything when the number of visitors to the web site changes within the diapason of its tolerable load)

The Control Dimension of Connectivity Patterns

This describes the responsibility for changes in connectivity as well as the form of control over such changes. It can take the following main forms:

- **Managed** control with varying involvement of dedicated (or dynamically elected) managers (can be done by computers in distributed systems) imposing centralized control enforcing the result on the system
- **Affected** control, when control centers are well distributed and/or are strongly sensitive to their clusters of influence, like elected committees are sensitive to distributed electorate opinions or group decision making
- **Self-organized** when all components of the connectivity can **evolve on their own** without any control or management including membership, roles, procedures, etc. Example: any sports game when patterns of connectivity among team members during the game are not managed by a special controller but rather evolve to adequately match new unfolding situations, like flocking birds, the wisdom of the forest and Nature in general are capable for self-organization.

Possible Strategies From High-Cost and High-Control Connectivity to the Viable Future

Resulting Types of Connectivity form a nine cell matrix and include the following combinations:

- fixed and managed (FM), fixed and affected (FA), fixed and self-organized (FS)
- scalable and managed (SM), scalable and affected (SA), scalable and self-organized (SS)
- dynamic and managed (DM), dynamic and affected (DA), dynamic and self-organized (DS)

The paths to the future of connectivity (similar for sensitivity and interpretational abilities) can be seen on Fig. 9.

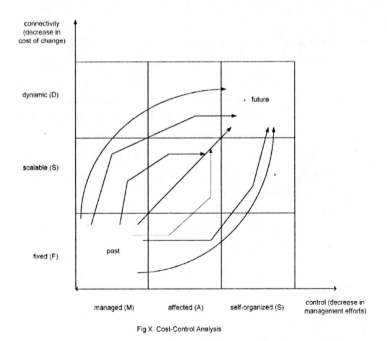

Fig X. Cost-Control Analysis

The further analysis of the particular paths from FM to

DS as a goal of AHS strategic development allowing the easiest adjustment to the flow of changes and supporting the optimal LCA—the form and the position show the possible strategic approaches. In the examples below we can see the logic of some of these strategies.

1. The FM-SM-DM-DA-DS path chooses the way of decreasing transactional costs (probably via intensive use of automation and technology), which is supposed to allow for control relaxation later
2. The FM-FA-FS-SS-DS path attempts to relax control first (e.g. starting with administrative reorganization), which was seen as a way to offer more power to the local decision makers and intelligent processes in using proper technologies to decrease transactional costs
3. In FM-SA-DS path the strategy cost and control are being curbed simultaneously
4. Other non-reversible ways from FM to DS explore the remaining possible strategies (where control and cost of change can only decrease)

Examples of Connectivity Patterns

At the current level of connectivity, most of the changes with cost-control involvement are in the area concerning the improvement of the existing patterns of connectivity and the support of the new ones. Some of the e-business examples include the main objects of business structure and functionality like products, customers, organizations, etc. But the increased connectivity among them creates the effect of DPCS evolving in a communication context of mutual sensitivity, making these objects more fuzzy and dynamic.

Examples of e-business connectivity patterns can include:

• **Products-to-customers** (with the following subpatterns: searching connectivity, ordering capability, the physical connectivity of the product delivery, connectivity to product support, help, etc.)

- **Business-to-customers** (with details on specs, satisfaction, demand patterns, etc.)
- **Customers-to-their-past-choices** (a shopping cart, the history of previous orders, the history of browsing— intelligent prompts in the browser, etc.)
- **Business-to-developers/employees** (the conditions of contracts, benefits, feedback from extra efforts, suggestions about improvements, etc.)
- **Business-to-business** (order fulfillment, the collaboration efforts through seeing each others changes, etc.)

Some connectivity characteristics used for the better analysis of connectivity patterns include: information flow characteristics, security, the topology of the connections, membership, bandwidth and general connectivity efficiency, the quality of service, payment methods, other requirements to connectivity. The variety of particular connectivity characteristics and implementation problems can be seen as layers of abstractions where each layer describes connectivity from the point of view of only some class of aspects and problems. Such layered representation of connectivity is called connectivity protocols and could be understood not only in a networking engineering sense but much more generally. Then protocols will be commonly accepted aspects of connectivity with standard interfaces to the other classes of connectivity problems/solutions.

Patterns of Sensitivity and Interpretation

Once we understand the method of connectivity pattern analysis in the cost-control diagram as cost-control analysis (CCA), the same procedure with the same nine sectors and paths could be created for sensitivity and control. All CSI-patterns, in order to support optimal LCA features, have to end up in the same upper-right corner, minimizing the costs of the adjustment of their various characteristics and scalability, as well as decreasing the need for control effectiveness which becomes impossible with CUI growth.

Any specific application of CCA in strategic development is based on the acceptance of the methods of the HE, the UVO, and the understanding of the CSI role in harmonization dynamics. The knowledge of harmonomics showing various patterns and forms of harmonization with their features, and the understanding of CSI role as the basis for all harmonization results, lead to the use of CCA as a strategy directed toward the increased viability and efficiency of AHS in turbulent environments. The flexibility and efficiency of CSI adjustments create the foundation for the successful use of all necessary types of adaptive behavior and desirable DPCS forms. The shift from numerous controllers, theories, and models to the use of the creative power of the harmonization processes allows for standardized development and improvement of CSI technologies and processes as the main tool of systems development.

Method of Pattern Evaluation

Pattern evaluation is one of the most important processes in the design methodology of holistic engineering. The result of the evaluation is a plan for action in terms of enhancements and distribution of connectivity, sensitivity and interpretational abilities. The approach to CCA has two aspects: the evaluation itself and the supporting methodology of holistic engineering as it is shown below:

- Detect one of the CSI patterns (start with the ones with highest value) in the analyzed entity/phenomenon (pattern of connectivity, sensitivity, or interpretation).

Find situations where DPCS could be developed with the biggest volume of feasible HHz which determines a Hz Schema.

- Explore and build its super and sub-patterns, as well as patterns strongly affecting it and each other. Build a DPCS structure of pattern's links and sub-clusters.

- Evaluate the position of each main pattern on the CSA chart and its possible development. Find the patterns of internal influence that can lead the Hz in the right direction, allowing other LDPCS to tune to them instead of the environmental situation.

- Assess the readiness and efficacy of going along the one of the viable directions. Assess their Hz abilities and sufficiency of the CSI levels. Make a conclusion about the next change. Choose the future direction of their evolution.

- Check if such changes are still valuable (and competitive) See if other harmonizers could be more competitive since the HHz law is also a law of Hz competition—the better the Hz, the more powerful it is.

- Find the movement of the other patterns, considering their own CSI development and leadership of the new evolving Hi. Find the degree of VM where internal leading LDPCS guide the development of other components more then their local external sensitivity.

- Reevaluate the New state of the system. Start all over again. Find several scenarios (remember Rubik's cube when the optimal future could be achieved through sub-optimal intermediate steps) and choose the tactically feasible and strategically effective way.

The described steps of the CSI-pattern analysis allow to forecast the future evolution in complex dynamic situations that are difficult to analyze using "hard" models. Here we offer the method of looking into the future of complex evolutionary developments and choosing the best tactical and strategic directions.

Generality and Universality of UFO and UAHS

UFO

The essence of the HE could be seen as the behavior of active AHS/MSOS in the search/engineering of the AES, using the adaptive CSI changes and providing the longest period of successful holistic harmonization at the highest possible (supporting optimality of its Rx) level of the Hi. This goal is another way of saying that properly designed organizations have the most efficient way of coevolving with the possibility of the maximum use of free harmonization energy. The natural trend of Hi maximization is mainly limited by the necessity of keeping optimal Rx (as the proper features of the limit cycle) supporting long-term harmonization abilities and the best discovered harmonies. But Rx optimality is based on the stability and adequacy of the environment to the Hi. The proper choice/design of such an environment by designing the proper area of external sensitivity (we can think of it as the field of organizational engagement, market, sub-industry, etc.) allows for Rx existence, which will limit Hi growth less. In such a context, an organization becomes a Macro Maxwell Demon hunting for external DPCS that, being "consumed", can support or properly readjust its internal Hi.

Building an organization according to such a vision will allow for the use of the HE, harmonomics, universality and simplicity of the UFO-based on the UVO. This is important, since if an organization is disharmonic in the pursuit of the overall coevolutionary goals, then it cannot use the energy of free harmonization, but will rather fight against it. This is why seeing harmonization as a goal is an important part of successful UVO implementation. The high cost of operations is often a symptom of the poor match of the internal harmony to the external one. In order to properly align internal harmony and all organizational processes as going along natural harmonization lines, holistic engineers have to use the UVO and its T-mode vision. Harmonomics shows the real sources of the problems or the success in a context of proper sailing: with natural harmonization "winds" and "currents" and not against them. The latter creates a danger of increasing inadequacy and a final destruction under the harmonization pressure of the environment.

In this sense, the use of UVO not only allows for improved communications and collaboration but changes company's orientation, goals and methods, showing the dangers of disharmony and the previously invisible resources of free harmonization energy. The adoption of UVO is connected with the move toward a more consistent rethinking and retooling of all structures and processes according to the Universal Framework Organization using:

1. General methodology of the HE based on harmonomics and the T-mode of vision
2. Generalized architecture, strategic processes, methods and instruments of the HE for all types of MSOS/AHS
3. Universal technology of the vision management system (VMS)

Obtained universality allows for the development of something like a "system-out-of-the-box" which could be used by any organization. Such a system will include know-how, methodology, supporting technology, initial design, AES-connection and Rx-balancing services with subsequent training in the H and the HE.

The adoption of the UVO and the switch to the UFO will generally allow for much more efficient organizational dynamics on all internal and external levels, like mergers and acquisitions, restructuring, alliances and so on, made easy due to the possibility of smooth and continuous management adequate to the level of the necessary mutual sensitivity. Big conglomerates will be able to manage the orientation of all sub—MSOS, based on the UVO aligning them along the global outlook concerning holistic harmony. Small companies will be able to grow at the speed of their vision and harmonization abilities. Peer-to-peer clusters will find the way to joint harmonization and free growth based on mutual sensitivity and not on management models of "good behavior." UVO will allow multiple participants (people, systems) to form new organizational DPCS-like structures.

Yes, there is a catch. All existing methods of economic regulation are based on OO/C vision and require a well-defined corporate identity. This has to be re-thought and re-adjusted for the new DPCS reality. Such changes should affect, at a minimum: accounting, the legal area, taxes, ownership and others. It's quite a change, but reality posts PO/H problems into the OO/C minds of organizations more and more often. For example, the discussion about human cloning and stem cell research touches the very foundation of the established vision of life, good and bad, the human role and purpose and many other fundamental matters that will be affected through the chains of OO/C causality and logic, making all models, definitions, and taboos fuzzier, more dynamic . . . and more harmonic.

UAHS

Advancements in the HE and the H should lead to the universal AHS capable of the best evolution in the HHz. Once designed and implemented, they are supposed to do the job. Such universal AHS (UAHS) is the next generation of matter (DPCS) evolution—becoming the most advanced creatures of the evolution.

Such AHS will use generalized **Methodology, Vision Training** (for human and auto forms), **VMS** and proper **Initial Design** (for the **right Hz schemas, AOS** in their environments). Starting as specialized AHS harmonized for particular environments and Hz schemas, they will evolve 'into more general AHS clusters and super clusters. Here is the need for more advanced AHS to manage the growth of more specialized ones in order to coordinate their involvement into more global AOS/environments.

This makes UAHS a universal product/system, which can serve as building blocks or whole designs. At the same time macro AHS design (like the whole organization) is capable of affecting all sub-systems and neighboring MSOS. The proliferation of UAHS will serve the growth of harmonic development versus the growth of control and disharmonization of the environment.

Chapter 6

UFO TECHNOLOGY

Evolutionary Changes in IT/IS

Vision management based on the methods and approaches of holistic engineering offers new ways of using technology in the development of organizations and sensitive systems in general. The role of information technology in e-organizations and especially in holistic organizations is going to change. From being a keeper and a caretaker of information objects "as assets," IS/IT is gradually switching to its role as an inter—and intra-organizational glue, connecting more stable components with their fluid contexts. The rapidly growing sensitivity of e-business greatly contributes to the need for this new role for technology.

Several fundamental changes in the way computers and IT are being used affect the further evolution of information and communication technology. The most important changes include the globalization of computing, ubiquitous computing, mobility, always-on connections, increasing requirements toward interactivity, communication, information and interpretation richness, and the fight with the complexity of system design and support.

Global Computing

The enterprise model of computing, which was adopted not so long ago and which resulted in very effective internal organizational systems, is gradually moving toward a global computing model. The necessity to integrate systems among all supply, sales and collaboration channels, and hubs posts a problem for isolated voluntarily decisions about the choice of object design platforms like COM+, Java Beans, CORBA, agent-oriented solutions and some others. The world of objects which was born by the OO/C vision is facing the challenge of inter-object cluster harmonization, where different system responsibilities can be assigned to various types of components and realized in a coherent manner across all types and locations of computing resources. Global connectivity has to be independent from local implementations of encapsulated Hi.

Ubiquitous computing

Ubiquitous computing adds more profound, broadband, rich, and dynamic sensitivity to more environmental areas, ranging from traditionally connected entities to dynamically evolving DPCS. The list of new parts of our Real World joining artificial computing processes is constantly growing. It already expands from nanotechnology, smart pills and wearables, to the huge variety of household, enterprise and environmental entities. Combined with methods used in distributed systems, the term computing is gradually losing its meaning. Indeed, if all resources could be shared, then any set of resources capable of collaborating with other resources is a part of distributed computing. It is not about microprocessors anymore. For example, something like an ingestible M2A Capsule, the size of a large pill, which includes a color video camera, a miniature transmitter, and is connected to the personal data recorder/processor worn in the belt, becomes a system which, since it is connected to a remote computer(s), just expands connectivity and sensitivity of existing DPCS. Another example is Java-based in-car wireless services developed by Sun Microsystems for Fiat Auto, where a special type of a telematics service provider (TSP) is created that provides services and applications to telematics-ready cars.

The ability of telemetry to always know the user location and be able to adjust the user system and information to particular environmental systems and information is an important step toward local harmonization processes. For example, any user can get, at any given moment, the best possible adjustment the environment can offer, ranging from local sales coupons and deals to targeted services for people (and non-human users and DPCS).

Given existing Internet and private/public network expansion, we see a growing codependence of various aspects of reality to each other—the times of global connectivity and sensitivity allowing for the extension and amendment of the process of natural harmonization on the natural connectivity of the physical world. These attempts require the understanding that it is not about computing now available here and there, but about the changes of the tissue of the World, consisting of connectivity and sensitivity and its creative evolution, which gives birth to all the forms of DPCS harmonization.

Wireless

Wireless interactivity is springing around with Bluetooth, 3G and 4G plans and initial implementations. The possibility of being connected at any location at minimal cost of such ad hoc connection shifts the concept of networking as the design of specific connectivity to the more important problem of sensitivity handling. Whom and what do you need to be connected to? Whom are you sensitive to? These are becoming very important questions now. Wireless LANs and Web services delivered on their basis become the Protoforms of the fully functional DPCS.

Mobile

The mobile aspect of computing in the wireless context just enhances the previous possibilities, practically eliminating specific location connectivity costs. Anyplace is the place! Connectivity is based not on the space closeness and locations, but on mutual sensitivity itself as the only necessary condition for connectivity evolution in the CS-dynamics of mutual harmonization.

Another aspect of mobile computing is the existence and evolution of clusters of connectivity (channel DPCS) that are used by others to get connected. The dynamics of such clusters and mobility does not allow for the old OO/C-controlled style of network design, when the topology and specific connectivity are controlled and fixed. New processes will dynamically seek, see and recognize the best ways, paths and parties to be connected to.

Always-On

The always-on property just enhances the previous possibilities, eliminating not only location connectivity costs, but the management of the moment such action takes place. Any time sensitivity demands enhanced connectivity - it will be ready. This leads to highly interactive configurations of CS-dynamics. For example, Nortel Networks and Research in Motion (RIM) have formed a strategic marketing and technology alliance, designing and supporting "Always On,

Always Connected™": Internet for the wireless delivery of interactive, digital information and services to mobile consumers.

Interactive

The ubiquity of computing together with wireless, mobile, and always-on connectivity rapidly creates the foundation for the new PO/H vision connected, via UVO, with the previous concept of Turing "machinery." It is becoming more appropriate to talk not about computing, delivered services and information products, but about highly reactive, almost alive tissues-carrier for multiple forms of DPCS that can exist and influence us invisibly, until the new vision will allow us to see them, account for their existence, use them in the model based on CSI—layers based on technology that already is capable of supporting all the dynamics of harmonomics and using all methods of holistic engineering.

Devices, processes, people, networks and groups increasingly use connectivity and sensitivity as the tool for their evolution, versus programming logic and data structures responsible for "capturing" reality in computing models. Interactivity decides, demands, and creates always-on, always there, always mutually sensitive with varying connectivity patterns.

Communication, information and interpretational richness

A number of new interesting concepts and theories reflect the aspects of quality, richness, influence, and their measurements and improvements in dynamic and sensitive contexts like *communicative economies* (Reder, 1988), *media space* (Fish, 1993, p. 48-61) and (Bly, 1993, p. 28-47), information richness theory (Daft, 1984, pp. 191-233), social influence theory (Fulk, 1990, pp. 117-140), and a number of others.

The existence of connectivity, per se, doesn't mean a solution for evolving sensitivity. Example can be seen in switching from rigid supply channel management to c-commerce models that, in addition to general connectivity, offer the ability to influence and respond to specific aspects of collaboration with sufficiently dynamic and rich forms of communication matching the complexity of sensitivity maps. Another feature of rich communications is their openness to current environments that respond to the communication situation influencing it (in a simple form, this might be seen as the influence of the current social, workgroup, and economic factors on the way, form, and content of communications).

Advancements in the ability to organize sufficiently rich communications directly competes with the advantages of local communications and communication intermediaries tailoring information and its interpretation to local specificity. Local interpretations, reformatting, and different communication regimes justified their existence in supporting the structure of connectivity matching the dynamics of sensitivity. Not anymore. Some manufacturers, like Dell, offer rich interaction with end customers eliminating retailing tailoring. Dynamic Web content, a new generation of browser sensitivity to users via DHTML, XML, scripting coupled with manufacturing capability to match such communication richness (which is an important factor of rich communications as back-end processes) allows for a shift of the discussion about the degree of centralization to the degree of harmonization of parties, mutual connectivity and sensitivity of the needs and accompanying dynamics of evolution.

The growing average level of CUI in socio-economic

context puts organizations, at least, in the middle level of the VO-pyramid. It means there is a possibility of using OO/C and PO/H methods as an everyday mix. OO/C methods in turbulent environments tend to move toward machine and organizational learning methods and technologies under the umbrella of adaptive control. Within such a framework, technology assists in faster learning and adaptation to the uncovered patterns of the past. With CUI growth, such a past is being taken as a very recent one and treated only as a tactical solution, which might deviate from the strategic optimum, but supports everyday viability. Also, what was previously considered as noise is getting increasing attention, avoiding being filtered out by the strict models of "reality."

A further increase in CUI makes the assumption "that there is what to learn and adapt to in the past (even recent past)" more and more inaccurate. The PO/H methods of immediate response and vision management guided by the **current** or **approaching** situation start making more sense. Instead of concentration on models and means of propagating their control, IT started developing CSI solutions, supporting the connectivity and dynamic sensitivity of various organizational clusters. The dominating role of environmental evolution becomes easier since systems started exposing features of holistic complexes (DPCS) doing the job of coevolving internal harmonies fast and easy, responding to forthcoming impacts. Growing sensitivity (strength, breadth and depth) puts emphasis not on the recognition of the past patterns but on detection, integration, and interpretation of the signals of forthcoming events (driving by the windshield view).

The Threat of Complexity

The previously discussed trends in IT contribute to the problem of the growing complexity of systems and the speed of their changes in evolving high CUI environments. As a result, we can see growing system development and maintenance costs as well as the growing risk of decreasing viability and quality of service. Harmonization, usually, is performed by **external** (to the system) human efforts that have to be much faster and more precise then human model/logic design methodologies can offer within a given price/risk compromise. Simply speaking, after a system reaches a certain level of complexity it becomes unmanageable for OO/C control. Such limitation poses a great danger for further economic growth or general system evolution that are based on IT/IS effectiveness and efficiency.

The problems of specific model development and management in the OO/C approach were discussed many times and finally became the basis for DoD and IBM calls for concerted efforts in conquering the complexity of system design, implementation, and support based on constant model/logic redesign. This problem can be seen as the growing complexity of a system's connections in high CUI environment with no implemented means of self-harmonization.

Additional pressure is put on systems development/ support by the emergence of DPCS-like entities that are difficult to handle by traditional IT-engineering means. Among these are:

- The dynamic creation of user groups, decision groups, experience groups
- The dynamic clustering of web documents according to their topic closeness, application use, origin, and so on, for the purpose of group VS creation for group orientation in such document space
- The clusters and changes in Internet and database connectivity
- The changes in connectivity of s/w components
- System sensitivity to configuration and its changes

- Rich transaction interpretation different in different systems' sensitivity clusters (thread restart, replication or migration mechanisms, ultimate protective measures, etc.)
- The interpretation of malfunction in configuration (internal and external environment)
- The connectivity fields of wireless communications enhanced with a multiplicity of possible entities and processes getting into such clusters, creating mutual sensitivity clusters of people and devices
- Dynamic multi-agent clusterization for intelligent routing, creating a connectivity layer independent from physical reality and capable of spreading over all possible means of connectivity, agent grouping for content processing for mutual knowledge harmonization, etc.
- The identity of communication agents connected with an IP address is being blurred into patterns of collaboration/competition of communicating parties with networks of IP-referenced sites as shared resources in a distributed system
- Changing user sensitivity, preferences, attitude to products, product groups and clusters, services and service type clustering and networking
- The patterns of organizational vulnerability and security
- The dynamic clusters of collaboration relationships in supply, design, sales chains and networks
- The dynamic wireless connectivity and smart matter sensitivity clusters
- Complex distributed transactions in dynamic context
- Harmonization in virtual clusters of multi-agent systems

Overall, requirements of continuous Business Functionality, Viability, Scalability, and Modifiability lead to the problem of DPCS identification in order to support, distribute, scale, or replicate them during dynamic changes imposed by the named requirements. In OO/C methodology such identification is based on the logic and structure of the whole system, as well as its components, in order to provide the necessary model adjustments supporting the system's viability and QoS. Such an approach leads to the necessity of determining the meaning of all processes in the changing context of their internal and external sensitivity in order to find out if the occurred change is a symptom of systems' sickness or a normal process of reacting to incoming changes where everything will be OK. The capabilities of controlling such environments with a sufficient level of proof that the model, the system is representing, is correct in all its aspects and that it is adequate to the current situation are dramatically diminished with the system's growth in size and interactivity. This requires more radical (even revolutionary) changes in the attempts at gaining ground in IT/IS development and support.

Revolutionary Changes in IT/IS

All these changes prepare IT/IS for the new role it is pushed to by e-business and the need in PO/H vision that is springing up in almost every area of human activities. In order to follow our previous approach to e-business analysis in the first part of the book, we have to address the revolutionary changes necessary in IT/IS to meet the needs of radical reproaching the task of IT/IS—stimulated organizational development.

The task of VM development and switching from MBA to CBA (or more precisely to MBA/CBA balancing with much more attention to CBA then before) discussed on an organizational level translates in the IT/IS domain into a different approach to systems development and support. It is generally acknowledged that, on the one hand, information technology can be used for the purpose of supporting and enforcing enterprise architecture (Davidow, 1992; Drucker, 1992; Peters, 1992; Snow, 1992) and, on the other hand, as improving sensitivity of its communicational abilities (Jarvenpaa, 1994; Nolan, 1995; Rockart, 1991). It means that just intensification of technology use can serve both positively and negatively, depending upon the approach to its use. Our previous analysis shows that instead of using IT as a support for overall control processes domination based on predetermined models (algorithmical and data), the use of vision sources for guidance and adaptation will be the main focus of IT employment. Remember driving by the windshield view . . .

Just as in the case of organizations, in systems development it means the switch of the design from enterprise architectures (EA) to dynamics enterprise architectures (DEA). On a more detailed systems level it is a switch from systems architectures (SA) to dynamic systems architectures (DSA). The move from MBA and SA to CBA with dynamic enterprise architecture has several stages. In each successive stage the practice of vision management and CBA is substituting for OO/C development methodologies more and more:

1. Structured model-based development
2. Object-oriented model-based development
3. Human-oriented communication-based development
4. Technology-oriented communication-based development
5. UVO based holistic engineering

Structured Model Based Approach

An example of the model-based approach is SAD (Systems Analysis and Design) with its systems development life cycle (SDLC), otherwise called a waterfall development method. The assumptions allowing the use of this method are:

1. The **CUI is low,** meaning the environment, and eventually the system, can achieve static harmonization by capturing the main patterns of the environment and interpreting them as internal Hi (systems design), also supporting He (value for users)
2. It is possible at the stage of the systems analysis and the feasibility study **to capture** these environmental patterns, as well as persistent internal harmonies (structures), and determine a long lasting harmonization schema
3. **Effective and efficient implementation** (design and embodiment harmonization) is possible and the presence of the new DPCS—as the system itself—will not upset the proposed harmonization process

The problem of complexity is handled in a reductionist manner when the system is split into smaller well-defined units with well-defined interfaces (stable and fixed). Then all the pieces are assigned design and management responsibilities. Architectural guidelines, goals, policies, and style are supposed to keep it all together, capturing a meaning which cannot fit any isolated unit, but belongs to the whole system. This is how the problem of the whole being bigger than the sum of its parts is approached in this method. Such tools are pretty much fixed too. Afterwards, supporting technology is also a fixed design choice.

The resulting layered architecture—see its good description in Buschmann et al (1996)—and interfacing of all kinds are the methods separating changes in one area from influencing others dealing with them locally. The goal of such interfaces is to prevent sensitivity from spreading around, keeping it all as prefixed connectivity patterns. Such an approach, though stabilizing the system, prevents the existing sensitivity from paving its way by enforcing the necessary connectivity changes and advancements. The system is kept prisoner by the original design, which is the only time in systems life when an external designer's vision is being used. This is an example of how vision organizations in the lower part of the VO-pyramid tend to move to the very bottom because they cannot support continuously changing adequacy at higher levels. It is also becoming clear why it is so difficult to move out of the lower left sector in the CCA diagram. The vision utilization step is so aligned with the whole OO/C process that it is pronounced a mystery, an art and is discussed only in structured goal terms, leaving the mechanics of the process itself totally unaddressed, and left out of nicely laid plans and blueprints.

Under the growing CUI pressure, the MBA approach of systems design started moving toward stage 2, using the growing practice of **end-user involvement** in ALL aspects of development as the "seers" of the final value, making the development more sensitive to the existing WHOLE situation (and not only internal engineering problems). Overall sensitivity was enhanced with the increasing use of so-called pilots as early sensors of the way the new harmony works. These smaller project implementations played the role of DPCS, opened to external and internal sensitivity and consisting of all involved parties. They can be much more sensitive to the situation through their design and applications in live processes (by connecting them to all real world aspects). Another aspect of pilot sensitivity is based on the possible rapid reaction by the developers that can easily modify these small systems "on the fly."

The shift to the upper levels of VO, better suiting dynamic operating situations, continued with the use of *best practices* and *design patterns*. When it became obvious that, in addition to the structures forming a system's stable components (software and data), there is a huge area of designers' (including "end-users") sensitivity, with its evolving patterns of connectivity capturing discovered harmonies, the new movement labeled "knowledge management" took off. Its goal was to externalize these structures and solutions that had the necessary sensitivity to their environment (context-sensitive "solutions"). This resulted in a huge investment into "best practices" and various "design/solution patterns." The practices and design patterns are somewhat different from design and implementation rules, models and control methods. They are not as much controlling, but rather "influencing," the design process, leaving room for a particular vision, knowledge, current and specific sensitivity, offering an attempt to harmonize local vision with more global and stable (abstract) vision existing elsewhere. Despite its radicalism, these methods were still oriented toward "solutions" (tactical and strategic) as final fixes of connectivity maps.

Object-Oriented Model-Based Approach

With CUI growth, the *waterfall* model becomes more like a *fountain* model, showing sensitivity and harmonization relationships between project steps. Such inter-step sensitivity is not handled well or naturally with Structured Analysis Paradigm (Yourdon, 1989) based on repeated decomposition into subcomponents. Why did it work in low CUI and is useless in situations with high CUI? The answer can be found in the differences of OO/C layering and PCCE design. If the goal of the first is layer insulation, separation from internal harmonization inside other layers, PCCE decomposition seeks holistic carriers and environments based on clusterization of sensitivity, and not on the classification of connectivity into abstract levels, communication between which is treated in a reductionist manner. All steps and phases in Structured Analysis are supposed to produce an intermediate result developed as a kind of descriptive **model**, capturing discovered stabilities as final harmonization solutions.

Once sensitivity grows and internal/external relationships are much more interwoven in the process of holistic harmonization, the influence of changes inside project phases started affecting other phases/models. Phase/step decomposition stops working. This is when a new idea has emerged that, instead of grouping stabilities around large model types or levels of abstraction, it might be better to group them around custom made clusters of connectivity (not sensitivity yet). Such clusters do not deal with artificial level separation, but rather with more natural connectivity that has roots in real world situations and, therefore, carry some *meaning* (or, rather, *sense*). Such units were called objects (as if to remind us of the continuing OO/C quest).

The development of the meaning out of such units of sense is done in object-oriented (OO) paradigm through inter object sensitivity harmonization. Instead of going from a very general meaning (of system value) and then making sense of elements of its decomposition in multiple testing and pilots, the OO approach suggests the opposite way of meaning creation out of units of sense discovered by designers. The management of small changes in such sense-components is much easier, faster and, to a certain extent, naturally insulated from changes in other sense-objects of sense-impacts (SI). At the same time designers try to find more precise SIs by "playing" with their sense and seeking more stable and interrelated features, weeding the rest out. Such a process is called *generalization* in OO analysis, and leads to the design of more general SI that can survive certain environmental changes, meaning that captured Hi will be sufficiently stable and worthy dealing with.

Such knowledge/sense capturing abilities necessary for the smallest components of captured encapsulated Hi has its roots in frames—although some differences between them exist—proposed in the context of knowledge processing studied, at that time, in AI domain (M. Minsky, 1975). A frame represents a concept which uses connectivity and sensitivity features where structured stable elements (data, procedure logic) play the role of connectivity while behavioral, experiential features play the role of sensitivity (such as external and internal interfaces as well as the ability to be initiated and assigned the most appropriate attributes by anyone with knowledge of interface implementation).

It is important to realize that the systems development project is an AHS of its own. Technology plays the role of a carrier, business value becomes environment and implemented and modified systems become DPCS of interconnected issues influencing each other. It means that IT/IS development is moving toward the same VCP-architecture instead of waterfall phases, where all stages and phases are blurred into vision (V), control (C), and physical (P) levels. The vision level is what the analysis was considered before, and is currently evolving under the OO-analysis paradigm, moving beyond it. Analysts or V-level designers have to keep track of sensitivity patterns among all DPCS, talk to end-users of all kinds (including so-called internal users) and consistently produce the current S-map (or a kind of analysis description—if it is properly done). C-level developers are doing actual harmonization of all sensitivity into patterns of connectivity or some stable elements, concepts, processes. This also has to be done on a continuing basis. Finally, implementation is the P-level of IT/IS AHS. "Implementors" are trying to maintain the viability of functioning systems. Their attempts in the component/object-based approach are based on the assumption that all the problems are not vision-level but implementation-level problems, and can be resolved by proper mapping of upper level harmonization solutions onto the current situation.

The described approach is more adequate for higher levels of CUI then in a pure MBA case. It is good for prototyping, for responding to changes in objects and their harmonization within whole system functionality via a messaging mechanism. Instead of the classical eight stages of the waterfall design paradigm, we have only three that are more clearly distinguished than other suggested activities, practically blurred into the three VCP levels represented by analysis, design, implementation macro activities.

Human-Oriented Communication-Based Development

With further CUI and sensitivity growth in the design and implementation environment, the ideas of capturing all the requirements, during even the most sensitive process of analysis as some kind of fixed He and then harmonize them with the current Hi state of IS, seem not feasible. The analysis and design phases cannot exist separately any more. Changes in requirements become the norm of the process, which can hardly be called development. Rather, it is a process of continuous external/internal sensitivity harmonization where sensitivity cannot be separated from the connectivity of the design as uncovered "solutions," capable of holding their validity/value for a long time. Sensitivity and connectivity are becoming more and more interwoven in their Yin/Yang dance and mutual transformation.

The need to inject sensitivity in all of its incarnations into the everyday design process has led to new approaches forming according to Fowler's expression "human oriented" development approach as opposed to object-oriented one. People as the main sensors/harmonizers and V-level carriers play a much more active role in such new approaches as

Extreme Programming (Beck, 2000), Adaptive Software Development (**Highsmith, 1997**), SCRUM, Feature Driven Development (Coad, 1999), Dynamic System Development Method (Stapleton, 1997), Agile Software Development (Cockburn, 2001) and some others.

The search of ways to activate human sensitivity and harmonization abilities and inject it into the continuous analysis-design-implementation loop iterations serves the goal of adding vision to the system development/existence process. Such a loop should remind us of the LCA loop, where harmonized sensitivity of vision and communications leads to the findings of more stable patterns that attempt to curb the original sensitivity, which then has to be supported in its revitalized role, leading to the next iteration.

Our previous LCA analysis shows that the loop should be small enough and rotate fast enough to stay viable. Similar to LCA, the above mentioned human-oriented (we will call them vision-oriented) methods and development frameworks require short development iterations (from one month to one week) with a complete cycle, including micro-implementation and testing, allowing external sensitivity to affect the internal harmony of the project.

Another line of efforts is based here on the desire to use the human body/mind carrier for vision evolution, inter-LVS harmonization and interaction with higher VS levels. This leads to more integral responsibilities for each developer while concentrating in one person most of the jobs previously distributed along the control pyramid.

Unfortunately, using small cycles, a lot of human interaction and integration of many vertical functions and responsibilities in one developer has its limitations which, practically, have been reached already. Proper human incorporation in project development as a part of the VM approach is a necessary but insufficient measure for project/process viability and full realization of the CBA approach. A big and well connected logical OO-project cannot be effectively split into many microcycles of microimplementations reconnected in super effective communications and internalization of vertical functions. Even an important move away from the development models and toward a more flexible language description (like UML), when the language could be used in any suitable way, doesn't deliver much without totally switching to the CBA approach and VM methodology. Yes, certain improvements will be achieved, but without good chances of keeping pace with CUI growth and the need in smaller and more efficient LC loops of AHS. There is a visible limit to the further shortening of the iterations and the size of micro-projects that still have to carry end value, as well as external sensitivity delivered in such way.

Technology-Oriented Communication-Based Development

Human-oriented development was the first conscious declaration of war against the cult of stability and control, leading the way to increased sensitivity and fighting stability, similar to the management catastrophe described in part 1. Self-organization, CBA and VM are the directions of further development.

The major problem in systems development is in the word "system" as a goal of such development, as a final value and product the customers look at and pay for. Once the system is seen as a product, it falls under legal and psychological rules, practices and expectations of dealing with products that were built according to an order. Such products should be well described, capable of carrying, for a long time, the name, the fixed distinctive attributes and other features of OO/C. Legal and accounting practices are created around such products determining the fair payment and pricing as well as customer and producer protection rights. All this is in OO/C terms while the reality is already far away in PO/H sphere. Such a situation is the source of problems in creating a development methodology for systems and software products that are not really systems or products anymore. It is similar to the obsession of Western medicine with pill-packaged "solutions" versus continuous holistic treatments/therapies like Tai Chi, yoga, and others.

No matter how well the design evolves, it will always be separated from the implementation and the user value assessment side in legal, accounting and cultural aspects of OO/C vision, until we somehow break away from this situation. What are the options?

Actually, a new approach to systems development is already working. This is the switch from focusing on IS to efforts in IT. Even in the job market they already are not looking any longer at particular languages and databases, but at the knowledge of various technologies. Information technology or, often, simply technology is becoming the main attraction and the talk of the town.

Technology, basically, is a system of protocols, interfaces, and means of communication allowing for the support of connectivity, sensitivity, and interpretational aspects of the real world life of information and communication processes and "objects." It includes software in various forms, hardware solutions, some math methods and algorithms implemented in hardware, handshake and routing decision making, etc. The main distinction of IT from IS is not actually in its formats and implementations, but in the philosophy behind its valuation. An IT solution is a value by itself which might not be translated into a final user's value. The possibility of emailing each other is important even if the company doesn't see real money-making projects based on it immediately. It is a behavioral advantage. This understanding of the pure value of increased connectivity, sensitivity and interpretational abilities becomes a design in reverse, where the users will have to adjust to the new reality thinking of how to add value to their organizations having such and such technology available. But once the value is found, the specific implementation can come fast, matching the dynamics of a particular need.

Thus the design is separated, to a great extent, from reactive behavior on the business level, with its analysis and quick and cheap implementation. Such separation allows very large and lightly connected groups to compete for technological perfection and new developments, while the business public competes concerning the best use of such products and services. By unofficially declaring the new market of CSI, such separation is even more significant because it means living according to its own logic (influenced, of course, by the needs of the users, but not in a contractual way requiring management coordination). It is a step toward product-age catastrophe, resulting in the pure value of CSI and a possible DPCS evolution based on it (see the discussion in the following section).

Technology, or we can call it *techware* in order to create a reference to its new value-carrying ability, usually incorporates some software components like objects, scripts, etc., thus filling the shells of newly developed CSI—features. For example, the global acceptance of TCP/IP, HTTP, and HTML led to the phenomenal search of value and its creation within WWW universe. More specific technologies offer various means of connectivity to these tools as well as sensitivity, and interpretation of their formats during communication sessions. The growth of the modern company is going not only *outside-in* (as it was previously discussed) but *upside-down* when, often, technology paves the way to inventions and new ways of getting value out if it (business models).

The explosive interest in Web services, SOAP, XML, Common Runtime for various languages, and other of the latest technologies is based on the shift of attention from "ends" of communication processes to the patterns of connectivity and sensitivity, allowing for new DPCS to evolve somewhere in between (see far fetched philosophy behind BizTalk and similar ideas of the. Net), as a major processing area versus end-user computing. Such DPCS-in-between could evolve and exist purely on their own and be recognized and supported by various groups and organizations. See as an example Napster and the pure peer-to-peer arrangements of the evolution of various clusters, groups, and relationships based on mutual sensitivity which results in more advanced connectivity and interpretational procedures.

The use of techware also means the shift to the new programming, when code doesn't exist as a sequentially executed chunk of logic, but has to be distributed as filling into various technological components and processes that provide vehicles of macro-engineering for such code, and add immediate meaning and value being utilized in any particular business model or its part. Techware is becoming a special concurrently distributed type of algorithms, languages, and various modeling and controlling tools in a healthy mix with CSI processes, adding flexible ad hoc experiences, sensitivity maps and evolutionary dynamics based on possible reuse in a variety of business configurations responding to actual situations. If we look at all the code existing in scripts, objects, services and protocol processors on hosts, routers, switches, mobile agents, and so on living in modern Web based distributed system, we can see a merger of the software, hardware, human technological intrusions and automated evolution of CSI patterns into techware phenomena, blending into each other and coevolving with each other. Becoming not MBA-based but a CBA-dominated form of "driving by the windshield view", a form of *Environment Driven Computing* (EDC) which will get its full bloom on Stage 5 described next.

Web services are more a connectivity/sensitivity solution then a program modeling/control. The main achievement here is in the ability to use the Internet as a connectivity layer with sensitivity hidden inside object functionality at service ends. The need in something else results in connection with the different service. The big problem is a rigid interface not allowing for full CSI interaction when some new needs cannot be dynamically addressed as a mutual adaptation of the two sides of one service. Until end node flexible participation in service will be achieved and service will be able to modify itself, UDDI and WSDL should be supplemented with some kind of search engine where new needs will result in just new service. More advanced adaptability moving to the channel according to LH3 leads to some kind of interpretational services that can be used when an intermediary, having connection to both sides (client and server), can "repackage/reinterpret" the service in SOAP (or the like) according to the changing needs of the client, with possible involvement of other services dynamically included into such service "harmonizer/interpreter."

Other types of techware can use different methods and technologies of CSI enhancement. This includes wireless, non-Internet networking, and a variety of software additions to various parts of current technologies "softening" their CSI properties, making them more flexible moving to the upper-right corner of CCA-diagram. For example, DHTML with scripting, various client-side downloaded objects and applets can dramatically increase browser sensitivity to the user of software attached to it. ASP, JSP, Perl, and other server-side technologies increase server sensitivity to client needs and capabilities. ATM, cable modem, ISDN and other networking technologies increase connectivity of hosts to external networks and, in some cases, sensitivity of such a connection offering variable bandwidth for variable sensitivity needs. Software can be inserted into routers, switches, hosts, firewalls, intermediate servers and gateways, etc. Each technology still has its own CSI value, can be tested separately, and can be enhanced through the proper softening by software and analog computing. Analytical or intelligence services added internally or being Web-based, represent an example of interpretational layer processes harmonizing external sensitivity seen as data, with some internal DPCS or its CSI-process (like CRM, SCM, etc.).

Techware, as the future way of IT/IS design, can be formalized (which is beyond the scope of this book) into a particular methodology based on the ideas and value of CSI-engineering. The main ideas of the techware approach include:

- Value wrapping, independent from any system contract or development
- Testing independence
- Open-ended possibilities of coupling it with other types of techware through the use of common standards, interfaces, easily interpreted procedures and the logic of the work
- Development independence and cooperative possibilities with other groups based on the clear formula of connectivity or sensitivity or the interpretational value
- Independence from programming languages and tools allowing for input from a variety of developmental platforms
- Potential value (which has to be constantly uncovered) for organizational and human life, but without specific models of how it will be "plugged in."

Web services are a new evolving technology form something more then connection and signal transfer. It is an entity with a life of its own that can be processed BETWEEN the objects, when objects become just weights on its ends. Once the coherent system of services in their dynamics, adaptability and sensitivity is developed, objects just feed it and can be replaced and modified. This initiates *Object-Independent Development* versus OO-Development as a more CSI—consistent type of engineering.

 · The possibility to openly switch to CSI-engineering, forming a sufficiently independent development industry, will allow the organizational designers to become new business model initiators, perfectly understanding the capabilities of new technologies and the ways of tweaking them to the need of particular CSI-based value idea. Such tech-based (CSI-based) ideas are very active, stimulating a large number of participants that can think of their use in simple CSI-terms without getting into implementation details forming the DPCS of the current and future harmonization. Such DPCS can be realized as automated complexes, agreements and organizational forms of specific practices.

CCA diagrams can play an important role in laying out a further course for technological development. The final goal is, then, not a system as a product but an effective and efficient care of a LCA loop life cycle, while dynamically responding to various external and internal changes. Such a CBA approach leads to dynamic, constantly evolving architecture, which is the main result of using CSI-technologies. Coevolution and self-organization of necessary patterns within an organization becomes AHS. This translates into the following three-section VM-methodology of using CBA approach VMS:

- Comfortable Live Space versus Live Controlling Model
- CCA strategy
- LCA—driven goals and values

Space Versus Model: The Cube

Further advancements along CSI—techware lead to the need for a common language or, rather, vision, allowing for all technologies to smoothly get along. Discussed UVO as such a universal vision approach forces the switch from IT/IS to Vision Management Technology/Systems (VMT/VMS). Basically all development decisions/evolving go along the following coordinates in the development space of the main options:

1. VCP levels instead of users-(business rules/objects)-middleware-data architecture
2. CSI interacting layers where harmonization of sensitivity enforces connectivity through the appropriate interpretation of preexisting C-maps
3. SCT approaches to the ways external sensitivity forms internal patterns

These three coordinates form the Space of systems populated with DPCS with their life and evolution. Choices along VCP allow the placement of efforts and resulting techware into domains of V-level, C-level, or P-level. These decisions consider the role of technologies as effectively evolving and sensitive ones, capable of capturing and supporting the main vDPCS with their evolution, or that would be a controlling/interpreting coordinating logic on C-level, managing more stable and, therefore, less adaptable technologies of P-level.

CSI techware provides both the carrier and harmonization on it with full CS-dynamics, using interpretational richness. CSI solutions could be used on any level (V, C or P) with proper balance between stability and sensitivity that, actually, decide which level it is going to be.

SCT-decisions choose the way external sensitivity will be interpreted into internal DPCS harmony. The choice is between external vision management (EVM) done by the analysis team and then converted (C-level) by the design team into the P-level of models ("solutions") in S-mode manner, or organically embodied vision into all DPCS done T-mode way, where no external entities offer Vmods and their evolution is explicitly included in system life as internal VM (IVM), or choosing something in between, such as the C-mode approach.

The described space of the system development/ evolution choices forms the Cube representing all 27 fuzzy areas of all CSI/SCT/VCP combinations. The important feature here is the substitution of model designing and their following implementation with the evaluation of the precision of such implementation as a measure of value and success for the designing of the Space of the system's life and evolving, which has to be comfortable enough to allow for the easy movement and reshaping of various evolving DPCS within such space of features. Another goal is in the proper distribution of efforts and resources supporting the Cube functionality. In particular, more have to be used in the slice containing V-level and Tmod technologies. The proper interaction between connectivity and sensitivity has to be improved where higher or lower sensitivity between parties follows LH3 and results in higher or lower connectivity between them. Dynamic interpretation of sensitivity onto the evolving C-map is another area requiring serious improvements.

CCA

The possibility of DPCS to comfortably (effectively and efficiently) evolve and move in the Cube space is based on the flexibility of used techware, and could be planned and assessed using the CCA-diagram discussed before. The movement to the upper right corner of CCA diagram will result in less controlling efforts and the cost of used resources necessary to accommodate the changes in DPCS development within the Cube.

LCA

. The final section of CBA methodology includes LCA-driven goals and values. Not the satisfaction of precaptured "requirements," but the viability of the closed loop circling process of the LCA-diagram is becoming the goal, and the value of the holistic engineering substituting for analysis-design-implementation systems modeling.

All three components of the CBA methodology: Space versus Model, CCA-strategy and LCA-driven goals and values change the philosophy and the meaning of the IT/IS design/support, making it a VMS/VMT effort. It means the design (intentional or evolving) has a different structure: instead of elements, attributes, and their functionality in methods and interfaces directed toward Lego-like building, we have space for possible forms and features that can live and evolve in this space, being unrestricted in their specific shapes at any particular moment. Such space should be hospitable as a live world for our evolving creatures and sufficiently complete. The Cube space and CCA play the role of a road map of the evolving path toward space improvement (as a strategic goal). An improvement to the extent that it will be a "pleasure" for the new DEA/DSA to evolve and live there, maintaining the optimal pattern on LCA.

The reality of global connectivity and sensitivity leads to the evolution of business models that, if inadequate, die out fast. They have to respond to this new invisible hand which is becoming harder every day. So why not to start designing such an Invisible Hand, as well as giving it some Vision abilities in order to see what it is doing?

Stage Five: UVO-Based Holistic Engineering

Further enhancement of VM effectiveness and efficiency can only continue with growing automation of the human-performed tasks in VM architecture, which leads to full UFO as it discussed before. Among the tasks analyzed in the previous chapters of HE, the most challenging is the task of switching from External Vision Management (EVM) done by a group of people working according to Smod methodology to Internal Vision Management (IVM), predominantly using Tmods.

The S-mode approach is based on the separation of sensitivity from connectivity as two different stages. Whatever the developers see during the analysis phase is captured, preharmonized and packaged as "solutions" or other model-type controls on the design stage to be later industrially embedded (interpreted on the implementation stage) into the current/new system.

Tmods, if you remember, have to provide for the holistic connection of the sensitivity/connectivity mutual interaction based on external sensitivity directly, and working on the Hi of existing DPCS, similar to animals capable of performing perception and reactive acts in their natural interrelated manner (or any other life form to that extent). No external designers are involved and the situation manages coevolution in a structural and behavioral sense. Such an approach allows for very efficient complex behaviors supporting small LC diameter (on a LCA-diagram), leading to fast and inexpensive adaptive reactions.

It is important to note that VCP and CSI architectural solutions can be used in all types of Vmods (Smods, Cmods, and Tmods). The specificity of the situation any subsystem is in, its CUI, and some other features might prove better performance of any one of Vmods or a particular mix. But since currently Tmods are almost non-existent a lot of work has to be done in giving them the leading role with emergence of appropriate technology. This is what we meant speaking about the proper effort and resource distribution in The Cube development.

The switch from EVM to IVM is necessary for higher efficiency and better interconnection of CSI-layer dynamics.

An intermediate solution is possible when, instead of the full internalization of Tmods embodied in all processes and sub-areas, we go only for the automation of VCP-levels of interaction. V-level, in many cases, could be implemented, technically, on a different carrier and in a different place, providing it has the ability to properly participate in dynamic exchange with C—and P-levels. Modern communication technology rapidly makes the notion of "embodiment" more of a logical interaction nature then a distance property.

Although it seems like serious work has to be done in order to offer Tmods their leading role, the use of Cmods as an intermediate solution has already started. Examples include Fuzzy Logic and Neural Network implementations and some additional soft-math methods. Both Fuzzy Logic (FL) and Neural Networks (NN) might be used in their further development as Tmods, like in self-organized maps (Kohonen, 2001) as well as Cmods, the most widespread use now. In Cmods they attempt to sense external patterns and implement the evolving C-map as an encapsulated (but largely insulated for Se) Hi. For example, membership function in FL designs (like point-and-shoot cameras) capture either human or NN sensitivity which then, in its already unchanged form, is connected to the logical part performing the action. NN in many cases are pre-trained (when connectivity patterns are emerging out of past sensitivity from collected data) and then again used as harmonization "solutions." The more often NN trains or FL modifies their membership function, the more actual their vision is. The future path to Tmods using these tools, in particular, is in the formation of the continuously working process of vision management with the CSI version, like cycles working smoothly as Yin/Yang pair in optimal LCA.

A number of other evolutionary technologies, including Artificial Life, Genetic Algorithms, patterns of the evolution of multi-agent systems, recurrent NN with temporal processing features, other adaptive Cmod technologies and their combinations form a new type of computing—Environment Driven Computing (EDC). They create a competition for current model-driven (Smod type) computing as EDC moving toward Tmod technologies. This new type of computing combined with techware, which has the ability of adding particular implementation experiences and values in a different way then Tmods, will supplement each other in a new HE methodology.

EDC as a software methodology and VM (driving by windshield view) as a general approach require proper movement along CCA and redistribution inside The Cube. One of the promising technologies of the future that potentially can support interwoven dynamics of CSI-layers is the abstraction from connectivity, as circuit/packet switching, and substituting it with virtual connectivity, sensitivity, and interpretation, interacting as distributed mobile intelligent multi-agent systems (MAS) and multi-agent environments (MAE). The tasks of sensing the environment and communicating SI to other agents, regardless of the distance, is a matter of coupling rapidly evolving MAS engineering with modern communication technologies (Vengerov, 2002). This new carrier/harmonizer will be independent from hardware and software implementations, potentially becoming a live conceptualized universal framework for the evolution of particular methods of harmonization, harmonic transform, and CSI-interaction. Combined with nanotechnology and ubiquitous EDC as UVO implementation, the new Universal Framework Organization can play a major role in systems and the business revolution of the future.

Universal VMT/VMS

UVO implementation in its Universal Framework Organization (UFO) is the path of effectiveness and efficiency of HE. The need for the free evolving of DPCS within The Cube architectural space requires universality of methods, tools and technologies in all locations, on all system levels, and in every cell of The Cube, which is the only way for a comfortable choice of the evolutionary path as a regular *modus operandi*. H-engineering should be ubiquitous, evolving and unbinding. Every little area where some harmony is being encapsulated should enjoy the same Cube space as all other contenders, including the system as a whole. This is why universality is very important.

The current trend in Web services shows that any universal communication technology, in order to serve its purpose, has to be the same inside organizations, departments, or between different conglomerates. Although there is a long way to go toward full UFO implementation, the philosophy, orientation and methodology of systems analysis and development should start preparing for its ubiquitous universality. The conceptual implementation of CSI layer interaction, availability of the Cube space for every process and area requiring it, CCA-progress and efficient management of LCA together with other HE methods and approaches should serve the successful implementation of UFO.

The existence of universal system solutions and their grounding into actual environmental situations is, by itself, a revolutionizing factor for IT/IS and e-business. Such universal products/services coupled with universal methodologies, approaches and practices can create a super **mass production** industry again, supported by included self-harmonized components **automatically** tailoring systems (in **self-customization** fashion) to particular situations. Such a combination of mass-production with self-customization based on the Universal Vision Organization can increase the economic effectiveness manifold, gradually moving toward the use of measurements, goals, and principles of harmonomics in the H-engineering of sensitive systems of all kinds.

Conclusion

The continuous development of the World Economy, being hopelessly restricted by practically all tangible resources from energy to "human capital," has the only chance in the growing effectiveness of technological stimulation and support. But already in 1968 NATO saw the limits in further technological development sponsoring a conference addressing the problem of the "software crisis" that threatened the economic health and military adequacy of the West. The discovered solutions only postponed the growing threat of complexity capable of making even the best technological advancements of systems development too costly and risky. Mr. Horn from IBM calls the complexity problem the industry's "next grand challenge." Researchers from all over the world more and more realize the vital importance of finding a way to support the further evolution of technology as the major resource of the global well-being in spite of the systems complexity stonewalling such efforts.

Scientific methods, and the OO/C vision organization in general, are showing the limitations and the lack of solutions to the stated problem just postponing the coming crisis of systems inadequacy. The crush of tech companies in the beginning of the XXI century was a symptomatic demonstration of the growing disappointment in existing OO/C methods following the hype and the promise of technological advancements without the consideration of the following raise of the ghost of complexity acting with increased vengeance and frequency. The path of the reappearance of new technological miracles that can save the world is becoming less and less believable with every disappointment in uneven battle with Complexity, which grows even faster.

In this book we see a cure in a more radical activity—changing the whole vision system, which we all were trained in and which is so widely used in current business and engineering practices. The new vision offers better orientation and adaptivity. But what is more important, it offers the sources of friendly power comparable with the power of complexity. The same way as holistic problems of systemic disorders in human health are better treated by holistic approaches and medicine and not by strong pills with specific local effects—the holistic problems of system's complexity, uncertainty and instability should be treated by holistic engineering, leading to higher harmony in our economy, society, and world.

P.S. the discussion of the book and the additional materials could be found on the author's web site: **www.holosticengineering.com**

Bibliography

Aghion, P. and P. Howitt (1992). A Model of Growth through Creative Destruction. *Econometrica*, 60, 2, pp. 323-51.

Akao, Y. (Ed.). (1990). *Quality Function Deployment*. Cambridge MA: Productivity Press.

Allen S. Lee, Ojelanki K. Ngwenyama (1997). Communication Richness In Electronic Mail: Critical Social Theory And The Contextuality Of Meaning. *MIS Quarterly*, Volume 21, Number 2, 145-167

Allport, A. (1985). The historical background of social psychology. In Lindzey, G. and Aronson, E. (Ed.), *Handbook of Social Psychology* (3rd ed., Vol. 1, pp. 1-46). New York: Random House.

Anderson, Philip W., Kenneth J. Arrow, and David Pines, eds. (1988). The Economy as an Evolving Complex System. *Santa Fe Institute Studies in the Sciences of Complexity*, vol. 5. Redwood City, Calif.: Addison-Wesley.

Argyris, C. and D.A. Schon (1978). *Organizational Learning: A Theory of Action Perspective*. Reading, MA: Addison-Wesley.

Argyrus, C. (1990). *Overcoming Organizational Defenses: facilitating organizational learning*. New Jersey: Prentice Hall.

413

Ashby W. R. (1964): *Introduction to Cybernetics.* Methuen: London.

Ashby W.R. (1958). Requisite Variety and Implications for Control of Complex Systems. *Cybernetica* 1, p. 83-99.

Bagby P. (1958). *Culture and History,* London: Longmans, p.109

Bak, Per, and Kan Chen. (1991). Self-Organized Criticality. *Scientific American,* January, 46-54.

Bandura, A. (1971). *Social Learning Theory.* New York: General Learning Press.

Bargh, John A. (1994). First Second: The Preconscious in Social Interactions. Presented at the meeting of the American Psychological Society, Washington, DC (June)

Beck, K., (2000). *Extreme Programming Explained: embrace change.* Addison Wesley.

Bentham, J. (1839). *The Rationale of Judicial Evidence.* Edinburgh: William Tait.

Bertalanffy, Ludwig Von (1968). *General System Theory,* New York: George Braziller

Bly, S., Harrison, S., & Irwin, S. (1993). Media spaces: Bringing people together in a video, audio, and computing environment. Comm. ACM, Jan., p. 28-47.

Bonarini, Andrea, (1997). Anytime Learning and Adaptation of Structured Fuzzy Behaviors. *Adaptive Behavior Journal,* 5.

Brown J.S. and Duguid P. (1991). Organizational Learning and Communities-of-Practice: Toward A Unified View of Working, Learning, and Innovation. *Organization Science,* Vol. 2, 40-57.

Brown Lester (1996). *Acceleration of History.* State of the World. Ed by Lester R. Brown and Janet Abramovitz, W.W. Norton & Company, New York.

Buschmann F., R. Meunier, H. Rohnert, P. Sommerlad, M. Stal. (1996). *Pattern-Oriented Software Architecture: A System of Patterns.* John Wiley and Sons Ltd.: West Sussex.

Candace Pert, Michael Ruff, Richard Weber, and Miles

Herkenham (1985). Neuropeptides and Their Receptors: A Psychosomatic Network. *The Journal of Immunology*, vol. 135, no. 2, pp.820-26.

Capra, Fritjof (1988). *The Turning Point: Science, Society, and The Rising Culture.* Bantam Books: New York.

Carpenter, Gail A., and Stephen Grossberg (1987). A Massively Parallel Architecture for a Self-Organizing Neural Pattern Recognition Machine. *Computer Vision, Graphics, and Image Processing,* Vol. 37, pp.54-115.

Charles Bidwell (1986). *Complex Organizations: A Critical Essay.* 3rd ed., New York: Random House

Chin-Teng Lin and C.S. George Lee, (1996). *Neural Fuzzy Systems: A Neuro-Fuzzy Synergism to Intelligent Systems.* New Jersey: Prentice Hall.

Coad, De Luca, Lefebrve (1999). *Java Modeling in Color with UML.* Prentice Hall.

Cockburn, Alistair (2001). *Agile Software Development,* Addison-Wesley Pub Co.

Cournot, A., (1927). Researches into the Mathematical Principles of the Theory of Wealth. (N.T. Bacon Trans., original work published 1838), (Macmillan, New York).

Daft, R. L., & Lengel, R.H. (1984). Information richness: A new approach to manager information processing and organization design. In "Research in Organizational Behavior," B. Staw & L. Cummings, Eds., Greenwich, CT: JAI Press, pp. 191-233.

Daft, R.L., Lengel, R.H. (1986). Organizational Information Requirements, Media Richness and Structural Design. *Management Science,* 32(5), 554-576.

Dahleh M.A., Ignacio J. Diaz-Bobilllo (1995). *Control of Uncertain Systems. A linear Programming Approach.* Prentice Hall.

Dale Neef (1998). *The Knowledge Economy.* Woburn, MA: Butterworth-Heineman.

David A. Schum (1994). *Evidential Foundations of Probabilistic Reasoning.* New York: John Wiley & Sons.

Davidow, W.H. and M.S. Malone (1992). *The Virtual Corporation.* New York: Harper Collins.

Davidson D., (1978). What metaphors mean. *On Metaphor,* ed. Sheldon Sacks, 29-45. Chicago: University of Chicago Press

De Medio, C., Oriolo, G. (1991). Robot Obstacle Avoidance Using Vortex Fields. In S. Stifter and Lenarcic (Ed.), *Advances in Robot Kinematics*: Springer Verlag.

Deneubourg J.L., Goss S. (1989), *Collective patterns and decision-making,* Ethology & Evolution, 1, 295-311.

Derrida, Jacques (1981). *Positions,* trans. Alan Bass. London: Athlone Press.

Dreze, J. H. (1987), *Essays on economic decisions under uncertainty.* Cambridge: University Press

Drucker, P.(1988). The Coming of the New Organization. *Harvard Business Review,.* January—February, 45-53.

Economides, N. and W. Lehr (1995). The Quality of Complex Systems and Industry Structure, Quality and Reliability of Telecommunications Infrastructure. In: W. Lehr ed., (Lawrence Erlbaum, Hillsdale NJ).

Economides, N. (1994). Quality Choice and Vertical Integration. Discussion Paper EC-94-22, Stern School of Business, N.Y.U.

Economides, Nicholas and Charles Himmelberg (1995). Critical Mass and Network Size with Application to the US Fax Market. Discussion Paper no. EC-95-11, Stern School of Business, N.Y.U.

Extricity Software. Adaptec. Retrieved June 19, 2002, from *http://www.1185design.com/multimedia/final_sites/extricity/lib_adaptec.html*

Fish, R. S., Kraut, R. E., Root, R. W., & Rice, R. E. (1993). Video as a technology for informal communication. *Commun. ACM,* Jan., p. 48-61.

Fulk, J., Schmitz, J. A., & Steinfield, C. W. (1990). A social influence model of technology use. In Organizations and communications technology, J. Fulk & C. Steinfield, Eds., Sage, Newbury Park, CA, pp. 117-140.

Gail A. Carpenter and Stephen Grossberg (1990). Art3: Hierarchical search using chemical transmitters in self-organizing pattern recognition architectures. *Neural Networks*, 3:129-152.

Gifford and Elizabeth Pinchot (1994). *The End of Bureaucracy and the Rise of the Intelligent Organization*. San Francisco, CA: Berret-Koehler

Goodwin B.(1994). *How the Leopard Changed Its Spots*. London: Weidenfeld & Nicolson.

Goodwin, R.M. (1967). A Growth Cycle. In Feinstein, C.H. (Ed.). *Socialism Capitalism and Economic Growth*. Cambridge: Cambridge University Press.

Gould, S.J. (1989). An Asteroid to Die for. *Discover,* October, 69.

Granovetter, M. (1985). Economic Action and Social Structure: the problem with embeddedness. *American Journal of Sociology*, 91, 481-510.

Habermas, J. (1979). *Communication and the Evolution of Society*. London: Heinemann Press

Habermas, J. (1984). *The Theory of Communicative Action: Reason And Rationalization of Society*. Boston: Beacon Press

Hangos. K.M. (1993). Complexity of Dynamic Models for Intelligent Control. *Mutual Impacts of Computing Power and Control Theory*. New York: Plenum Press.

Hans-George Gadamer (1977). *Philosophical hermeneutics*. U. of California Press.

Highsmith, Jim (1997). Messy, Exciting and Anxiety-Ridden: Adaptive Software Development. *American Programmer Magazine*, April

Hodgson, G.M., (1993). *Economics and Evolution*. Cambridge: Polity Press.

Huber, G. (1990). A theory of the effects of advanced information technologies on organizational design, Intelligence, and decision making. *Academy of Management Review*, Vol. 15, No. 1, 47-71.

Huber, G.P. (1991). Organizational Learning: The

Contributing Processes and the Literatures. *Organizational Science*, 2(1), 88-114.

Ives, B., and Jarvenpaa, S. (1991). Applications of Global Information Technology. *MISQ*, 33-47.

Jarvenpaa, S.L. and B. Ives (1994). The Global Network Organization of the Future: Information Management Opportunities and Challenges. *Journal of Management Information Systems*, 10(4), 25-57.

Jean-Jacques Laffont (1990). *The Economics of Uncertainty and Information*. The MIT Press

Jennifer Stapleton (1997). *Dsdm Dynamic Systems Development Method: The Method in Practice*. Addison-Wesley Pub Co, 1st edition

Jorgenson, D.W. and K.J. Stiroh (2000). Raising the Speed Limit: U.S. Economic Growth in the Information Age. *Brookings Papers on Economic Activity*, 2000:I, pp. 125-211.

Joseph LeDoux (1994). "Emotion, Memory and the Brain," Scientific American, June.

Katsuki Sekida (1985). *Zen Training*. New York: Weatherhill.

Katz, M. and C. Shapiro (1985). Network Externalities, Competition and Compatibility, *American Economic Review*, 75 (3), 424-440.

Kauffman, S. (1995). *At Home in the Universe. The search for the Laws of Self-Organization and Complexity*, Oxford University Press: New York, NY

Kelly, K. (1998). *New Rules for the New Economy: 10 Radical Strategies for a Connected World*. USA, New York, NY: Penguin

Kiesler, S., Siegel, J. & McGuire, T. W. (1984). Social psychological aspects of computer-mediated communication. *American Psychologist*, 39(10): 1123-1134.

Kohonen T. (2001). *Self-Organizing Maps*. Springer

Kroeber A. L. (1952). *The Nature of Culture*. Chicago: University Press, p.403

Kuhn, D. (1972). Mechanisms of change in the development of cognitive structures. *Child Development*, 43, 833-844.

Kuhn, T. S. (1962). *The Structure of Scientific Revolutions.* Chicago: University of Chicago Press.

Lakoff, George, and M. Johnson (1980). *Metaphors We Live By.* Chicago: University of Chicago Press

Langton C. (1991). *Computation at the Edge of Chaos: Phase-Transition and Emergent Computation.* Ph.D. dissertation, University of Michigan.

Langton, Christofer G. (1989). Artificial Life. *Santa Fe Institute Studies in Sciences of Complexity,* vol 6. Redwood City, Calif.: Addison-Wesley.

Laszlo, Ervin (1973). Ludwig Von Bertalanffy and Claude Levi-Strauss.Systems and Structures in Biology and Social Anthropology. In *Unity Through Diversity,* ed. by William Gray and Nicholas D. Rizzo, New York: Gordon and Breach.

Leifer, R. (1989). Understanding Organizational Transformation Using A Dissipative Structures Model. *Human Relations,* 42 (10), 899-916

Lewin, K. (1951). *Field theory in social science; selected theoretical papers.* D. Cartwright (Ed.). New York: Harper & Row.

Lotman, Y. M. (1988).The semiotics of culture and the concept of a text. *Soviet Psychology,* vol.XXVI, no.3.

Marcel Danesi (1994). Messages and Meaning: An Introduction to Semiotics. Toronto: Canadian Scholars' Press.

Mark Weiser (1993). Hot Topics: Ubiquitous Computing. *IEEE Computer,* October.

Marshall Van Alstyne (1997). The State Of Network Organization: A Survey In Three Frameworks. *Journal of Organizational Computing,* 7(3)

Michael J. Mandel and Christopher Farrell (1998). The Economy. *Business Week:* May 25.

Mill, J. S. (1865). *A system of Logic: Ratiocinative and Inductive.* 6th ed. Longmans, Green: London

Mills, D.Q.(1991). *Rebirth of the Corporation.* New York: John Wiley & Sons.

Minsky M. (1975). "*A framework for representing knowledge.*" In P. Winston, editor, *The Psychology of Computer Vision.* McGraw-Hill.

Mintzberg, H. (1994). *The Rise and Fall of Strategic Planning.* London: Prentice Hall.

Mizuno, S. (Ed.). (1988). Management *for Quality Improvement: The 7 New QC Tools.* Cambridge MA: Productivity Press, Inc.

Morgan M. Granger and Max Henrion (1990). *Uncertainty. A Guide to Dealing with Uncertainty in Quantitative Risk and Policy Analysis.* Cambridge University Press.

Mosekilde, Erik, Javier, Aracil, and Peter M. Allen (1988). Instabilities and Chaos in Nonlinear Dynamic System. *System Dynamics Review,* vol. 4, pp14-55.

Munther A. Dahleh, Ignacio J. Diaz-Bobillo (1995). *Control of Uncertain Systems.* New Jersey: Prentice Hall

Murray, D. E.(1991). The composing process for computer conversation. *Written Communication,* vol.8, no.1.

Nagel, R.N. and Dove, R. (1992). *21st Century Manufacturing Enterprise Strategy.* Iacocca Institute. Bethlehem, PA: Lehigh University

Ngwenyama, O.K., Lee, A.S. (1997). Communication Richness In Electronic Mail: Critical Social Theory And The Contextuality Of Meaning. *MIS Quarterly,* 21(2), June, 145-167.

Nitin Nohria and Robert G. Eccles (eds.) (1992). *Networks and Organizations: Structure, Form, and Action.* Boston, MA: Harvard Business School Press.

Nolan, R. and D. Croson (1995). *Creative Destruction.* Boston: Harvard University Press.

Nonaka, I. (1988). Creating Organizational Order out of Chaos: Self-renewal in Japanese Firms. *California Management Review,* 30(3), Spring, 57-73.

Parasuraman, A., V. A. Zeithaml, and L. L. Berry (1988). SERVQUAL: A Multiple-Item Scale for Measurement

Consumer Perceptions of Service Quality. *Journal of Retailing*, Spring, Vol. 64, No.1, pp.12-40

Perelman C. and L. Olbrechts-Tyteca (1971). *The New Rhetoric: A Treatise on Argumantation*. University of Notre Dame Press. London

Peters, T.(1992). *Liberation Management: Necessary Disorganization for the Nanosecond Nineties*. New York: Alfred A. Knopf Inc.

Pincus, Steve, Waters, L. K. (1977). Information Social Influence and Product Quality Judgments. *Journal of Applied Psychology*, Vol. 62, No. 5, October, p.615.

Polya, George (1990). *Mathematics and Plausible Reasoning*. Princeton Univ. Pr.

Porter, Michael E. and Millar, Victor E. (1985). How Information gives you Competitive Advantage. *Harvard Business Review*, July/August 1985, 149-160.

Powell, W.W. and DiMaggio, P.J. (Ed.). (1991). *The New Institutionalism in Organisational Analysis*. USA: University of Chicago Press.

Powell, W.W.(1990). Neither Market Nor Hierarchy: Network Forms of Organization. *Research in Organizational Behavior.* 12, 295-336.

Price, Linda L. and Feick, Lawrence F. (1984). The Role of Interpersonal Information Sources in External Search: An Informational Perspective. *Advances in Consumer Research*, Vol. 11, pp. 250-255.

Reder, S. (1988). The communicative economy of the workgroup: Multi-channel genres of communication. *Proc. CSCW '88* (Portland, Sept. 26-29), ACM Press, pp. 354-368.

Robert F. Stengel (1986). Optimal Control and Estimation. New York: Dover Publications

Robert Scholes (1982). *Semiotics and Interpretation*, Yale University Press.

Rockart, J. and J. Short (1991). *The Networked Organization and the Management of Interdependence, in The Corporations of the 1990s.* M.S. Morton, Ed., 189-216.

Rockart, J.F. and Short, J.E. (Winter 1989). IT in the 1990s: Managing Organizational Interdependence. *Sloan Management Review,* 7-17.

Romer, P.M. (1989). Endogenous Technical Change. *Journal of Political Economy,* 98, 5, pp. 71-102

Rosen D.L. and Olshavsky R.C. (1987). The Dual Role Of Informational Social Influence: Implications for Marketing Management. *Journal of Business Research,* 15, pp. 123-144.

Schein, E. H. (1961). *Coercive Persuasion.* N.Y.: Norton

Senge, P. (1990). *The Fifth Discipline: the art and practice of the learning organization.* USA: Currency/Doubleday.

Slavin, R. E. (1990). *Cooperative Learning: Theory, Research and Practice.* USA: Prentice Hall.

Smolensky, P. (1988). On the proper treatment of connectionism. *Behavioral and Brain Sciences,* 11, 1-74.

Snow, C.C., R.E. Miles, and H.J. Coleman (1992). *Managing 21st Century Network Organizations.* Organizational Dynamics. 20(3), 5-20.

Stacey, R. (1995). The Science of Complexity: an alternative perspective for strategic change processes. *Strategic Management Journal,* 16, 477-495

Sun, R. (1996). Hybrid Connectionist-Symbolic Models. A Report From The IJCAI'95 Workshop on Connectionist-Symbolic Integration IJCAI'95 Workshop on Connectionist-Symbolic Integration. University of Alabama, Department of Computer Science.

Talcott Parsons, E. Shils, and K. Naegele, (eds.) (1961). *Theories of Society.* New York: Free Press

The Internet Economy Indicators. Review. Retrieved June 19, 2002, from *http://www.internetindicators.com/execsummry.html*

Thompson, John W. (1995). The Renaissance of Learning in Business. In Fred Kofman & Peter Senge's *Learning*

Organizations: Developing Cultures for Tomorrow's Workplace. Productivity Press, Portland Oregon.

Tsoukalas, Lefteri H. and Uhrig R. E., (1997). *Fuzzy and Neural Approaches in Engineering.* New York: John Wiley & Sons.

Van Valen L. (1973). A New Evolutionary Law. *Evolutionary Theory* 1, p. 1-30.

VanLehn, K., and Ohlsson, S. (1994). Applications of simulated students: An exploration. *Journal of Artificial Intelligence in Education,* 5(2), 135-175.

D. Vengerov, H. Berenji, A. Vengerov (2002). Adaptive coordination among fuzzy reinforcement learning agents performing distributed dynamic load balancing. *IEEE International Conference on Fuzzy Systems (FUZZ-IEEE), May.*

A. Vengerov (2001). Evolution of Electronic Business as a Sensitive System, *Ecommerce Research Forum of the Center for eBusiness at MIT and Institute for Operations Research and the Management Sciences (INFORMS),* #146.

A. Vengerov, S. Klein (2000). EQAL Approach to the Design of Learning Technology in Dynamic Information Contexts. *Proceedings of the Fifth Annual Northeastern Conference of The Consortium for Computing in Small Colleges.*

A. Vengerov (1999a). Toward the Design of Dynamical E-commerce Architectures. *Tenth Annual Conference of the International Information Management Association.*

A. Vengerov (1999b). Continuous V-Management and Planning under Environmental Discontinuity. *Sixth Annual Conference of ASBBS,* Las Vegas.

Vygotsky, L.S. (1978). *Mind in Society.* Cambridge, MA: Harvard University Press.

Waldrop, M. Mitchell (1992). *Complexity: The Emerging Science at the Edge of Order and Chaos.* New York: Simon and Schuster

Whittington, R. (1993). *What is Strategy—and does it Matter?* London: Routledge

Wilkins, H. (1991). Computer talk: long-distance conversations by computer. *Written Communication*, vol.8, no.1.

William E Halal, et al (1991). *Internal Markets.* New York: Wiley

William Raft Kunst-Wilson and R.B. Zajonc (1980). Affective Discrimination of Stimuli That Cannot Be Recognized. *Science*, February

Yourdon E. (1989). *Modern Structured Analysis.* NJ: Yourdon Press.

Zeghal, K., Ferber, J. and Ecreau, J. (1993). *Symmetrical, transitive and Recursive Force: A Representation of interactions and commitments.* Paper presented at IJCAI Workshop on Coordinated Autonomous Robots, Chambery.

Index

263, 264, 265, 266, 267, 268, 269, 270, 271, 272, 273,
274, 275, 276, 277, 278, 279, 280, 283, 285, 286, 288,
289, 290, 292, 293, 294, 295, 297, 298, 299, 302, 304,
310, 315, 316, 317, 318, 320, 322, 323, 324, 327, 328,
329, 333, 336, 343, 347, 348, 351, 354, 355, 362, 371,
376, 377, 382, 383, 384, 386, 387, 388, 390, 391, 392,
393, 395, 396, 398, 400, 401, 404, 409, 410, 412, 413,
414, 415, 416, 417, 420
DPI 205, 206, 207, 209, 218, 233, 255, 265, 288, 289, 295,
309, 337, 347, 348
DVI 206, 218

E

e-business 22, 23, 31, 32, 39, 40, 46, 62, 68, 69, 91, 115,
117, 143, 161, 250, 295, 309, 368, 378, 382, 389, 398,
421
e-businesses 49, 63, 64
evolving 12, 13, 23, 28, 32, 35, 36, 37, 41, 44, 49, 57, 63,
65, 77, 78, 80, 81, 82, 84, 86, 87, 89, 91, 98, 101, 105,
118, 119, 123, 124, 135, 141, 142, 147, 152, 153, 155,
160, 161, 162, 164, 166, 171, 176, 181, 184, 185, 199,
204, 209, 210, 217, 220, 221, 230, 233, 234, 241, 242,
247, 252, 264, 270, 275, 282, 287, 295, 298, 300, 304,
311, 313, 318, 319, 322, 323, 329, 332, 339, 341, 358,
359, 360, 361, 362, 363, 367, 371, 373, 375, 382, 385,
390, 394, 396, 402, 404, 413, 414, 415, 416, 419, 420
external harmony 165, 176, 191, 217, 330
external sensitivity 41, 64, 68, 119, 123, 124, 140, 165, 166,
167, 174, 184, 185, 193, 203, 216, 227, 244, 253, 255,
276, 295, 301, 302, 412, 417

F

fuzzy boundaries 84, 169, 379

H

L

LCA 355, 356, 363, 364, 366, 368, 381, 383, 406, 414, 416, 418, 419, 421

LCh 198, 199, 215, 216, 259

LDPCS 178, 180, 183, 184, 185, 190, 203, 209, 210, 219, 223, 233, 384, 385

LH1 153, 159, 162, 174, 181, 187, 189, 191, 193, 194, 197, 211

LH2 174, 181, 184, 185, 186, 187, 191, 193, 194, 197, 202, 211, 226, 230, 251, 276, 330, 343, 347

LH3 186, 188, 189, 190, 195, 197, 201, 203, 210, 211, 215, 217, 229, 231, 232, 252, 297, 312, 317, 336, 341, 348, 411, 416

M

MBA/CBA 359, 362, 363, 364, 366, 367, 374, 399

MDPCS 178, 179, 180, 181, 182, 183, 184, 185, 186, 190, 191, 192, 199, 201, 202, 203, 206, 208, 209, 210, 211, 218, 222, 223, 233, 276, 280, 294

meaning 19, 33, 42, 65, 66, 67, 69, 70, 71, 76, 77, 78, 79, 80, 81, 82, 83, 84, 89, 91, 92, 93, 95, 96, 98, 102, 111, 114, 123, 137, 139, 141, 143, 144, 153, 156, 158, 205, 217, 220, 269, 270, 284, 289, 305, 307, 308, 310, 322, 325, 326, 330, 334, 336, 354, 360, 366, 376, 390, 398, 400, 403, 410, 416

MHHz 247, 281, 282

MLS 264, 280, 282, 283, 285, 288, 292, 303, 304, 305, 308, 316, 317, 321, 342, 347, 353

MSOS 212, 222, 223, 224, 225, 226, 237, 246, 247, 248, 250, 251, 252, 253, 254, 255, 258, 263, 265, 266, 268, 274, 276, 277, 278, 281, 283, 285, 286, 287, 288, 289, 290, 293, 294, 296, 299, 300, 306, 307, 308, 309, 311, 312, 313, 314, 317, 318, 328, 329, 330, 332, 336, 337, 338, 339, 340, 348, 351, 355, 376, 385, 387, 388

multilevel holistic harmonization 281

Multilevel Rx balancing 267

N

network externalities 15

O

object-orientation 48, 83, 92, 109, 110
object-oriented 31, 50, 56, 71, 73, 83, 155, 270, 275, 290,
  353, 403, 406
old economy 14, 15, 18, 46, 52, 143, 377
OM 214, 215, 220, 247, 255, 259, 260, 261, 263, 264, 281,
  282, 287, 293, 294, 296, 308, 309, 310, 311, 314, 317,
  318, 338, 340
OO/C 66, 67, 68, 69, 82, 87, 88, 89, 91, 92, 93, 94, 95, 97,
  102, 103, 109, 114, 116, 117, 118, 120, 121, 122, 126,
  129, 130, 131, 133, 134, 135, 137, 138, 139, 140, 142,
  143, 146, 148, 150, 156, 168, 170, 176, 192, 199, 238,
  253, 259, 265, 267, 275, 279, 284, 289, 292, 304, 311,
  313, 315, 316, 319, 320, 326, 327, 328, 344, 347, 350,
  351, 352, 353, 356, 359, 387, 390, 392, 395, 396, 398,
  399, 401, 403, 408
Orientation 64, 83, 100, 213
OS 214, 247, 259, 260, 261, 264, 293, 311, 314, 315, 345

P

P-level 206, 207, 208, 209, 210, 211, 212, 213, 214, 215,
  218, 219, 222, 224, 225, 227, 233, 248, 257, 258, 265,
  281, 283, 285, 286, 287, 291, 300, 309, 313, 314, 318,
  319, 320, 321, 323, 324, 328, 338, 339, 340, 348, 353,
  405, 415
pattern 18, 29, 35, 41, 49, 53, 56, 69, 80, 84, 89, 90, 123,
  128, 129, 142, 147, 153, 159, 160, 163, 164, 165, 166,
  167, 168, 169, 171, 172, 173, 175, 176, 178, 179, 180,
  182, 184, 185, 187, 192, 195, 196, 200, 201, 204, 222,
  224, 228, 229, 231, 234, 240, 253, 256, 260, 268, 270,

T

T-mode 121, 124, 125, 142, 146, 147, 148, 158, 162, 230, 233, 234, 246, 251, 267, 305, 319, 320, 323, 328, 334, 350, 351, 352, 386, 387, 415
TB 170, 171, 172, 173, 176, 177, 190, 215, 216, 217
techware 409, 410, 411, 412, 414, 415, 416, 419
the Cube 415, 416, 421
Tmods 124, 125, 140, 141, 142, 146, 251, 275, 279, 280, 305, 323, 339, 343, 345, 354, 417, 418, 419

U

UAHS 385, 388
UFO 143, 144, 238, 350, 385, 386, 387, 389, 417, 420
UVO 98, 101, 117, 120, 125, 126, 127, 133, 134, 135, 137, 139, 140, 142, 143, 144, 146, 147, 156, 233, 237, 245, 250, 251, 263, 264, 267, 279, 280, 296, 297, 315, 316, 323, 324, 350, 351, 352, 354, 355, 383, 386, 387, 393, 400, 414, 417, 420
UVO Use Schema 352
UVO use schema 137, 323

V

V-level 206, 207, 208, 209, 210, 211, 212, 213, 214, 215, 216, 217, 218, 219, 220, 222, 223, 224, 225, 229, 233, 243, 244, 248, 250, 255, 256, 257, 260, 261, 263, 264, 274, 280, 281, 282, 283, 285, 286, 287, 288, 290, 291, 293, 294, 295, 296, 301, 302, 303, 304, 306, 311, 313, 314, 318, 319, 320, 321, 322, 323, 324, 328, 329, 330, 333, 336, 337, 339, 343, 348, 353, 404, 406, 415, 418
V-management 244, 257
V-modes 120, 121, 139, 140, 141
VCP decomposition 284, 318, 349
VCP-architecture 284, 294, 404
vDPCS 206, 207, 208, 209, 210, 211, 212, 215, 216, 217, 218, 221, 223, 233, 256, 263, 264, 267, 270, 274, 279,

ANDER VENGEROV

279, 280, 304, 352, 358, 395, 401, 402
VO-plane 113, 116
VO-pyramid 112, 113, 115, 116, 117, 123, 139, 147
VO-space 111
VS 114, 115, 116, 212, 213, 214, 217, 219, 220, 221, 222,
249, 250, 251, 253, 254, 255, 256, 257, 262, 267, 268,
276, 278, 282, 287, 291, 294, 295, 299, 300, 301, 302,
303, 304, 305, 306, 307, 308, 309, 310, 311, 312, 314,
320, 322, 324, 329, 330, 331, 332, 333, 336, 337, 338,
339, 340, 341, 342, 343, 344, 345, 346, 348, 353, 397,
406

Y

Yin/Yang 162, 326, 406, 419

Printed in the United States
790300001B